Democracy and Exclusion

Democracy and Exclusion

PATTI TAMARA LENARD

OXFORD
UNIVERSITY PRESS

Oxford University Press is a department of the University of Oxford. It furthers
the University's objective of excellence in research, scholarship, and education
by publishing worldwide. Oxford is a registered trade mark of Oxford University
Press in the UK and certain other countries.

Published in the United States of America by Oxford University Press
198 Madison Avenue, New York, NY 10016, United States of America.

© Oxford University Press 2023

All rights reserved. No part of this publication may be reproduced, stored in
a retrieval system, or transmitted, in any form or by any means, without the
prior permission in writing of Oxford University Press, or as expressly permitted
by law, by license, or under terms agreed with the appropriate reproduction
rights organization. Inquiries concerning reproduction outside the scope of the
above should be sent to the Rights Department, Oxford University Press, at the
address above.

You must not circulate this work in any other form
and you must impose this same condition on any acquirer.

Library of Congress Control Number: 2023934155

ISBN 978-0-19-758581-8

DOI: 10.1093/oso/9780197585818.001.0001

Printed by Integrated Books International, United States of America

Contents

Acknowledgments	vii
Introduction: Democracy and Exclusion	1
1. Subjection and Democratic Boundaries	23
2. Deportation and the Excluded Undeportable	38
3. Citizens Abroad: In or Out, of What?	55
4. Revoking Citizenship Status	71
5. Visa Issuance and Denial in an Unequal World	87
6. Deserving Citizenship?	108
7. Resettling (LGBTQ+) Refugees	132
8. Cultural Accommodations and Naturalization Ceremonies	153
Conclusion: Inclusion Remains Out of Reach	175
Notes	179
Bibliography	189
Index	211

Acknowledgments

This book was drafted while COVID-19 precautions made travel difficult. Many friends and colleagues responded to my desperate request for virtual talks on portions of early chapters, even though the format is less than ideal. I am very grateful to many people for responding so generously.

Alex Sager and Brad Berman invited me to give a talk about skills-selective migration policies at the Portland State University Socratic Society. Georgiana Turculet and Ricardo Bravo Santillan invited me to speak to the Polemo working group at the Central European University, about the merits of citizenship oaths. Christine Sypnowich put me on the schedule for the Queen's University's Political Philosophy Reading Group, to discuss citizenship oath ceremonies. Juri Viehoff invited me to speak about visas at Manchester University's Faculty Colloquium in Political Theory. Kieran Oberman and Mollie Gerver invited me to give a talk about whether exceptional contributions were grounds for citizenship at the University of Edinburgh's Migration Ethics Workshop. Annamari Vitikainen invited me to give a talk on the resettlement of LGBTQ+ refugees at the University of Tromsø, Norway's Globalizing Minority Rights consortium. Benedikt Buechel gave me a spot at the Normative Theory of Immigration Working Group, to talk about the rights that citizens remain entitled to even while abroad. Martin Ruhs, Rainer Bauböck, and Julia Mourao-Permoser invited me to give a talk on travel bans for would-be labor migrants to the Gulf States.

Many colleagues and friends participated in these workshops, asking questions and offering comments. I am indebted to all of you: Laura Santi Amantini, Henriet Baas, Peter Balint, Esma Baycan-Herzog, Eilidh Beaton, Ali Emre Benli, Chris Bertram, Michael Blake, Benjamin Boudou, Rebecca Buxton, Shuk Ying Chan, Avner de-Shalit, Sue Donaldson, Jamie Draper, Melina Duarte, Magnus Skytterholm Egan, Andreas Føllesdal, Mollie Gerver, Anca Gheus, Kerah Gordon-Solomon, Daniel Guillery, Gina Gustavsson, Stephen Hood, Kevin Ip, Eszter Kollar, Meena Krishnamurthy, Dragan Kuljanin, Will Kymlicka, Nikola Lero, Kasper Lippert-Rasmussen, Andrew Lister, Matthew Lister, Terry MacDonald, Alistair Macleod, Andrew Mason, Zoltan Miklosi, Andres Moles, Alasia Nuti, David Owen, Serena

Parekh, Devyani Prabhat, Miriam Ronzoni, Lukas Schmid, Daniel Sharp, Sarah Song, Clara Sunderlind, and Agnes Tam.

Several people were generous enough to read through most or even all of the manuscript. I would like to thank Christine Straehle for organizing a manuscript workshop "at" the University of Hamburg, and Phillip Cole, Valeria Ottonelli, Matthias Hoesch, Felix Bender and Georgiana Turculet for participating in it. The "whole picture" comments I collected at that workshop were invaluable to my final stage of writing. At the last minute, Rainer Bauböck jumped in to comment on the first two chapters of the book, which I appreciated very much. Jacob J. Krich and Margaret Moore (and a very helpful anonymous reviewer) also read and commented on the full manuscript; both Jacob and Margaret have discussed nearly all the ideas in this book with me, sometimes more than once, and I am very lucky that neither of them (said they got) tired of doing so!

My academic home is the Graduate School of Public and International Affairs, University of Ottawa, and my colleagues provide the most collegial environment in which to work that a political theorist could wish for. As I wrote this book, the School was directed by Gilles Breton, who made it clear during his tenure that he was on all of our sides as we struggled to teach and research during the many difficult COVID-19 months. I am grateful for his advocacy and support. Many graduate and undergraduate students at the University of Ottawa provided research assistance as I wrote the chapters of this book. Thank you especially to Engi Abou-El-Kheir, Madeleine Berry, Anne-Marie Chevalier, Stéfanie Morris, Charles Takvorian, and Jeanette Ghislaine Yameogo.

My commitment to taking a clear-eyed view about how immigration and integration policies can be improved in the direction of justice, even if these improvements are slow and incremental, stems in large part from the work I have done with a community organization I co-founded, with Elizabeth Bolton, called Rainbow Haven. This organization works to sponsor, settle, and advocate for LGBTQ+ refugees and asylum seekers. This in-the-community work has shown me clearly that even small changes in the direction of justice can have a monumental impact on the lives of those who benefit from them. We should, as I argue in this book, take the victories where we can and press on.

Angela Chnapko and Alexcee Bechthold at Oxford University Press welcomed this book and sheparded it through the various stages of publication with kindness and enthusiasm. Evan Murtadha designed the stunning cover, and more than that, she and her wife Samar taught me so much about what it means to be included in a democratic society on full and equal terms. I am, and will always be, thankful that they have included me in their journey.

For every political theorist who writes a book, there is a family (some chosen) that gets the job of surviving the ups and downs of manuscript writing, and I am delighted to be able to thank my own team here. They are Jacob J. Krich, Elisa and Gavi Krich-Lenard, Harriet and John Lenard, and Angela Kaida.

Introduction

Democracy and Exclusion

Exclusion takes many forms in democratic states, some obvious, intentional, and permanent, and some implicit, unintentional, and temporary. Convicted criminals, who are jailed for a period of time, or who are denied the right to vote temporarily or permanently, are excluded from regular society for the duration of their incarceration, and possibly also from the political process. Immigrants who are deemed unsuitable for naturalization, or would-be immigrants who are deemed inadmissible to a state, are excluded from membership and even from that state's territory. Citizens whose rights remain unprotected—as the Black Lives Matter and Indigenous Land Back movements have highlighted in gruesome detail—are excluded from many of the basic goods that democratic societies are meant to protect, in equal measure, for all citizens, regardless of race, religion, or sexuality. *Democracy and Exclusion* examines these forms of exclusion to examine if and when they can be justified.

A genuinely just democracy aims to include all citizens, in some form, in the central decision-making procedures that govern it. However, all real-life democracies struggle to meet the demands of inclusion to which, in principle, they are committed. This book argues that too many people are unjustly excluded from various goods to which they are entitled, and it examines the mechanisms by which democracies exclude, from their membership and from their territory, to assess when and where exclusions are permissible. Even in democracies that are characterized by injustice across multiple domains, progress towards justice can be made in important, although sometimes incremental, ways. By exploring a range of specific exclusion cases in detail, the analysis in this book suggests that exclusion in its myriad forms is rarely justified, and it proposes mechanisms by which to move from exclusion towards inclusion. My hope is that my analysis will prove genuinely action-guiding in democracies as they struggle with whom to include, when, and under what conditions.

Two major questions have traditionally occupied the political theory of migration—first, whether states have the right to exclude migrants from their territory and, second, whether people have a basic human right to move—Amy Reed-Sandoval has referred to these two questions as central to the "classical immigration debate" (Reed-Sandoval 2016). On the one hand, open border advocates defend the right of would-be migrants to cross all borders, including international ones, and they often argue for the dismantling of borders altogether (Oberman 2016; Cole 2000; Carens 1987; Kukathas 2021). Usually, this argument makes the economic inequalities between states, sustained by unjust international institutions, central; sometimes, the suggestion is that the right to move freely can alleviate at least some of these economic inequalities, and sometimes the suggestion is that, so long as inequalities exist, certain rights restrictions, including with respect to the right to move, cannot be justified. On the other hand, so-called closed border advocates emphasize the right of states to refuse entry to would-be migrants, citing other important values that may thereby be undermined, including the erosion of national cultures, the welfare state, and social solidarity, as well as the right to freedom of association and democratic self-determination (Miller 2016c; Blake 2019; Wellman 2008; Song 2018). They typically do not agree, moreover, that the right to move across borders is a basic human right.

Although these questions remain central to ongoing migration debates, I think it is fair to say that the theoretical domain has been well mapped out. Newer political theory is more likely to be focused on questions raised by distinct forms of migration, including temporary labor migration, refuge-seeking, human smuggling and trafficking, family reunification, economic migration, and so on. Recent work in the political theory of migration tends to begin with a brief account of the author's overall position on the so-called classical debate, and then moves quickly to applying a preferred theoretical position to the various main streams of migration, including for example refugees, temporary foreign labor migrants, and economic (including business and investment) migrants. Typically, they dedicate a chapter to these distinct migration streams, discussing how they each raise their own normative questions, before proposing resolutions to each one and showing how those resolutions are consistent with or inevitable from within the theoretical framework with which the author began (for books structured broadly this way, see Carens 2013; Song 2018; Miller 2016c; Brock 2020).

Often these streams are treated in isolation from each other, without attention to the way in which migrants move between and among them, or the way in which the global migration regime forces would-be migrants to select the migration stream that they believe will be most likely to gain them entry, rather than the one they prefer or that makes the most sense of their own situation. Moreover, more normatively complex questions are typically left unaddressed, including how to treat stateless peoples, citizens abroad in moments of unexpected humanitarian emergency, those who have committed terrorist acts at home and abroad, and asylum seekers whose refugee claims have failed but who have genuine reasons to fear deportation to their home country.

Another strategy taken by more recent political theory of migration is explicitly contextual (Modood and Thompson 2018; Kukathas 2004; Lægaard 2019). As Joseph Carens explains, a contextualist methodology recommends moving between theory and practice, using each one to interrogate the other (Carens 2004).[1] Such movement highlights how best to achieve certain moral objectives given the constraints of a particular case, and it demonstrates that principles can and do operate differently in specific contexts. All democratic states are committed to freedom of expression, for example, but the parameters of that freedom vary across them. Carens recommends the contextual methodology for applied political theory in general, and then spells it out in some more detail in his recent work on migration (Carens 2004, 2013). There he suggests that it is important, when evaluating challenges that are presented by the fact of migration, to identify the normative questions at stake, to consider specific constraints that are unique to the context in which the questions have arisen, and then given those constraints, to propose resolutions that are genuinely possible within that context. When Jeffrey Howard and Jonathan Wolff call for taking a similarly "engaged" approach to evaluating public policy, the result is meant to be first and foremost the production of a range of feasible policy options, with specific attention to the context in which they are being recommended, alongside the arguments in favor of and against them (J. Howard 2020).

The method might be interpreted uncharitably as conservative—Wolff describes the approach as having a status quo bias, for taking very seriously the considerations that have led to a particular policy's adoption and support (Wolff 2020, 76)—but such an interpretation gets the project wrong. Those who adopt an engaged, contextual method intend rather to encourage scholars to see that policy makers always operate under a wide range of constraints and that pressing forward the project of immigration justice requires understanding them and taking them seriously; as a result, proposing options and resolutions to press states to move towards more justice in the space of immigration will require a deep understanding of and sympathy to these constraints, and a willingness to celebrate incremental changes in the direction of justice.

A contextual or engaged approach requires a kind of intellectual openness to considering abstract, theoretical, principles *and* the specific contextual conditions in which they will, in practice, be applied, at the same time (Carens 2000, introduction; Lægaard 2019).[2] For most of the questions I tackle in this book, it would not do to ask simply whether a particular policy furthers or harms the right to move across borders, for example, or whether a state is justified in excluding particular migrants. Rather, a fair response will require considering a range of factors, including whether options facilitate or encourage movement, certainly, as well as whether they support or undermine other values that are widely shared. Some of these values apply globally, like the importance of resisting and combatting discrimination and the legacies of colonialism, or remedying global inequalities, and others apply domestically, like the importance of treating all members of a democracy with equal respect. In the cases that occupy my attention in this book, it will sometimes be the case that a trade-off among values has to be made. Outlining the trade-off in fair and honest terms is part of my objective here, so that the harms of exclusion can be weighed against the goods that are alleged to accompany it.

A contextualist approach does not require, or even imply, the abandonment of political and moral principles (Miller 2013, ch. 2); rather, it requires attention to how they play out in practice and in specific cases. For some critics of a contextualist approach, it is too often incapable of offering principled guidance in real-life cases, in part for being unable to achieve the critical distance that is sometimes needed in order to evaluate them well (Lægaard 2019; Kukathas 2005). However, it is attractive as a strategy for the way in which it recognizes that our principles may not operate in practice as we hope, or expect, and therefore may require modification in specific contexts. Correspondingly, a contextual approach encourages deep thinking about when and how to prioritize certain values and objectives in a particular context, if they cannot all be respected or achieved right away. As a result, a contextual approach can generate policy recommendations that are attentive to the constraints and opportunities presented by a particular context, and in so doing makes it more likely that—although incrementally—movement towards justice can be made. For these reasons, I adopt a contextual method in this book.

Democracy and the Harms of Exclusion

In what follows, I treat democracy as a requirement of justice. Democracy is, at its most basic, a strategy for collective decision making, which presupposes a fundamental equality among those who are party to these decision-making procedures. For most scholars of justice, *equality* is at its heart; and justice typically refers broadly to the proper, that is equal, distribution of resources, economic, social, and political, in a society. As Laura Valentini observes, however, a society that is characterized by a reasonably equitable division of economic and social goods, but is governed by a "wise sovereign, or a small enlightened elite" rather than democratically is not fully just (Valentini 2013, 181); it is not fully just because political participation is not treated as a resource that is subject to equal distribution, just as are economic resources. So, a fully just society must be democratic in some form.

A commitment to justice as equality constrains the policies that may be chosen in democratic states, in general and in the context of migration and diversity that are the focus of this book. It requires the protection of many basic human rights and a commitment to protecting them for all citizens and, as I shall argue in Chapter 2, all residents on an equal basis. Such a commitment protects against the possible harms of majority rule, by ensuring that a range of basic rights are protected against violation by the majority. These rights are typically thought to include a range of very basic rights, including rights of due process, as well as the rights to freedom of conscience, speech, association, and political participation. To borrow language from Thomas Christiano, democratic authority in decision-making is limited by the requirement that these rights are protected for all, on an equal basis (Christiano 2004).

Carrying out this project that I describe in more detail below relies on distinguishing between what justice requires and what justice permits (Carens 2005). There are many nitty gritty questions of immigration and diversity policy that do not press up against the constraints that justice imposes, and the result is that a wide range of policies in this space can be compatible with justice, and are thus permissible. To take one example: immigration justice requires (as I will articulate below) that long-term residents be able to access citizenship in time, but it does not explain how quickly such access must be granted, or what sorts of obligations can be imposed on those who aim to access it. A naturalization period that is three years long and one that is seven years long may well both be compatible with justice, as a result, even if those who are in favor of more open borders to both membership and territory prefer the shorter time. Answering policy questions requires outlining both what justice requires and what is permissible within the boundaries of what is required.

So, readers may wonder, if trade-offs must be made, and if I am recommending an ecumenical philosophical approach to the challenges posed by immigration, is there a danger that my proposals will ultimately be arbitrary? I hope not. Rather, I begin with a conviction that guides the analysis that follows, and that conviction is that exclusion requires justification. This book is, at its core, a rejection of unwarranted and unjustified exclusion.

Let me say more about the wrong of exclusion, and what I mean to signal by making this wrong central to the analysis that follows.[3] Exclusion is usually harmful, but not always morally wrong. To say that something is harmful is to say, in general, that it sets back or damages one's interests, whereas to say something is wrong is to make a claim about the failure to respect someone's status as a moral equal (Lazar 2009). Most of us have the experience of knowing that friends have arranged to get together, for a drink or dinner, but have not invited us. We may be hurt by that but we are not wronged. Likewise, if the person we wish to marry does not wish to marry us, we may be harmed in the sense that our interests may be set back, but we are not wronged. Yet, it remains the case that people do not like to be excluded, and so we ought not to do it if it can possibly be avoided, even when the exclusion is merely harmful and not wrongful.

To make matters just slightly more normatively sophisticated, in many of the cases I consider in this book, exclusion makes it more difficult for those who are excluded to meet their needs, achieve their objectives, and shape the contours of their lives according to the priorities they have set themselves; even this form of exclusion may not always be wrongful, even if it is certainly harmful. And so, if exclusion is to be justified—and in what follows, I will suggest it rarely is—the justification must explain why it is that individuals can be prevented from meeting their needs, achieving their objectives, or shaping the contours of their lives. The justification must highlight what *goods* can be achieved if the proposed exclusion is permitted. Rarely will these goods be sufficient to justify exclusion in a particular case. I have framed the statement as I have deliberately: often, political theorists offer robust and persuasive views about the importance of democratic self-determination, and the mechanisms by which such collective self-determination can justify certain forms of exclusion (Song 2018). Similarly, although more controversially, worries about cultural integrity and the challenges of integration, the environmental impact of overpopulation in a particular jurisdiction, and economic well-being, drive arguments in favor of a state's right to exclude would-be migrants (Miller 2005; Pevnick 2009; Macedo 2011; Orgad 2016). But, as I aim to show, such views do not offer much philosophical guidance in the nitty-gritty challenges posed by migration as it is actually experienced in democratic states. Democratic states face urgent questions with respect to how they should treat migrants who are on their territory or who aim to gain access to it on a temporary or permanent basis. Highlighting the wrong of exclusion, and the harms it generates in particular cases, is a more fruitful way forward, I aim to show. The choice to exclude nearly always generates more harm than good; the harm, moreover, is specific and clear, whereas the good to be gained tends to be general and rather abstract.

This position puts me in some tension with scholars like Christopher Heath Wellman who ground their views in the importance of freedom of association and therefore adopt, as their starting point, a state's right to presumptively exclude (Wellman 2008). For Wellman, it is sufficient to notice the deep importance of the right to associate at the individual level and to observe concomitantly that this right to associate is only valuable if it includes the right to disassociate or at least to refuse association in some cases. To demonstrate the importance of association—and the right to refuse unwanted association, that is, to exclude—he considers marriage, noting that it is essential to marriage that it is freely chosen by both parties and exclusive. By analogy, he continues, democratic states are in effect an instantiation of the right to associate (among members) and the right to refuse association; that is, to exclude those who might otherwise desire to join. A similar intuition, that states can presumptively exclude, drives Michael Blake's analysis and so also leads him to conclude that it is often permissible for states to refuse admission to those for whom it does not want to take responsibility, where they desire to gain entry and even in many cases where they have, surreptitiously, gained entry; certainly, he suggests, it is wrong for individuals to *coerce* states into providing them protection by entering or staying irregularly (Blake 2014). I join others in rejecting the analogy between democratic states and marriages or clubs (Sarah Fine 2010). Democratic states are large, heterogeneous, and not in any meaningful way an organization of freely associated individuals, even if they do self-govern via democratic institutions; there is little of practical value in treating them this way, with respect to the localized and specific questions raised by migration presently.

On the contrary, the recent political presence and electoral successes of anti-immigrant, populist political parties demonstrate why we ought to be wary of, simply, declaring that democracies can, in general, permissibly exclude others. Of course, as a matter of politics, it is quite important to be attentive to the ways these parties constrain the choices that governments may have, if they aim, despite these parties' anti-immigration stances, to pursue immigration justice (Macedo 2020; Efthymiou 2020). This attention is key to the engaged, contextual, approach I take in what follows. But it is also a mistake to lean too heavily on views that treat democratic states as freely associating individuals whose choices about whom to admit or exclude are presumptively valid, thereby closing the discussion of what is normatively permissible and appropriate in the space of immigration admission, both to territory and to membership. Ultimately, in my view, both Blake and Wellman leave ample room—in my view, too much—for democratic states to exclude large classes of potential migrants or even to break their ties with already-present residents (and possibly even citizens, as I will consider in Chapter 4), simply because they want to do so. In the chapters that follow, I shall aim to find the balance between taking the constraints of specific political contexts seriously and proposing and defending policies that press states towards more rather than less inclusion.

The Moral Relevance of Inequalities Across Borders

Central to most political theory of migration is the fact of deeply unequal distribution of wealth that borders between states sustain. In 1987, when Joseph Carens wrote his foundational defense of open borders, he described the borders dividing states as protecting a kind of feudalism in which wealthy states retain their wealth and relatively poorer states struggle to provide for the basic needs of their citizens (Carens 1987). The historical arbitrariness of border placement in some cases, and the colonial imposition of borders in others, suggest to many scholars that those states that benefit from them have no good moral reason to refuse entry to those who hail from states that do not (Cole 2000). For some scholars, the fact that wealth inequalities persist, and that present-day borders operate to reinforce them, requires defending open borders as fully as possible. There are at least two reasons for this position. One reason is that freer movement across borders appears, in many cases, to reduce wealth inequalities. For example, this sort of argument is made in the context of whether or not to expand opportunities for temporary labor migration, and if so under what conditions (Lenard and Straehle 2012b): often, arguments for increasing temporary labor migration highlight its contribution to wealth redistribution in general, and more specifically, to the development of Global South states (Ruhs 2010; Pritchett 2006).

A second reason is broader, arguing that border controls cannot be morally justified so long as wealth inequalities of the kind that describe our global space are in operation. On this view, it simply cannot be that wealthy states can refuse entry to migrants who are leaving behind severe poverty in the hopes of making a better life for themselves and their families. For scholars with this view, although there may be conditions under which states can legitimately control their borders, the vast wealth inequalities that separate the wealthier states from the relatively less-wealthy states are such that *presently* border control cannot easily be justified, even if it is possible to imagine a future where it might be.[4]

In what follows, I, too, take for granted that questions of exclusion and inclusion of migrants must be understood in the context of global inequalities of wealth. These inequalities of wealth are severe, and in general impose substantial obligations on those who live in wealthier countries to do our parts in remedying them, as individuals and as members of states. I leave aside questions of the source of these duties, and their content, here (but see Gilabert 2012; Ackerly 2018; Brock 2009). Although these inequalities are key to understanding many of the challenges that migration appears to pose, they largely remain in the background of the questions I examine in this book. I operate with the premise that one should always give extra scrutiny to decisions about inclusion or exclusion that consign people to poverty that they could otherwise leave behind, as well as to whether certain structural features of the global migration system are such that they systematically disadvantage migrants from poorer states. For the analysis that follows, this understanding leads me towards accepting many inclusion claims, especially in cases where there is substantial evidence that the persistence of structural racism intersects with poverty to disadvantage would-be migrants; this framework will prove to be especially relevant in my assessment of the visa-issuing regime, which I consider in Chapter 3. The other cases I consider are not straightforwardly infused with worries about inequalities, even if inequalities are related to the movement that has led to the specific question I am considering.

For example, in Chapter 8, I ask whether states may legitimately deny citizenship to immigrants who refuse to participate in certain aspects of the host state's naturalization ceremony—at the time of writing, the case that is best known is of a Lebanese-origin doctor who refused to shake the hand of the female German officiant who would have declared him a citizen, on the grounds that his religious commitments forbade physically touching women outside of his family (Embury-Dennis 2020). I consider the legitimacy of naturalization requirements in Chapter 8, and while wealth inequalities are not central to that question in the moment, the migrant in question chose to migrate to Germany from a relatively poorer country in which he had fewer employment prospects. As it happens, most migrants to Germany who might have religious or cultural objections to shaking hands with members of the opposite sex have also migrated from relatively poorer countries. So, although questions of wealth inequality will not always be central to the questions that occupy my attention in this book, they are often in the background, in the sense that they influence the choices that migrants and states make, and they will often impact fair evaluations of the consequences of exclusion and inclusion.

Although the analysis that follows will proceed with attention to the ways that economic inequalities shape migration choices, I do not believe that the mere fact of inequalities, some of which are severe, is sufficient to undermine the claim that states can, sometimes legitimately, exclude would-be migrants from their territory and from their membership. I also do not believe relatively less-well off migrants must automatically be granted permission to enter as a matter of justice. Rather, a more promising approach is one that highlights the importance of securing, at least minimally, legitimacy across the global migration regime, and also domestically.

Recent political theory of migration has considered more deeply the conditions of legitimacy that the state system must meet, as a whole, for border control to be justified (for a review, see Sharp 2020). In this literature, the general thought is that a state's legitimacy—and its right to control borders—hinges on there being a fair global migration system to which each state contributes, and where it is not in place, to which they contribute in the form of constructing and developing the conditions under which it can be sustained (for variations on these arguments, see Owen 2020; Brock 2020). None of the scholars offering this sort of an argument is under any illusions: moving towards such a system is a long-term venture because the deep injustice of the starting point is well-acknowledged. I am in broad agreement that state legitimacy is connected in important ways to the fairness of a global migration system. Although as I will show, there are a great many cases where additional considerations will also be relevant to determining the legitimacy and permissibility of exclusion and inclusion, I will treat five legitimacy criteria, at the level of the state, as necessary (but not sufficient) conditions for exclusion to be justified. These necessary requirements for permissible exclusion are quite basic, although they are rarely (if ever) robustly met in current democratic states.

First, states may not adopt overtly discriminatory admission and exclusion policies. Although this criterion is widely agreed, the basis for the prohibition against discriminatory admission policies has been disputed recently among political theorists (Brock 2020; Miller 2016c). Here I simply aim to affirm that admission policies that explicitly refuse entrance to specific groups, based on ethnic, racial, and cultural characteristics, are impermissible. For example, Poland's choice to admit thousands of Ukrainian refugees while allegedly refusing entry to African-origin international students who had been studying in Ukraine is impermissible for being overtly discriminatory, no matter what one's explanation for the wrong of discrimination is (United Nations 2022). Second, states must respect the duties imposed by the Geneva Convention on Refugees, in particular, the duty of "non-refoulement," that is, to avoid returning asylum seekers to states in which they may face persecution before their claims are heard, and it derives in part from a global commitment to respecting international law with respect to refugees and asylum seekers (Gibney 2004). At least among political theorists, this duty also includes the duty to admit asylum seekers in the first place, to assess their claims fairly, and to offer them protection, if their claims are found to be valid. Third, states must respect the right to family unity for those whom it does admit, and this inevitably entails admitting at least immediate loved ones of admitted migrants, including children, partners, and parents—it may also require expanding the definition of who counts as family perhaps in general, and at least in specific cases. Fourth, states must have a strategy by which to regularize long-term non-citizen residents, whether they are present regularly or irregularly. Although the precise policy implications of these criteria will be a matter of disagreement, they are widely held to be defensible among political theorists of migration.[5] Fifth and finally, states must always permit the return of their own citizens, regardless of the length of, or reasons for, their absence.

These criteria are, as I said, minimal, and while adhering to them would not generate the open borders utopia that some hope to see, it would substantially change the global space for migration. They have an additional advantage, given my project here, which is that they are *widely* accepted, at the level of principle, even among democratic states that aim to control their borders; adopting a starting point that identifies principles that are by and large accepted is recommended by the contextual, engaged approach I adopt in this book. More specifically, their widespread acceptance among many democratic states, and most political theorists, suggests that they are a good basis for doing the work of this book: to evaluate specific cases, and to propose ways to resolve them fairly, with the expectation that democratic states can be persuaded to adopt morally justifiable policies with respect to would-be and current migrants.

My objective in this book is aimed at resolving specific migration dilemmas that are faced by, and often caused by, diverse, democratic states, under non-ideal conditions (Bauböck et al. 2022). Currently, democratic states face a whole range of questions focused on when and how to exclude both would-be migrants as well as long-term non-citizen residents, with regular and irregular statuses. These questions require some deep thinking, so that they can be resolved fairly *right now*, and the normative issues they raise are—as this book will show—often surprising and generally multidimensional. Rarely will the dilemmas I consider be resolvable with statements decrying the injustice of global migration governance and its colonial roots, or the unfairness of wealth inequalities and their colonial roots, even though these are both facts with which migrants must contend (Lu 2017; Cole 2000). Although I am deeply sympathetic to the voices that call for remedies in the form of fully open borders, correctly declaring that "no person is illegal," the demand to open borders is not often a feasible policy response—in particular, it will fail to resolve several of the dilemmas I will discuss—to the cases I examine in this book.

The Status of the Right to Move

While I do not believe that the right to move, especially across borders, must be treated as a basic human right, or one that should always be maximally prioritized among other rights, I do believe that movement is of deep importance to many people (but see Oberman 2016; Kukathas 2021). It therefore merits moral consideration. Yet, it is also important not to overstate how many people desire to move away from their homes; even though the number of people who do move is increasing and has been doing so for many years, globally the overall proportion of migrants has not changed substantially in recent years, from 2.8 percent in 1995 to 3.5 percent in 2019 (Edmond 2020).[6] However, I am of the conviction—sometimes maligned as "sedenterist"—that mostly people prefer to stay home, and mostly do so despite what may be perceived to be better opportunities in other places, and more would remain home if local conditions were better. This claim, if true, does not remove the importance of treating people who desire to move fairly, or who have moved with the hope of residing elsewhere either temporarily or permanently; the interest that people have in being able to move across borders is important *enough* that it merits substantial, if not absolute, protection, and I hope that my attention to its importance will be in evidence as I consider the cases that animate this book.

The book will be centered on four distinct ways in which democracies can and do exclude others. In what follows, I suggest four clusters of exclusion cases—a kind of typology of exclusion—with the purpose of outlining the specific wrongs they raise and outlining potential remedies. To explain them, let me begin by noticing two distinct ways to conceptualize democratic exclusion that are central to this book. One way to think about exclusion is in terms of *what* people are excluded from: democracies exclude people from gaining access to their territory and they can exclude people (who have gained access to their territory) from accessing citizenship. A second way to think about exclusion is in terms of *who* is excluded: citizens or non-citizens.

I think the first distinction, between exclusion from territory and exclusion from membership, is clear enough. Democracies typically control their territorial borders in such a way that only some can gain entrance. This control often takes place at borders, but as many before me have noted, it also takes place before migrants arrive at borders, at embassies and consulates, where would-be migrants apply for visas to gain entrance, and also by carriers, including airplanes, trains, and ferries, that are required to validate travel documents before they transport would-be migrants abroad (Shachar 2020; Gibney 2006). Democracies also control access to their membership, before and after migrants arrive on their territory. Perhaps the most obvious way that democracies control access to their membership is via the adoption of naturalization requirements, which aspiring members must meet. These requirements vary by country and can include security assessments, language tests, or citizenship tests (or both), proof of employment, and so on (Favell 1998; Bloemraad 2006; Calder, Cole, and Seglow 2009; Koning 2011). They often also involve formal citizenship ceremonies, which migrants must participate in as a final step towards naturalization. Migrants can be excluded from membership temporarily or permanently, in many states, for failing to meet these requirements. These two forms of exclusion, from territory and membership, are not always neatly distinguished in practice, however. For example, and as I will consider more deeply in Chapter 5, democracies also control access to membership by issuing visas to some migrants, for example, to tourists or temporary labor migrants, who are permitted temporary access to their territory, for a specific reason, but who are legally denied the right to apply for citizenship.

The second way to think about exclusion is about who—whether citizens or non-citizens—is excluded, rather than from what they are excluded. It is easier to see that democratic states regularly engage in the expulsion of non-citizens from their territories, sometimes forcefully via deportation, or sometimes merely coercively by issuing visas for temporary visits only, and connecting future opportunities for temporary visits to timely departures before the relevant visa expires. More controversially, democratic states engage in practices of expelling *citizens* from their membership and then from their territory, in the form of denationalization and denaturalization. Although formally on the books as a legal option in many states, the practice of banishing citizens on a permanent basis had been largely abandoned since the right to citizenship was formalized as a basic human right in the 1948 Universal Declaration of Human Rights. Recently, however, many democratic states have reclaimed the power to denationalize terrorists, as a form of punishment, or would-be terrorists, to protect national security. As well, exclusion persists even among those who are admitted to both territory and membership. Citizens can be excluded by systemic racism and discrimination that renders minorities, and in some cases majorities as in Apartheid states, unable to access the rights and benefits that should, in principle, be available to all citizens on equal terms; often, the existence of persistent racism translates into the adoption of policies that deliberately target minorities in ways that are intended to make their inclusion a struggle, as for example where laws demand the removal of facial and head coverings in public spaces. As I was putting the final touches on this manuscript, for example, a Hijabi teacher was fired in Quebec on the grounds that wearing head coverings in certain spaces (including in public schools) has been rendered illegal. Although great strides have been made in accommodating the specific needs of many minorities in democratic states, many citizens remain excluded from the goods that democracies are supposed to protect for all of them, in multiple ways. The Black Lives Matter movement, to which I return in the conclusion, is a grass-roots effort to recognize and remedy the persistent, structural exclusion of citizens and to press for their genuinely equal treatment.

If these two ways of understanding exclusion—as exclusion from membership or territory, and as exclusion of non-citizens and citizens—are treated together, then there are four clusters of exclusion and these four clusters form the backbone of the analysis that follows: (1) non-citizens can be excluded from territory, via the denial of entry at the border or by the refusal to issue them visas; (2) citizens can be excluded from membership, via the revocation of citizenship, the denial of voting rights while residing abroad, and the systemic and structural discrimination that persistently faces certain minority groups; (3) non-citizens can be admitted to territory but denied access to membership, as with tourists and international students, and more controversially with temporary foreign labor migrants and refugees with forms of temporary protected status (rather than permanent residence or citizenship); and (4) citizens can be excluded from territory, via deportations that follow from denaturalization, that is, the removal of citizenship from individuals who acquired citizenship via naturalization, or denationalization, that is, the removal of citizenship from individuals who are citizens in virtue of birthright citizenship laws. Let me elaborate each of these clusters, briefly, following a figure delineating each of them:

		Exclusion from territory		Exclusion from citizenship
	Chapter		Chapter	
Non-citizens	2	Deportation of irregular migrants, short- and long-term	2	Stateless peoples
			4	Tourists and citizen labor migrants abroad
	3	Visa issuance and denial	6	Laboring for citizenship
			7	Resettling (LGBTQ+) refugees
			8	Naturalization requirements
Citizens	4	Rights of citizens abroad, including children of foreign fighters	4	Rights of dual nationals
	5	Denial of return to foreign fighters	5	Denationalization, including of adult foreign fighters
			Conclusion	Persistent structural racism

The first cluster of exclusion cases the book focuses on are non-citizens who are excluded from territory. At first glance, this case appears easy, at least if we accept that states have a right to exclude at least some would-be migrants. That is to say, it is normal that states adopt immigration policies—and so long as they meet the minimal standards of justice I have outlined—they can permissibly exclude some people who would, otherwise, prefer to enter. Would-be visitors, workers, and permanent migrants, must all submit material in order to attain the right to enter, and a state is permitted to assess this material to determine whether a non-citizen may enter and for what reason. States ask would-be visitors to provide information about their connections to their home country, whether they are employed, and how much money they have in their bank account, for example, to determine whether someone requesting a "visitor" visa in fact intends to return home. Those who are permitted to enter are granted visas, which specify the terms of their admission. So long as these terms are justice compatible, they may be applied and, if need be, enforced against those who are granted temporary visas.

This latter statement, about the permissibility of enforcing the conditions of temporary visas, highlights a conceptual error that was made in early political theorizing of migration, namely, that the justice or injustice of immigration was merely a matter of who may enter and who may be denied entry to a state. In fact, however, as more recent political theory has demonstrated, admission and exclusion policies are also *enforced*, not only at the border, but also before would-be migrants arrive at the border, as well as once they have crossed the border and entered the territory (Mendoza 2015; Sager 2017). The border has perhaps always been more than a physical line dividing one state from another. But as is clearer than ever, would-be migrants now must confront the power of a state's border well before they arrive at its physical location.

As Mathew Gibney has highlighted with frightening clarity, many liberal, democratic states are perfecting strategies by which to ensure that certain clusters of would-be migrants—generally, poorer migrants whose home countries are struggling with poverty or violence—cannot gain entrance to them, at least not without putting themselves at significant risk. These so-called non-entry policies range from carrier sanctions—penalties imposed on airlines that permit the boarding of individuals who do not possess an appropriate entry visa—to "territorial excisions," where states declare that arrival on certain parts of their territory (the airport, distant islands) does not count as official arrival, and so is not sufficient grounds to claim asylum (Gibney 2006). Combined with extensive surveillance practices of migrants, which Ayelet Shachar describes, the actions that states take to *exclude* would-be migrants now extend beyond merely delineating admission policies and then implementing them, and they extend beyond the physical border of the state (Shachar 2020). These forms of extra-territorial border enforcement are coupled with border enforcement on a state's territory, focused on identifying non-citizens who have over-stayed visas or managed to arrive in irregular ways (i.e., not at a designated point of entry), and deporting them from the state. So, the point is, the exclusion of non-citizens happens in myriad ways beyond the mere delineation of an immigration policy. Non-citizens are increasingly denied the right to make a claim that they meet the admissions requirements—especially as asylees—and they are increasingly deported if they have managed in some way to circumvent standard admission procedures. Chapter 2, focused on the deportation of non-citizens, and Chapter 5, focused on the visa-issuing regime, both consider the permissibility of strategies that states take to exclude non-citizens from their territory.

The second cluster of cases focuses on citizens who are excluded from territory. Citizens can be excluded from territory in many ways, including if they are denationalized and deported to another country in which they retain citizenship status. But this form of territorial exclusion is not the only one to which citizens can be subject. As Elizabeth Cohen demonstrates in her brilliant *Illegal*, in its enthusiasm for deporting irregular migrants from the United States, hundreds, if not thousands, of American citizens were also deported, where they were not able to prove to the satisfaction of authorities that they were US citizens (Cohen 2020).

Additionally, complicated moral questions have arisen as so-called foreign fighters—individuals who have traveled to join foreign wars—have attempted to return to their countries of citizenship to find that in fact they have been denationalized while they are abroad and are not permitted to return. As well, their children, born abroad but legally entitled to the citizenship of their parents, are being denied the opportunity to return. Citizens can also be denied access to their territory if, having left the territory believing that their security was at risk, they sought asylum abroad. If this asylum is denied, then in principle the denying state is permitted to return the asylum-seeker to their country of citizenship. But that country must *accept* its citizen's return, and this acceptance is not always forthcoming. Individuals in these situations may prefer this outcome, but nevertheless it is an example of the denial of territorial entry to citizens. Chapters 3 and 4 consider when and whether states may deny their own citizens access to territory, as well as what duties states possess in relation to citizens who are abroad, for short or extended periods of time. Chapter 4 recognizes that those who travel abroad carry some rights of citizenship with them, which their state of citizenship retains the duty to protect, whereas other rights are protected by the state they visit or in which they are resident; the chapter's goal is to map these out, to show that the duty holder shifts from the state of citizenship to the state of residence over time.

The third cluster of cases, the exclusion of non-citizens from membership, raises separate normative concerns. This cluster of cases refers to those migrants who are admitted to territories but who are subsequently denied the right to apply for citizenship. Temporary labor migrants often fall into this category, that is, individuals who are admitted to fill acute labor shortages, on temporary contracts, after the completion of which they must either leave the country, or apply for an extension of their contract. These visas often travel with the stipulation that while those who hold these visas may apply for an extension of their *temporary* visa, they may not apply for permanent residency or citizenship. Similarly, long-term irregular migrants are often denied the right to apply for citizenship, although in this case the justification for the denial stems from their having violated the terms of admission in the first place, either by gaining entrance in an irregular manner or by overstaying a visa. Some states offer temporary residence—what in the United States is called "temporary protected status"—to individuals who are fleeing natural disasters. The "Canada–Ukraine Authorization for Emergency Travel" program is offering Ukrainians fleeing Russia's invasion three-year visas with work permits (Senyshyn, Tchern, and Maimust 2022). These visas are time-limited, on the expectation that eventually such individuals will return home. At the discretion of the hosting state, those with temporary status may have access to permanent status, but typically they do not, and, at least in the United States, they are generally only offered opportunities to renew the status on a semi-regular basis until even that opportunity is removed (Frelick 2020).

Non-citizens may also be excluded from membership by procedures that render attaining full membership difficult or impossible. Many states have recently adopted citizenship and language tests that are very demanding, such that all but the most dedicated of newcomers struggle to meet their requirements. In others, states have implicitly or explicitly adopted "cultural requirements" that they propose must be met. Earlier I described a would-be German citizen, with origins in Lebanon, who was denied German citizenship for his refusal to shake hands with the female officiant whose job it was to congratulate him, and France has recently denied citizenship to several women who have refused to remove face coverings (Breeden 2018; Bennhold 2008). These are *cultural* exclusions, which are adopted to deny membership to non-citizens who, otherwise, have met the requirements to attain citizenship. Chapters 6, 7, and 8 all consider the mechanisms by which states exclude migrants from membership, as they labor in temporary employment in the hopes that it leads to permanent status (Chapter 6); at various stages of their journeys, including as they begin to integrate (Chapter 7); and during the naturalization process (Chapter 8).

The final cluster of cases focuses on citizens who are excluded from membership. The (near) permanent expulsion from membership has a venerable history—the ancient Athenians practiced a form of ostracism, to exile citizens they believed had acquired too much power, although the exclusion was typically limited to ten years (Forsdyke 2009; Malkopoulou 2017). Similarly, the practice of exile as a form of punishment understood as less harsh than capital punishment has a long history (Kingston 2005). Increasingly, as part of the so-called war against terror, and also as part of the more general spread of anti-immigrant perspectives, more and more states are adopting policies that permit the denationalization and denaturalization of citizens. Denationalization refers to withdrawal of citizenship; denaturalization refers to the withdrawal of citizenship from an individual who has acquired that citizenship via naturalization. Denationalization has been deployed as a form of punishment, or deterrent, for those who have committed terrorist crimes, or who are suspected of intending to commit terrorist crimes. Where dual citizens are denationalized, their denationalization is followed by deportation to the country in which they continue to hold citizenship; the same is true in cases of denaturalization. It might be thought that the greater harm is the deportation—that is, exclusion from territory—that flows from denationalization (or denaturalization), but in these cases it is relevant that the exclusion from territory cannot proceed until the exclusion from membership is complete.

So, citizens can be excluded from membership in the form of having their citizenship revoked. As well, as I conceptualize it here, legal members of a state may sometimes be denied some of their membership rights, or they can struggle to gain the protection that is supposed to flow from membership or to exercise their citizenship rights on equal terms. For example, where citizens reside abroad, they may eventually be denied the right to vote in their home country's elections. In this kind of case, citizens retain citizenship but not the full set of rights to which membership typically gives rise. In others, there are subtle—and sometimes not so subtle—ways in which minorities are denied the protection that is meant to be afforded by equal citizenship or their attempts to deploy their rights in pursuit of that protection are dismissed or ignored. I consider this lingering challenge in democratic states in the conclusion to this book.[7]

Introducing Subjection

As I will argue in Chapter 1, all four of these clusters of cases include people who are *subjected* to the legal and political power of a state, and in some cases several states, without sufficient access to the protection that ought to flow from it. I will spell this out in some detail in Chapter 1, but for now the short version of my claim is that subjection, without appropriate inclusion, is a violation of democratic principle. In particular, over the course of the individual chapters in this book, I shall demonstrate where and when individuals in each cluster of cases are subjected to state power in ways that warrant inclusion, first, as protection from forced exclusion and second, with respect to the rights and privileges that permit individuals to protect themselves against this exclusion in its many forms.

I shall not conclude that every instance of exclusion is also an instance of subjection. Where exclusion does not travel with subjection, it is permissible. The book proceeds with the objective of assessing the various normative questions raised not by these clusters in general, but by key representative cases of each cluster. I begin, in the first chapter, by defending a version of the all-subjected principle as the best way to assess who is entitled to protection against exclusion in a democratic state. I defend it against a range of critiques to show that it offers a good guide to understanding and sorting out the moral dilemmas posed by the ways that democratic states attempt to exclude others. I do not, I want to highlight, argue that democracies must always include, although the commitment to inclusion is a key democratic principle. Rather, I will argue that wherever subjection is persistent and ongoing, inclusion is mandated—and by inclusion, as I will articulate in more detail, I do not mean the standard claim that citizenship confers a kind of equal status to its holders, but rather that those who hold the status of citizenship, or who ought to, must be protected from forcible exclusion from the political community. This argument includes an account of what citizenship status is, in my view, and what it offers its holders which is, to repeat, protection from forced exclusion, first, and access to genuinely equal citizenship rights, second.

The chapters that follow examine in some more detail the forms that exclusion from democracies take, broadly following the typology I described above. Chapter 2 considers the harms of deportation, especially for long-term irregular migrants. Chapter 3 considers what citizenship rights persist where citizens are abroad, either briefly or for a longer period of time. Chapter 4 considers the harm of citizenship revocation. Together these chapters are intended to demonstrate the importance of the status of citizenship, founded mainly on the importance of residential security. This first set of chapters examines, in sum, the ways in which democracies exclude those who are on their territory, from accessing or sustaining access to citizenship, as well as which rights do and do not travel with citizens when they voluntarily exit the territory of their state of citizenship, that is, from which rights they may be permissibly excluded, after long-term residence abroad.

The second set of chapters examines the mechanisms by which democracies control access to membership, which of course begins with access to territory in the first place. In particular, they highlight the challenges that arise as states make moves towards enabling the inclusion of some of those who are subjected to their power. Chapter 5 examines the mechanisms by which democracies admit or exclude migrants to their territory, by considering the normative questions that emerge when would-be migrants request entrance visas. Chapter 6 considers the permissibility of tying access to citizenship to *contributions* to a state, an issue that has special salience at the time of writing as some democracies consider their obligations to Afghan citizens who supported their military during twenty years of conflict. Chapter 7 turns towards a consideration of integration and what it demands of both newcomers and host states, with a special focus on the inclusion of resettled LGBTQ+ refugees. Chapter 8 focuses on the final step taken in the journey to access citizenship, namely the naturalization ceremony; it considers whether cultural and religious accommodations must be offered to those who desire to take a citizenship oath and have fulfilled all the prior conditions of doing so. The book concludes briefly with a discussion of recent movements focused on securing the equal protection of citizenship rights for those who have been, or continue to be, denied them.

1
Subjection and Democratic Boundaries

The proper boundaries of a democratic community are difficult to define. This chapter defends a variation of the all-subjected principle as a way to define the boundaries of the community. In particular, I argue that *subjection* to power, both formal and informal, entitles those who are subjected to access the status of citizen; or, more specifically, long-term, life-shaping subjection entitles subjects to protection against forcible and unwanted exclusion from both territory and membership in the form of citizenship status. As I will explain, the concept of subjection, and the way in which it is fleshed out inside of democratic boundary debates offers actionable guidance in the cases I consider over the course of this book.

To say that people are subjected to state power is to say that they can be compelled, against their will, to abide by rules and regulations issued by that state. Where they are not—indeed, where they are merely affected or even coerced—they can often be justifiably excluded from the decision-making procedures that determine the use of that power. The qualifier "often" is in place to recognize that although I am attempting to offer a general story to explain the relationship between subjection and inclusion, there are cases where the tight connection that I attempt to articulate between subjection and inclusion is not present; for example, asylum seekers are legally entitled to at least temporary inclusion while their claims are processed, and for longer if they are found to be refugees. But the basis of their inclusion claim is not subjection, but rather the duty that all states have to include those in search of safety as a result of (at least) persecution by their home state. So, I recognize exceptions to my general formulation of the subjection principle.

Nevertheless, what my formulation means, and what gives the concept of subjection its critical bite as well as its action-guiding potential in the chapters that follow, is that where individuals are subjected to power but not relevantly included, they are wronged: democratic exclusion is subjection without the attendant inclusion. I will begin below with a discussion of boundaries in general, and then turn to an account of subjection as well as of the rights and benefits that flow from it.

Boundaries in Democratic Theory

States are divided by physical boundaries. The historical origins of the boundaries that divide states are complex. Sometimes they follow geographic features, including mountain ranges and bodies of water, and sometimes they are the result of war, colonialism, or conquest. Theorists of territory are focused on articulating the best principles for identifying, and where necessary reshaping, these boundaries (Moore 2015; Kolers 2009; Espejo 2020). The boundaries of a specific territory, it is worth adding, can be justified or not, regardless of whether the community that resides on them is governed democratically. The appropriate procedures and principles for delineating the boundaries between territories are distinct from those that define who the people who merit full inclusion are. Leaving aside the question of identifying a state's legitimate physical boundaries, in this book, I am concerned with when those who are *on* a particular territory are entitled to be treated as full and equal members of the community that resides on that territory. This question emerges for the obvious reason that there are many individuals on a territory at any one time who are not "full and equal members" of the people; tourists to a state are perhaps the most obvious example here. But, and this commitment runs through this book, it is of vital importance that the boundaries of a political community are inclusive in the right way. In what follows I will defend the claim that the all-subjected principle is well-suited to explain who ought to be treated as full and equal members of a political community.

It is a familiar claim in democratic political theory that the people should rule themselves. It is just as familiar to point out, however, that before the people can rule themselves, the relevant collection of individuals who will be called "the people" must be identified. In principle, it ought to be the case that a democratic procedure identifies the relevant people—but, it seems, the proposal to use a democratic procedure to determine who the people are requires that the people who are permitted to participate in this procecure are already identified. This difficulty is called the democratic boundary *problem*, and is described by David Miller as follows: there is no "non-circular way of using a democratic procedure to settle boundary issues" (Miller 2016a, 48). In an attempt to resolve the problem, democratic theorists have turned to alternative principles, which are consistent with or derived from democratic commitments, as a way to explain who should be included in the demos and, thereby, who should be excluded. Two answers, both of which admit of many variations, are generally proposed: the all-affected principle and the all-subjected principle.[1]

In broad terms, the all-subjected principle says that where one is subject to—that is, bound by—a set of decisions made by a collective authority over an extended period of time, one is thereby entitled to a say in what these decisions are, including in particular with respect to who is elected to positions of power. To be bound by a set of decisions is to be required to abide by them, under threat of legal penalty. As advocates of the all-subjected principle observe, to be subjected by a law under threat of penalty is a violation of freedom.[2] The only way that this freedom violation can be rendered permissible is if those who are subjected to the law are offered a justification for it that they can reasonably accept. How can we know if a given justification is acceptable and, indeed, accepted? For advocates of the all-subjected principle, the answer is by granting those who are subjected to the laws a say in what they are, thereby giving them space to question the proposed justifications for laws and to object to those laws and propose others, if they find that these justifications are insufficient.

The all-subjected principle constrains the set of people who are entitled to inclusion to those who are subjected as I have described it above. By contrast, the all-affected principle states that all those who are affected by a given policy choice, including those likely or possibly affected, ought to have a say, both in decision-making procedures and in agenda-setting forums. There is strong, intuitive plausibility to the claim that where one's interests are affected by or are likely or even possibly affected by a given decision, one should be entitled not only to express one's view on the relevant decision, but to do so in the relevant decision-making forum. Choices made in one jurisdiction often have a real impact on other jurisdictions, and according to its defenders, the all-affected principle offers appropriate guidance for how to manage this impact in a democratic way. Its defenders celebrate the radically inclusive implications of adopting such a view by arguing that its logical conclusion must be some form of world government (Goodin 2007), and also that this conclusion is appropriate given increasing global interconnectedness. In response to skepticism that "mere" affect is sufficient to generate a right to have a say in the relevant decision-making forum, some propose a proportionality principle, dictating that the extent of one's "say" should correlate with how affected one is likely to be by specific decisions.

In the debates between those who advocate for the all-affected principle and those who advocate for the all-subjected principle, much hinges on how subjection is distinguished from affect. A skeptic might deny the difference, for example, by saying that to be subject to a law or authority just is one way to be affected by it; thus, the terms should be treated as more or less equivalent, morally speaking. Perhaps, the skeptic says, affect and subjection are distinguished mainly by subjection being a very important form of affect.[3] Indeed, I do not really intend to dispute this sort of an objection, as the parsing of the distinction matters less than does identifying a set of features that help to identify the kind of experience—what I am terming subjection—that requires political inclusion.

Coercion is also difficult to distinguish precisely from subjection, and indeed the two concepts sometimes appear to run together. For example, when Arash Abizadeh proposes that border coercion requires justification to those who are subject to it, he explains that "[t]he Principle of Democratic Legitimacy is true (in part) because of the truth of the Coercion Claim, that is, those subject to the state's laws have a right of democratic participation because such laws subject them to coercion" (Abizadeh 2010, 121). Similarly, Sarah Song defines the coercion principle as "all those subject to binding collective decisions should have a say in the making of those decisions"; those who must abide by such collective decisions can be described as "being subject to state coercion" (Song 2012, 50). This usage conflates coercion and subjection, but these concepts should be distinguished in the following way. Coercion is a violation of freedom where, using threats of force or violence, one agent attempts either to stop another from doing something she would otherwise do, or to force someone to do something she would not otherwise do (for more, see Anderson 2021). So, coercion, at least as I will use it in what follows, is reserved for individual instances, as, for example, in the case of an individual who is mugged at gunpoint (see also Bender 2021, 60).

Where one is subject to coercion on a more general scale, as in the case of citizens and residents of a territory who are part of a "coercive network of state governance" (Blake 2001, 258), the language of "subjection" is appropriate. As I said earlier, citizens and residents of a state are properly described as *subjected* to state power, where they are subject to a wide range of laws and regulations over the course of their day-to-day lives, with which they are expected to abide, and where state representatives have the power to enforce compliance, when it is not willingly offered, with these laws and regulations. The expectation of willing compliance adds a normative dimension to subjection, which is not present in cases of coercion.[4] Those who are subjected are expected to follow the rules and regulations. Ideally, they would do so more or less willingly, rather than as a result of a threat or force.

Crucially, as I conceive it here, the experience of subjection is *life-shaping*: subjection "actually shapes a person's life by opening up (and protecting) options they might choose while shutting off others" (Miller 2020, 5). Where people are subjected, they are subject in particular to an institutional environment that provides the contours in which people live their lives.[5] Will Kymlicka describes a "societal culture" in just this life-shaping sort of way: a societal culture, he says, "provides its members with meaningful ways of life across the full range of human activities, including social, educational, religious, recreational and economic life, encompassing both public and private spheres" (Kymlicka 1996, 76). The lives of citizens and long-term residents are shaped in profound ways by the economic, social, and political institutions that govern a particular territorial jurisdiction. The choices citizens and residents make are shaped by whether childcare is accessible and available, whether health care is provided on a universal basis or purchased in the private market, whether public transportation is affordable and available, whether political leaders are chosen by first-past-the-post electoral systems or via proportional representation, and so on. These are the formal *institutions* that shape the choices citizens and residents make, both on a day-to-day basis and on a longer-term basis.

On a longer-term basis, the norms and values that characterize a jurisdiction are also life-shaping, norms and values that I have elsewhere described as a "shared public culture" (Lenard 2007; Scheffler 2007; Festenstein 2005). The content of these norms and values is contested, and the commitment to them by residents and citizens varies substantially—among political theorists, there is ongoing debate focused on whether it is good or bad that jurisdictions are defined by a shared public culture and how such a culture can or should be imparted to newcomers; I will return to this question in the final chapter of this book (but see Gustavsson and Miller 2020). It is helpful, though, to see that tourists and short-term visitors participate in the variety of norms that are specific to a jurisdiction to "experience the culture," for example, by dining late in Spain, by adopting local norms with respect to boarding buses and trains, by saying hello and thank you in the local language, and so on. These norms and values shape the lives of citizens and long-term residents nearly as much as do the formal institutions I described earlier.

The suggestion that informal norms and values are also subjecting may seem unexpected, but a failure to adopt the norms and values of a particular jurisdiction can produce penalties of various kinds, some of which are relatively minor but others of which can be more substantial. Newcomers for example must learn the norms associated with job seeking, ranging from resume preparation to interview skills, and the failure to do so can make it harder to find work. I highlight the informal norms stemming from a public culture not to evaluate their merits (political theorists disagree on their merits) but to identify that they are present and, for long-term residents and citizens, they are life-shaping. One might object that the subjection that is central to state power is not equivalent to the subjection generated by the presence of an informal and diffuse public culture because, among other things, it is only the failure to conform to state rules and regulations that carries the threat of legal penalties. However, although not a legal penalty, the threat of social ostracism for failing to conform to dominant norms and values is also life-shaping; and so, just as do formal institutions, the shared public culture *subjects* citizens and residents in profound ways. In later chapters, I will demonstrate in some detail the ways in which cultural norms and values operate to subject newcomers.

To be life-shaping, the subjection—to both formal institutions and to norms and values—must extend "systematically" over a substantial period of time (Erman 2014, 536), with the expectation that this subjection will continue into the future. One can be required to follow a particular law or set of laws for a short time, for example if one is visiting a country. But subjection—in the sense adopted by those who defend an all-subjected principle—is not a really temporary condition. Tourists are required to abide by the laws of the countries they visit, and their willingness to do so is in part the basis on which they are granted the right to enter in the first place. But it is false to say that tourists' lives are shaped by this voluntary acceptance of the temporary requirement to follow a state's laws; rather, their lives are affected and even coerced by it. The laws in the state that is hosting a tourist are relevant to her; they apply to her for the duration of her visit, and in that sense affect her. If she chooses to violate the laws while visiting, the state will coerce her to comply or inflict punishment for her failure to do so. Some may think that tourists are subject to laws in ways that grant them the rights the all-subjected principle promises to deliver, perhaps to show that the all-subjected principle does not work, but that idea contains an error. Namely, the rules and regulations that tourists are required to accept as a condition of their entry is largely legal (i.e., formal) and very short-term. But to be subjected, as I described earlier citing Will Kymlicka's account of a societal culture, is not simply to be required to abide by the law on threat of legal penalty, as sometimes appears to be suggested by advocates of the all-subjected principle; to be subjected is to find one's life shaped by a range of legal and policy choices that apply across a range of formal institutions and which impact the norms and values that shape interactions among citizens and residents of a particular jurisdiction.

One way to know if subjection is life-shaping in the right way is by considering how long one is subjected, although focusing only on time may not seem sufficient to distinguish the tourist from someone who is subjected. One reason to think seriously about what counts as "long enough" is that some people enter a country as tourists or other forms of temporary visitors, with the intent to stay on once their visa expires. What if such an individual manages to evade authorities and therefore deportation for a long enough time that she meets the "extended period of time" criterion I have attached to the notion of subjection? This question is important, and indeed many of the scholars who have defended the all-subjected principle have done so with the explicit intent of offering reasons to think that such non-status individuals—people who do not possess a legal right to reside, but who are nevertheless long-term residents of a territory—are, at some point, entitled to join the political community on fair and equal terms, even though a violation of admission regulations has taken place (Bosniak 2020; Song 2016). It is their *subjection*, over time, that gives rise to this right; gradually, they move from being merely affected by, and instead subject to, the laws and regulations in a state. In what follows, I will agree with this general argument, that those who are subjected over time are entitled to a range of rights and privileges (I will clarify what these are, below). But it is right to consider in some more depth how "enough time" can be determined, in a way that helpfully distinguishes between those who remain temporarily affected by a state's legal authority and those who are rightfully described as subjected to, well, life-shaping subjection.

The emphasis on "enough time" as a key component of subjection will be unsatisfactory to those who are seeking a concept that can explain why those who are abroad, and who have no hope of arriving "here," may be entitled to entry. Such individuals cannot avail themselves of a principle of subjection and thereby gain access to the rights that are thereby entailed (I consider what rights these might be in the following section); in Chapter 5, I consider the justice of the mechanisms by which visas are issued, which is the central legal way by which migrants can place themselves under the subjection of a state. In the case of thwarted would-be migrants, while the denial of migration options has a profound impact on their lives—one for which they are entitled to some sort plausible and appropriate justification (Abizadeh 2008)—the resolution is *not* full inclusion, as it will be in the cases that occupy me in this book, where lives are shaped by a robust institutional environment that enables and constrains choices across a wide range of domains. This way of treating subjection will not be perfectly satisfactory—and as the Introduction to this book highlighted, the global migration regime is in profound ways unjust.

I agree that denial of entry is an impactful moment, but one that is better described as "life-changing" rather than life-shaping. Many individuals have experiences that they describe personally as life-changing, for example, falling in love, having a child, or being diagnosed with a life-threatening illness. These personal experiences alter the direction of one's life in substantial ways: they can be significant and, therefore, life-changing. Interactions with other individuals or institutional agents can be life-changing as well, and not always in a good way. Migrants who are detained for extended periods of time in states that are not their own describe the experience as life-changing; the trauma of detention can have long-lasting impacts on the mental and physical well-being of detainees (Nethery and Silverman 2015). Where life-changing experiences are the result of unjustified coercion, as, for example, where migrants are detained without reasonable cause, they are owed compensation of some kind. There may even be cases where full inclusion is warranted—migrants detained for extended periods of time may well be entitled to full inclusion in the detaining state for compensatory reasons. The general point is simply that a significant and unambiguously life-changing experience is not sufficient to count as *subjection*. Some life-changing experiences can be significant, and some may require redress, without requiring full inclusion. The challenge is in identifying when and where an alternative form of redress is morally appropriate, and the line will not be a neat one.

However, I hope nevertheless that the account of subjection as life-shaping will helpfully advance the conversation with respect to how to identify those who are genuinely subjected to a state power, and what rights and entitlements are thereby owed to them. The key question will be whether an individual's life is subjected in a comprehensive and long-term way to a set of laws and policies, which govern a wide range of social, economic, and political institutions. Having offered some guidance to identify *who* is subjected in the right way to a particular legal and political jurisdiction's coercive authority, to what are they then entitled? I turn to that question next.

What Are Subjects Entitled To?

One proposal is that subjected individuals are entitled to justification for that subjection. On this view, subjection is a problematic violation of personal autonomy, unless it can be reasonably justified to those who are, in fact, subjected. As Sarah Song characterizes this view, "subjection triggers justification": "what triggers the need for justification is that one is bound by or subject to the collective decision" (Song 2012, 50).

However, for democratic theorists who are focused on the nature of subjection, it is not sufficient that decision-makers offer justification. A second proposal is that, in light of subjection, there must additionally be a mechanism by which those who are subject are able to engage with that justification in some way, e.g., to object to it as insufficient to justify the relevant subjection. So, those who are subjected are entitled to access some sort of deliberative political process, in which those who are liable to subjection can participate, and in which the reasons for and against the proposed subjection can be publicly weighed and accepted or rejected.

One way this participation is described is in terms of having a "say" in the political decisions to which one is subject. For example, Sofia Näaström describes that "all those subjected to political rule within its [the state's] boundaries ought to have a say in its making" (Näsström 2011, 117). The precise meaning of "a say" is ambiguous, but one interpretation is, simply, as the vote. Although Robert Goodin does not endorse the principle himself, he writes that "proponents of the All Subjected Principle hope that, by extending the franchise to . . . only those who will be *subject* to the laws of that jurisdiction, they can justify keeping the franchise broadly within its conventional bounds" (Goodin 2016, 368). Others adopt a more an expansive interpretation of "a say." For Abizadeh, for example, "all those subjected to the exercise of political power [must] be included in the demos, that is, granted a right of democratic say over political decisions" (Abizadeh 2012, 878). Elsewhere, he explains that on his view, the procedure of justification transpires via political participation, which in turn ought to be understood as whatever is "required for persons to be able to see themselves as the free and equal authors of the laws to which they are subject" (Abizadeh 2008, 41). Ludvig Beckman, in a dissection of the many possible ways to understand who is subject to a set of binding laws, assumes that once the "subjects" have been successfully identified, they are entitled to not merely the franchise, but also to a broader cluster of "participatory rights" in the making of laws (Beckman 2014, 257). These participatory rights include the right to vote and to run for elected office, as well as the range of actions that constitute political participation, including the rights to associate, speak freely, mobilize, raise money for political candidates, and lobby political actors. Of these latter, it is worth noting that most are among the most basic of human rights, and thereby not granted on the basis of subjection in particular.

Political theorists sometimes characterize the political entitlements that flow from subjection, very slightly differently, in terms of "inclusion." Usually, where emphasis is placed on inclusion as the entitlement that flows from subjection, inclusion is interpreted in practice to mean access to the set of political rights described above. In his account of subjection, for example, David Miller writes of the subjection that "gives rise to a claim for political inclusion" (Miller 2020, 5), and then continues, "once we have a decision-making body with the power to enforce its decisions over a particular area, we can ask who is and who is not subjected to those decisions and therefore has a right to be enfranchised" (Miller 2020, 5), and similarly that "being coerced by a demos does generate a claim for inclusion" (Miller 2009, 221). When Sofia Näsström characterizes the all-subjected principle, citing Robert Dahl's earlier formulation, she notes his observation that the demos must *include* all relevant adults, and then interprets this inclusion by making the following statement: "This proposition—that all persons subject to rule should have a democratic voice at their disposal—is what we henceforth shall refer to as the all-subjected principle" (Näsström 2011, 119). And, in her critique of current accounts of the all-subjected principle, Eva Erman notices that to have a say is not necessarily sufficient to ensure that one's say is meaningful and argues instead that the all-subjected principle entitles subjects to "equal influence" over binding decisions. The equal influence principle that she endorses is that, "all those who are systematically and over time subjected to the exercise of political power (authority) and to its laws, political decisions and rules, should systematically and over time have an equal influence in the decision-making" (Erman 2014, 536).

In summary, advocates of the all-subjected principle typically argue that subjection entitles subjects to some form of inclusion, usually spelled out with respect to participatory democratic rights, understood most frequently in terms of access to the vote for political representatives. Often, there is an assumption that these participatory democratic rights travel *with* citizenship—and thereby that in arguing for the right to vote, one is also arguing that the state must provide citizenship to a would-be voter. But such is not always the case; rather, many of the scholars who defend the connection between subjection and the right to vote are attempting to move away from conventional views of democracy that simply tie voting to citizenship status.

I am in strong agreement that subjection ought to translate into political rights, broadly understood, and including the right to vote. I agree, in other words, that it is appropriate to sever the connection between citizenship and franchise; there are cases where it may be permissible to extend the franchise but *not* citizenship to certain residents of a state, and similarly where it may be permissible to deny citizens (generally, who are abroad for long periods of time, as I will suggest in Chapter 3) the right to vote (see the contributions to Bauböck and Orgad 2019). Indeed, there is some indication of a global trend towards extending the franchise towards residents of a state under some conditions. For example, the Maastricht Treaty in Europe granted all residents of a state, of European origin, the right to vote in local elections in their state of residence (even where they are citizens of a different European state). Some Commonwealth citizens are permitted the right to vote in local and even national elections in the United Kingdom without gaining citizenship status.[6] In Canada and the United States, there have been largely unsuccessful attempts to extend at least municipal voting rights to permanent residents (Lenard and Munro 2012; Hayduk 2006), although in December 2021, New York City's city council voted to extend local voting rights to legal non-citizens residents (Mena 2021). Granting long-term non-citizen residents the right to vote in at least local elections is spreading, on the broad idea that *residence* rather than citizenship can be sufficient to generate the right to have a say in at least a subset of issues that are relevant to residents as well as citizens (Bauböck and Orgad 2019; Pedroza 2019).[7] I, too, have defended this severing, and especially its radical implication—if residence is the relevant basis for the vote, then, for example, temporary foreign labor migrants may become entitled to participate in the vote, even if they genuinely intend to remain in their state of residence only on a temporary basis (Lenard 2014; for an alternative view, see de-Shalit 2019).

It is certain that granting the (limited) right to vote offers some protection to those who gain access to it. Ultimately, however, granting the franchise, or even more extensive political rights, is not as protective as its advocates hope, for two related reasons. One reason is that the right to vote is part of a bundle of rights that work together to protect citizens from the harms of subjection, and it cannot easily be severed, or disaggregated, from those other rights (Celikates 2013). The meaningful exercise of the franchise requires not only the protection of a wide range of other rights, including the right to associate and to speak and think freely, it also requires that other material conditions are in place to enable would-be voters the time to assess options, communicate with potential representatives, and so on (Verba, Schlozman, and Brady 1995). A second reason is that to be even minimally protective, a voter must *feel* free to exercise her vote in line with her preferences. While it may be the case that enfranchised non-citizens gain some value from being able to vote in elections that may impact their lives in substantial ways, there are also reasons to believe that residents who are not secure in their right to stay permanently may not feel free to vote or participate more generally as they wish, for fear of reprisals taken in the form of exclusion from the territory.

The fear that voting "wrongly" will result in exclusion from territory is revealing. In particular, it suggests that granting non-citizens access to the vote, while valuable, may be insufficiently protective for subjected non-citizen residents. A too-narrow focus on granting the right to vote makes the mistake of failing to take serious account of who is at greatest risk of the harms of subjection and especially what they fear most. While the political theory debate that is focused on answering *who* makes up the people is aimed at delineating the appropriate boundaries of the political community, those who are at risk of exclusion are not worried about whether they can vote and thus have a say in the political decisions that affect their lives, but rather whether they can be excluded from those boundaries, without their consent, and without meaningful redress of any kind.

They would therefore not be satisfied with Rainer Bauböck's proposal. According to Bauböck's pluralist account of democratic inclusion, subjection grounds a claim to equal protection rights, but not obviously the right to vote. He says, "those who are subject to the jurisdiction of a polity have a democratic claim to equal protection under the law," and as such may have "a right to contest" the decisions made within that polity—short of the right to vote (Bauböck 2018b, 20, 49). Such individuals are distinct from those who "have a legitimate stake in participating in the self-government of a particular polity [and] have a democratic claim to be recognized as citizens," including not only the right to contest political decisions but also, crucially, the right to vote for political representatives (Bauböck 2018b, 20).

Most advocates of the all-subjected principle are, at base, worried about the freedom violations that stem from unjustified subjection. For them, political participation rights operate largely to compensate for them, by giving those who are subjected the right to defend or contest the violations and the justifications for them. Bauböck's move shifts away from this emphasis, towards a focus on the critical role that states play in protecting the rights of residents and citizens. This point is important, and one that I too wish to make. For Bauböck, and for me, the appropriate emphasis is rather on the protective role the state plays with respect to rights and entitlements; and so, *subjection* to state power is justified only where, as well, states take their protection job seriously.

Where Bauböck goes wrong, however, is in his insistence that subjection translates only to the rights of political contestation, a set of limited democratic participation rights that includes neither the right to vote nor the right to run for political office. For Bauböck, subjection does not translate into the right to access the very citizenship status that is required to ensure that rights are genuinely protected on an equal basis. Without citizenship status, subjected residents cannot fully protect themselves from the harms that subjection can generate; instead they are forced to hope that the state will protect them sufficiently. But, in my view, it is citizenship status that ensures that, well, citizens can themselves act in political spaces so as to secure the protection of their own rights. Insisting that subjection does not give rise to the right to citizenship, or even the right to vote, is a mistake, because of the way in which it fails to respond to the worries of those who are subjected—that they must rely on others for their rights protection rather than themselves.[8]

So, while I agree that long-term, life-shaping subjection to the formal institutions and informal public culture that together govern a state gives rise to an entitlement to political rights, it is my view that such subjection gives rise, as well, to an entitlement to *stay*. Without the entitlement to stay, the associated political rights cannot do the protective work that advocates of the all-subjected principle desire. So, to repeat, it is morally appropriate to extend political participation rights to all those who are subject to state power, certainly; it follows from the subjection associated with long-term residence that political participatory rights, including the right to vote, ought to be granted. But because political participation rights can be, and indeed in many cases ought to be, severed from citizenship status, the proposed response to subjection, in the form of political participation rights, does not capture what those who are subjected require protection *from*, which is forced exclusion from their preferred state of long-term residence.

The importance of protection against forced exclusion stems from the moral relevance of residence, and in particular the importance of protecting its security. Residence, to be residence, extends over time. During that time residents are subjected to the laws of a state, and the structure of these laws has a significant impact on the shape of residents' lives, as I have already described (Carens 2010a). Over time, they build their lives in substantial ways in the place where they reside, and in response to the opportunities that are available there; over time, unwanted disruptions from their place of preferred residence become increasingly costly to them. So, when someone is subject to forced exclusion from a territory in which they reside, their lives are upended and their interests are substantially set back. Granting the right to vote, as an entitlement in virtue of subjection, has some value, but it does little to protect the residential security that non-resident citizens seek. I will return to this observation in Chapter 2, where I consider the harms of deportation, which only citizens can be sure to avoid.

Concluding Thoughts

To summarize the view that I have defended above, and which I will flesh out in the coming chapters, subjection entitles subjects to protection against forced exclusion, on the grounds that residential security is of deep moral importance, and it is the state that is responsible for ensuring this protection. In most cases, the practical effects of this statement are, first, that subjection generates rights to political participation (including the right to vote), and second, to a right against forced exclusion; the latter is necessary to protect the capacity to deploy the former. That is to say, while I am in agreement that subjection cannot be justified without access to fair and equal participation rights, protection against forced exclusion is a normatively prior and more important entitlement of those who are subjected to state power. In the next chapter, I consider the harms of deporting long-term residents, to notice that it is *citizenship status* that best protects against forced exclusion. Because political participation can, in some cases, permissibly be severed from citizenship (and often should be), and because political participation does not guarantee the protection of those who are subjected to state power, subjection requires the granting of citizenship, followed by a commitment to supporting the development of equality of respect that attends this status.

Characterizing the entitlements of subjection as I do, in terms of protecting the rights of all residents, captures another reality—those who are at risk of exclusion, or who are victims of subjection without sufficient rights protection, are also least likely to be able to effectively use political participation rights as a way to protect themselves. That is to say, whereas I am in agreement with Eva Erman that it is crucial to protect the right of individuals to an equal influence over the political conditions that shape their lives, many of those who are subjected will not easily be able to use political participation rights to protect themselves in a substantive way. They require prior protection, which cannot be assumed to travel with political influence, against forced exclusion. So, while the all-subjected principle offers a principled justification for granting political rights to those who are subjected, it *also* and quite distinctly requires that such individuals are entitled to protection against forced exclusion. Because this protection can only be guaranteed by the status of citizenship, as I will argue in Chapter 2, and because citizenship status in democratic states typically travels with the right to vote, the result is that those who are subjected will gain access to political participation rights because they gain access to citizenship. But this connection is not necessary, in the sense that political participation rights, including the right to vote, can be extended to many who remain at risk of forced exclusion. What people who are subjected are entitled to, however, is the protection against the latter, in the form of access to citizenship status, which in turn permits the free and effective use of political rights.

In the chapters that follow, I focus on specific cases of exclusion, and deploy the concept of subjection—as life-shaping, over an extended period of time—to illuminate key moral questions and to inform morally appropriate policy responses to a whole range of dilemmas that emerge in diverse, democratic, states. One of the key contributions of this book is an examination of the hard cases generated by the combination of a belief in the state's right to exclude, in at least some situations, and the reality that there are cases where exercising that right is unjust. In general, the overarching theoretical claim in the book is that it is subjection that justifies a right *against* forced exclusion—that is, subjection justifies a right *to* residential security in the form of citizenship status—so that where subjection as I have defined it characterizes the relation between state and citizen or non-citizen, exclusion from territory or from membership is unjust.

2
Deportation and the Excluded Undeportable

In Chapter 1, I made the case that ongoing, life-shaping *subjection* to coercive law is at the source of the right to citizenship. The main point was that attention to the lived experience of subjection is a good guide to identifying who is entitled to the permanent right to stay in the form of citizenship. In this chapter I focus on if and when those who are not yet citizens can be rightfully deported from the territory to an alleged "home" country. Deportation is the forced, involuntary removal of individuals from the territory on which they are located, and on which they are often residing—in some cases, for many years. The right to deport is typically treated as a legitimate part of an immigration regime, for reasons I will elaborate in the first section of this chapter. I will then examine several reasons to think that deportation ought to be treated, in general, as a harm to be avoided where it can be. In a final section, I consider what these arguments against the widespread use of deportation mean for the conditions that face stateless peoples. In particular, the fact of stateless peoples—and the widespread awareness that the wrong they face is the lack of a state to protect their rights—demonstrates that immunity from the risk of deportation is not the only benefit offered by citizenship status. And so, through a consideration of what is owed to stateless peoples, I add to my account of citizenship as a status that protects its holders first from exclusion from territory and second from exclusion from membership.

Deportation and Border Control

In the abstract, it makes sense that states would claim the right to deport irregularly present migrants. If it is fair and legitimate that states control their borders, as many scholars believe—even if they must adopt policies that are consonant with key principles of justice to do so legitimately—then the right to deport those who manage to circumvent such policies appears to be an obvious and logical consequence of that right. Border control is, for one thing, imperfect; some people whom the state has deemed inadmissible, or who would struggle to produce legal documentation testifying to their admissibility, nevertheless gain entry by irregular means, for example by crossing into states at unmonitored parts of a border, or with support from smugglers. As well, many of those who gain legal entry at a border are issued temporary visas, which their holders allow to expire, so their territorial presence transitions at some point from lawful to unlawful. So, assuming for now that states have the right to develop and implement immigration admission policies, even if their choices are constrained by certain justice requirements, it seems reasonable to believe that they also possess the right to enforce them. And, if the implementation of admission policies at the border is imperfect, then it seems at least plausible that deportation, in at least some cases, is a right that states possess; it is a right that is derivative of their right to control borders in the first place. The distinction I have drawn here is between immigration admission policies and immigration *enforcement* policies; deportation is among the latter (Mendoza 2015; Sager 2017; Hidalgo 2019).

In the introduction to this book, I outlined the five basic principles that constrain the choices that states can make with respect to immigration policies, and they apply as well to the right to enforce such policies. Any enforcement undertaken by states in pursuit of border control must avoid discrimination and refoulement, and it must respect the right of long-term residents to stay, including especially where doing otherwise would break up families and separate children from their primary caregivers. There is more to say about what constrains enforcement policy, however: even if immigration policies themselves conform to the minimum requirements I have outlined, their enforcement cannot be pursued by any means desired. The pursuit of immigration enforcement is additionally constrained by a commitment to basic human rights more generally. If enforcement requires violating these, then the enforcement is not permitted, even if more generally it is agreed that (non-human-rights-violating) enforcement is.

Why is this statement important to clarify? One reason is beautifully explained in Ayelet Shachar's *The Shifting Border*, which in gruesome detail articulates the surveillance and violence to which especially asylum seekers (but also desperately poor migrants) are subject as they attempt to access safety (Shachar 2020). Shachar proposes that, at any moment where an entity assumes the right to control and coerce migrants, that same entity ought to be treated as in "effective control" of the relevant migrants and therefore also as responsible for the protection of their human rights. A second reason is that those who are charged with enforcing border control regularly violate the human rights of those whom they target. Considerable data suggest that rights violations are common elements of immigration enforcement: those whose status is questioned by law enforcement are the victims of racial profiling; legally present residents who cannot demonstrate their status to the satisfaction of law enforcement are unjustly detained, sometimes for extended periods of time; and migrants die in detention and during the process of deportation (Cohen 2020; Bowcott 2010; Menjívar, Cervantes, and Alvord 2018). In the face of evidence of persistent human rights violations during the process of immigration enforcement, Alex Sager has suggested that no enforcement regime appears able to function without human right violations—for him, that enforcement always violates human rights is a reason to defend borders that are as open as possible (Sager 2017). In the next section, I will focus in some detail on the range of harms generated by deportation in particular, but I will conclude nevertheless—against Sager—that deportation can be conducted while protecting human rights, at least in a small set of cases.

The Harms of Deportation

By definition, deportation is involuntary and, often, forced. Leaving aside for just a moment the question of whether deportation is permissible in general, or only in a small number of cases, being deported is always at minimum a setback of interests or plans for those who are deported. The involuntary aspect of deportation sets it apart, at least in principle, from so-called voluntary repatriation, where states support migrants with various statuses to return to their home state. European states in particular have experimented with encouraging irregularly present migrants, as well as failed asylum seekers, to return "home" by offering various incentives, including money and other material goods (Kalir 2017; Leerkes, van Os, and Boersema 2017; Kalicki 2020). Voluntary repatriation is sometimes thought to be the preferred option for refugees as well—if they have sought, and been granted, asylum in a state on a temporary basis, the status is sometimes granted up until it is reasonably safe for them to return home. Scholars of repatriation have well-documented that repatriation is not always as voluntary as political theorists might like, and it often enters into the realm of the coercive (Bradley 2008, 2013). Mollie

Gerver documents, for example, the "voluntary" return of migrants in Israel, who *choose* to return only because Israel threatens them with prolonged detention as an alternative (Gerver 2018). In some such cases, for example where migrants would return home to severe insecurity and poverty, their "choice" to return home is properly understood as coerced—it is deportation in all but name.

Political theorists have identified at least three distinct reasons to think that deportation is harmful and therefore, all things equal, should be avoided. All these reasons focus on the deportation of relatively long-term residents, rather than people who are turned away at the border or those who have recently crossed the border. I too will follow this convention of focusing on those who have been resident for some time and acknowledge that identifying the moment at which someone becomes a "long-term" resident is a complicated one, which I considered in Chapter 1. The reason to focus on those who are long-term residents is that these individuals have made lives for themselves—they have jobs, they care for families, they have social connections, all of which are severely disrupted if they are deported.

One reason to resist deportation highlights the harm of deportation itself. Barbara Buckinx and Alexandra Filindra suggest that the right not to be harmed—*jus noci*—explains why deportation should be avoided, where it can be. Deportation generates a whole range of harms, including social, economic, and psychological, especially for long-term and well-integrated residents, and the harm is especially acute for such individuals, not only because their lives will be disrupted, but also because they are likely to struggle to reintegrate into their "home" countries[1] in the event of deportation. So, their account focuses not simply on the harms of deportation itself—an act that can cut deportees off from their economic livelihood and the social relations that matter most to them—but also emphasizes the challenging experiences that a deported individual would face upon return "home" (Buckinx and Filindra 2015). Correspondingly, for Buckinx and Filindra, those who are not likely to experience substantial harm in the event of deportation can be permissibly deported, even if they would prefer to remain (Buckinx and Filindra 2015, 408).

A second reason to resist deportation as much as possible emphasizes the specifically psychological harm caused by the persistent *threat* of deportation. This claim is at the center of Antje Ellerman's argument in favor of regularizing the status of long-term irregular migrants. Ellerman points to the principle of legal certainty, which she says recognizes the right of individuals to "make long-term plans for their lives by requiring that state action be reasonably predictable and nonarbitrary" (Ellerman 2014, 294). This principle is at the foundation of the widespread commitment to "statutes of limitations" in the case of the vast majority of crimes—such statutes, which set a time limit on how long the state has to prosecute a particular crime, allow for people to make "long-term plans for their lives" and also to "demand that the state cut its losses and accept the consequences of its failure to act in a timely manner" (Ellerman 2014, 294). Such a time limit should also apply to the state's right to deport those who are present without status. Like Buckinx and Filindra, Ellerman is especially worried about those who are long-term residents of a state, for whom deportation would represent a substantial hardship. But she additionally worries that an emphasis on the harms to those who are well-integrated (rather than simply those who are present over the long-term) encourages an assessment of would-be deportees according to unfairly subjective metrics of what counts as integration, an assessment that can harm those who do not seem to meet the standards at the core of such assessments. Rather, says Ellerman, the harm of deportation stems from its arbitrariness, which imposes a harmful psychological burden on those who remain subject to it, at least in principle.[2] Constant threats to one's right to stay generate "existential insecurity" among migrants who must live with the worry that at any moment their lives will be upended (Ellerman 2014, 301).

The arbitrariness that worries Ellerman stems from multiple sources. I mentioned one source of deportation's arbitrariness earlier, that the wrong of irregular presence—usually associated with irregular entry or a visa expiration—is not subject to a statute of limitation as is the case for most other wrong-doing, and so those who are irregularly present are persistently threatened with deportation. In the United States in particular, the arbitrariness has a second source, namely, the rapid movement between the "blind eye" that is often turned towards irregularly present migrants, whose economic contributions are widely valued, and the aggressive pursuit of deportation of irregular migrants or some specific categories of them, including in particular those with a criminal record (Ellerman 2014, 300). Evidence for the blind eye strategy is in the numbers of deportees as a percentage of irregularly present migrants in the United States: at least in 2014, those without a criminal record faced a 0.8 percent chance of deportation per year. Whereas former President Donald Trump celebrated his successes in deporting irregular migrants (Department of Homeland Security 2017), the rates of deportation plummeted after the election of President Joe Biden, who is so far responsible for a record low number of deportations ("Lowering the Bar" 2021). Ellerman argues that the low rate of deportation represents a decision by the US state to allow employers to rely on irregular migrants, rather than its inability to identify those who (at least according to US law) are eligible for deportation (Ellerman 2014, 300). The "low probability" of deportation, alongside the unpredictability of the state's choice to aggressively pursue some (mainly with criminal records) irregular migrants for deportation together amount to a violation of the principle of legal certainty that ought to justify the regularization of long-term residents rather than sustain their liability to deportation (Bouie 2018; Youn 2019).[3]

A third reason to resist deportation as a strategy of immigration control is that its pursuit encourages racial profiling in ways that are especially harmful to legally present minorities, whether or not they have immigrant origins. In the United States, and more generally, both legal and irregular immigrants are often visible minorities, and the search for those who are irregular results in attention being directed at visible minorities *in general*. The impact of this additional attention is to reduce not only the subjective experience of security among visible minorities, who learn that their very appearance triggers suspicion. It also teaches them that they are viewed as in some ways outside of, or threatening to, the integrity of the state that has admitted them and in which they are a citizen or long-term resident. In her account of the dramatic immigration enforcement efforts taken by the United States, historically and also currently, Elizabeth Cohen details the number of American citizens who are approached by border enforcement agencies to prove their right to be present in the United States, and a smaller although not inconsequential number of citizens who cannot do so to the satisfaction of such authorities, who then find themselves mistakenly deported and struggle to return home (Cohen 2020).

Moreover, and as is well-documented, border enforcement authorities are often aggressive and threatening, and sometimes violent, towards those they target for questioning (Borger 2021). These facts together should warn against the use of deportation—and the targeting of visible minorities that often precedes it[4]—on the grounds that it encourages and permeates discriminatory treatment of minority residents and citizens, regardless of whether they have migratory backgrounds. This objection, that the permissive use of deportation in effect enables racial profiling, is not an argument against deportation itself, but rather to its mode of implementation (Lever

2016); it is in principle possible for citizens and residents of a community to be asked to provide evidence of their legal status without deploying aggression and violence, and without racial profiling to identify who can permissibly be asked to provide such evidence. For those who leave some room for permissible deportation, it is important that carrying it out is done in ways that are respectful of basic human rights, and with a recognition that its negative impacts will be felt not only by those who are deported but also by those who share visible characteristics with those who are deported. The importance of respectful deportation applies equally to those who are long-term residents and to those who have recently crossed the border (and those who have been turned away at the border itself).

These three reasons work together to warn against the liberal use of deportation as a strategy to control borders. Whatever the specific harm of deportation—whether it is located in the economic and social costs to would be deportees, the psychological harm of being persistently subject to the arbitrary deployment of power, or in the apparent permission it gives to those who identify potential deportees to engage in racial profiling—it undermines the residential security that, I argued in Chapter 1, is the first and most important benefit of citizenship status itself. Citizens are not liable to deportation, that is, to involuntary or forced exclusion from the territory on which they prefer to reside; so, at the risk of stating the obvious, one good way to protect irregular migrants from the harms of deportation is to grant them at least long-term residence visas, if not citizenship.

Among those scholars who object to deportation and who defend a right to stay, there is a notable reluctance to argue that the moral obligation to grant citizenship status thereby follows, however. Instead, many scholars defend what in my view is a "lesser" right to stay. The right to stay is just as it sounds: it is a right to remain resident on the territory in which one has made a life, without interruption, and with the expectation that one can continue to do so.

This view, that the right to stay can somehow be severed from citizenship and remain sufficiently protective, is widespread. Ellerman for example argues for "legalization," which can be citizenship, but which can also be respected with a visa that permits legal, long-term residence. Similarly, Buckinx and Filindra write, "While remaining agnostic about the question of full membership or citizenship, we argue that states may need to grant many of their residents a de facto right to continued territorial presence" (Buckinx and Filindra 2015, 395). Paulina Ochoa Espejo defends "a right to place"—which grounds a right to stay, defined as "a *pro tanto* right that a person has not to be forcibly removed from the place where she dwells—at least until she has been given the chance to fulfill all of her outstanding place-specific duties" (Espejo 2016, 68). The duties can be fulfilled without citizenship status, and so Espejo's account similarly does not connect the right to stay to the legal status of citizenship. Sarah Song proposes this strategy as well, saying that "we ought to consider an approach that disaggregates certain rights from the formal status of citizenship and extends them to noncitizens in virtue of their territorial presence" (Song 2016, 242).

Rutger Birnie proposes to rely on what he terms a "domicile principle of non-deportability," which is grounded in the "fact that someone has made the territory in which they reside the centre of their most fundamental life projects and attachments"—such a principle ought to protect non-citizens from deportation just as citizens are similarly protected, in virtue of the importance of protecting the "integrity of their geographically grounded life project, regardless of whether they choose to naturalise" (Birnie 2020, 383). In defending a "disaggregation" strategy, Birnie offers a series of reasons to think it is superior to offering citizenship to long-term irregular migrants. In particular, he objects to those who might be of the view that migrants who choose against naturalizing can be interpreted as refusing the membership opportunities made available to them, and therefore reasonably left in a position where deportation is possible. Rather, he says, we should not assume that migrants, even irregular migrants, desire citizenship; they may well have good reasons to avoid naturalization, even if it were easily accessible.[5] Birnie leaves readers largely in the dark with respect to what such reasons may be, however, and how they should be weighed against the protection that citizenship status offers. As well, he says, there may be naturalization requirements that are challenging to meet, such that the right against deportation ought to kick in before many candidates can meet the relevant naturalization requirements (Birnie 2020, 384). This latter argument, however, about the difficulty that some migrants have in meeting naturalization requirements seems to me to point to the importance of adopting naturalization requirements that can be met relatively easily rather than to the view that legal long-term residency is sufficiently protective and ought to be treated as such.

It is of course true that the proposal to grant citizenship to irregular migrants is controversial, as a matter of public policy, even for those who are sympathetic to the idea that such individuals should be permitted to stay.

One worry is that, following the announcement of an entitlement to apply for citizenship after a certain period of time, deportation efforts would in fact amp up in an attempt to identify would-be long-term residents before they gain entitlements to citizenship. A second worry is that such a policy would produce a moral hazard; that is, it would not only encourage more irregular migration, it would further encourage such migrants to remain underground and then to announce themselves as available for naturalization once the residency requirement has been met. But this "hazard" is an inevitable consequence of adopting just immigration policies, which, as I said in the Introduction, require that states have a mechanism by which those who are present irregularly can join the community in full. This so-called moral hazard—the possibility that an accessible procedure would encourage irregular migration—is in my view an acceptable price to pay for refusing to countenance the injustice of long-term migrants without access to citizenship. A third worry is that granting citizenship to irregular migrants who have evaded authorities for an extended period of time amounts to rewarding those who have committed a wrong-doing,[6] and correspondingly that granting them citizenship is not fair to those who are waiting patiently in an immigration queue to follow the proper rules of admission (for a discussion of these worries, see Bosniak 2013; Carens 2009; Hing 2007; Hollifield, Martin, and Orrenius 2014). These worries, however, press in favor only of taking care with respect to formulating the proper policy in practice, and doing so will not be easy. They do not offer principled reasons to deny the importance of transitioning long-term irregular migrants to citizenship status.

Permitting long-term irregular migrants to languish without status amounts to accepting the presence of what are effectively second-class residents of a state. Michael Walzer described the objection to long-term second class residents in his consideration of the post-Second World War German guest worker program, which invited mainly Turkish citizens to carry out crucial jobs but refused to grant them citizenship even as their temporary visas were repeatedly renewed (Walzer 1983; see also Chin 2007; Barbieri 1998). Walzer's examination focused on the denial of access to citizenship to long-term, legally present migrants, but his general point applies more broadly: the presence of long-term migrants, whether present legally or irregularly, without a clear and accessible procedure for attaining citizenship is unjust for the ways their rights are ignored, for the ways in which they cannot freely lobby in defense of their own rights, and for the ways it consigns key members of a society to, effectively, second-class status. I will return to Walzer's analysis of guest work programs, and his conclusions, in Chapters 5 and 6.

So far, I have signalled that I am in agreement with the scholars with whom I engaged just above that there should be a strong norm against deporting those who are long-term residents but who have not yet fulfilled the requirements for citizenship. However, I have suggested against most of them that the harms that attend deportation are so substantial that they demonstrate the importance of ensuring that long-term residents, whether irregular or not, have reasonable pathways to naturalization, rather than simply the right to stay legally.

But I have not declared a blanket objection to all forms of deportation, raising the obvious question of when it may be permissible to deport those who have not yet accessed the minimum conditions for eligibility to naturalize, but who have nevertheless begun to remake their lives on a particular territory. Most of those whom it may be permissible to deport are individuals who have recently crossed the border (although not those who have made asylum claims, which must be considered as a matter of international law). I am not going to articulate the precise mechanics of this procedure here (but see Lenard 2015), and will simply suggest that any fair deportation procedure must provide opportunities for those who are impacted (the deportees) to make a case that they ought to be permitted to stay, and legal representation must be provided to them to support them in making this case. One mechanism for doing so might be modeled on the Finnish Ombudsman for Non-Discrimination, which has legal standing to protect the rights of migrants across many matters, including with respect to deportation orders (The Ombudsman n.d.).

For those whose response to this proposal is that it is too favorable to irregular migrants, or that host states are somehow not responsible for protecting those who are present on their territory irregularly, let me note that the very fact of their being present on a territory gives rise to legitimate rights claims, even as their irregular presence may seem to generate a state's right to forcibly exclude them. This observation is Linda Bosniak's, who writes that, "[t]heir territorial presence is simultaneously the source of the offense that states invoke as a justification for illegalizing them, the basis for protections the migrants may claim against the state for basic fair treatment *while present*, and the ground for claims they make (or that are made on their behalf) to *remain present*—i.e., to stay in the territory" (Bosniak 2020, 55). As I will articulate again later in this chapter (and again in Chapter 4), the mere fact of presence on a territory generates claims for rights protection, and this protection applies to all those who are present. In the case of irregular migrants who have been present for some time, but not long enough to naturalize, the obligation lies with the state to ensure that deportation will not generate the harms listed earlier.

What About the Stateless?

The argument I have just defended examines the fair treatment of long-term migrants who, I suggested, are entitled to access citizenship status to protect them against forcible exclusion. Because long-term residents, regardless of their mode of entry, are eventually entitled to protection against forced exclusion, they are morally entitled to the status of citizenship which protects it. However, citizenship is not *only* about protecting people from deportation from territory, and to see why it must be about more than that consider stateless peoples—people without citizenship status at all. Stateless peoples present legal and moral challenges to a global environment divided into states: "Persons without a citizenship . . . are not simply lacking a privilege, they are fundamentally anomalous, and are accommodated in our state-centered world only precariously and in an ad hoc fashion" (Brubaker 1992, n31, 198).

Mostly, people gain their citizenship in one of two ways: either they are born on a territory and granted citizenship in virtue of that or they are legally entitled to the citizenship of one or both of their parents, or sometimes both (Carens 2013, ch. 2) . But the laws by which citizenship is granted vary sufficiently by country that some children are inadvertently born into statelessness: for example, children born to migrants on a territory that does not grant citizenship by birth can have trouble accessing the citizenship of their parents, if citizenship requires residence on that territory. Additionally, in as many as twenty-five countries, nationality law remains problematically gendered, denying the right of women to give their own citizenship to their children (European Network on Statelessness 2019). For example, there is presently a stateless population in Lebanon, composed of children of Lebanese mothers married to foreigners; they are stateless because mothers cannot pass on their citizenship to their children (Institute on Statelessness and Inclusion 2016). Statelessness can also emerge where borders between countries change, and new and restructured countries refuse to acknowledge or grant citizenship to some of their "new" citizens, whose citizenship in their prior state has been cancelled as a result of that restructuring (often the denial of citizenship is grounded in claims that the would-be "new" citizens do not share the ethnic background of the majority in their new state). States can also render their citizens stateless by simple declaration, as Nazi Germany did to its Jewish population in the 1930s, and as Myanmar did to its Rohingya population in 1982. The global stateless population is estimated to be roughly ten million, although this figure is also widely considered to be an underestimate as a result of the difficulty in identifying who is officially stateless (Cole, Bloom, and Tonkiss 2017).[7] The stateless are sometimes defined according to whether they are "de facto" stateless or "de jure" stateless; the former are those who have no state that recognizes them as a citizen, and the latter are those for whom their state of ostensible citizenship does not recognize that status and/or refuses to protect the rights that ought to flow from that citizenship status. What matters, ultimately, is "effective nationality"; that is, whether an individual legally possesses a citizenship that is recognized by the relevant state as entitling her to rights protection, which is in turn forthcoming (Siegelberg 2020, 231).

The harm generated by statelessness is clear and well recognized in international law. As Mathew Gibney explains, the imposition of statelessness is both unjust and cruel. It is unjust because it violates the right of citizenship, to which every person is entitled—Article 15 of the Universal Declaration of Human Rights states simply, "Everyone has the right to a nationality"—and it is cruel "because it may be a recipe for exclusion, precariousness, and general dispossession" (United Nations 1948; Gibney 2013, 651). The absence of protection offered to people in virtue of their status as humans was central to Hannah Arendt's analysis of the right to nationality, that is, a right to an entity that is formally charged with protecting one's rights (Arendt 1963). The harm of statelessness stems from the vulnerability to state power that stateless peoples face, against which they have no or nearly no protection. For example, the 1961 United Nations Convention on the Reduction of Statelessness recognizes the harm to those who do not have a state on which they can rely for protection of their basic human rights. Of course at least in principle, states are obligated to protect the basic human rights of all those on their territory; in practice, much of the protection provided to residents is tied to their legal status as citizens or citizens-in-waiting. Judith Shklar, in her analysis of the history of inclusion and exclusion from the United States, writes, because "every living person is said to have rights to protect and interests to promote as a citizen, then exclusion from public life is a denial of his and her civic personality and social dignity" (Shklar 1991, 39).

Consider the Rohingya population of Myanmar, whom I mentioned earlier. The Rohingya have been effectively stateless for generations, although in 1982 they were formally denied access to Myanmar citizenship with the passing of a Citizenship Law that formalized their statelessness (in general, see Rae 2018). Until 2017, most Rohingya lived in Myanmar, but especially aggressive state repression in 2017, including state-sanctioned burning of Rohingya villages and the seizure of their land, prompted nearly one million Rohingya to flee to neighboring Bangladesh (Ullah 2011; Milton et al. 2017). Only one-half million remain in Myanmar (Human Rights Watch n.d.). The global response has been one of horror, as Bangladesh struggles to provide for its Rohingya visitors, even with extensive international support. But nearly no state has offered the obvious solution: blanket citizenship status for the Rohingya.[8] It is clear enough to many onlookers that the situation for the Rohingya in Bangladesh, and in Myanmar, is deeply unsafe; their rights are not systematically protected in any meaningful way.[9]

The solution to statelessness, recommended by the 1961 UN Convention on the Reduction of Statelessness I previously cited, is for each state to grant naturalization to the stateless on their territory.[10] Signatories to that convention are in principle obligated to facilitate the naturalization of stateless people, although specific recommendations for ensuring their naturalization are not outlined. In many cases, at least in principle, states have procedures by which to prove that an individual is stateless, via a statelessness-determination procedure of some kind. As well, some states have procedures for granting stateless people legal status that is attended by a variety of rights, including the right to work and other socio-economic rights. Yet, barriers persist in accessing such procedures, as well as in attaining citizenship by following the mandated steps—among them, that the burden of proving one is genuinely stateless remains high (European Network on Statelessness 2021) and, of course, as in the case of the Rohingya in Myanmar and Bangladesh, the strong state resistance to the proposal that citizenship be granted to unwelcome minorities.

In some cases, states agree to resettle those who are stateless to another state elsewhere, with the intention that they naturalize to citizenship in time. In these cases, states typically treat stateless people more or less like other migrants, who can permissibly be asked to meet often quite demanding naturalization requirements. The principle underlying this thought is a reasonable one, that is, that incoming members can be asked to fulfill certain requirements as a condition of attaining citizenship. However, some naturalization requirements may be so demanding that they remain in practice unmeetable. In all of Denmark, the Netherlands, and the United Kingdom, for example, which each agreed to resettle a small number of Bhutanese refugees,[11] many remain without citizenship because they are unable to meet the very high naturalization requirements, usually with respect to language competence (Karki 2021). I will consider the legitimacy of key naturalization requirements in Chapters 7 and 8, including what makes certain requirements impermissible for being unreasonably demanding.

As I have said earlier, those who are subject to state power should be granted citizenship after a reasonable time has elapsed; and, after a reasonable period, those who remain subject to power without the option of full membership are unjustly excluded. It is of course morally relevant that in states that agree to resettle stateless people, such individuals possess the legal right to be present, which typically travels with an extensive package of rights. In such cases, the harm of difficult naturalization is comparatively less than the harm done to the stateless who have no pathway to naturalization or who are forced to remain in an irregular status. But, in my view, there is an additional imperative to ensure that citizenship is genuinely accessible to stateless peoples (otherwise the problem that statelessness poses is not resolved), and this may require that generally permissible naturalization requirements are eased for them in cases where the requirements are high enough to pose a barrier to their accessing citizenship. This additional imperative stems from the harms of statelessness itself, to which such individuals have been subject in the past.

Having articulated the particular importance of naturalizing stateless individuals, let me turn to something else that a consideration of stateless peoples demonstrates: although I am defending citizenship as centrally about protecting its holders from forced exclusion, immunity to deportation is not the only good offered by citizenship status. Among the main practical benefits offered by citizenship is a passport that enables travel: passports enable travel by confirming the identity of the traveler and identifying the state that is responsible for the traveler and thereby permitting that traveler to gain admission to another country, on a short- or long-term basis. It is not possible, in general, to gain legal entry to a state without a valid passport issued by one's state of citizenship. In Chapter 4, I examine the morality of visa-issuance, which is also key to gaining entry to other states, but gaining the appropriate visa is generally something that can only be done by someone who is in possession of a passport to begin with. Correspondingly, the legal deportation of those who are stateless is, in effect, impossible—rendering the stateless, uniquely among non-citizens, not liable to it. In the absence of a valid passport, no other state will legally admit them, except as part of an explicit scheme to resettle them. Paradoxically, then, stateless peoples are protected from one form of harm to which other non-citizens remain liable.

But this so-called benefit is cold comfort to those who remain excluded from the second benefit of citizenship status, namely the protection offered by an equal package of rights, or in the language I am emphasizing in this book, from *membership*. That is to say, while I have deliberately emphasized the component of citizenship status that protects its holders from forcible exclusion from territory, it is also a status that is meant to guarantee at least their formal inclusion into the benefits of membership. In the Conclusion to this book, I will highlight the importance of current political movements to ensure that inclusion is substantive for all members of a state. What a consideration of stateless people demonstrates, however, is that citizenship status offers protection from exclusion in two ways: from territory and *also* from membership. While the right to reside on a territory is prior, in the sense that its protection enables people to have the security of residence that is required to freely shape the life they want in the jurisdiction in which they live, the protection of this right travels with the protection of equal rights that is at the basis of full and formal membership.

Let me respond here to an objection, namely, that an emphasis on citizenship status as a right that must be protected for all those who are subjected to state power undermines progress towards a better solution, namely one in which citizenship status is *irrelevant*. This sort of a view underpins defenses of post-national or cosmopolitan citizenship, which look forward to a future (that at least some defenders believe is near) in which all people's rights are protected in virtue of their being human and not in virtue of citizenship status (Soysal 1994). This vision is informed at least in part by the rise in the number of people who cross borders, and who sustain multiple attachments as they do so.

However, in what follows, I insist on the importance of citizenship and the normative desirability of a world in which each individual possesses such a status. One reason is simply that citizenship matters in ways that have profound and deep effects on the lives of individuals around the world. To be a citizen of a state is to know which state is responsible for protecting one's rights. Beyond the mere practicality of citizenship, however, is the value that citizens get from being members of a community that is regulated by shared institutions and shaped by a shared public culture. However much it is wished otherwise, most people remain attached to the state they call home, and the particularities associated with living there. Their status as citizens is of substantial value to them, and the very fact that citizenship status is valuable to a state's members is a reason to protect it, even if, as many have noted, the construction of state boundaries is somewhat arbitrary and deeply historically contingent (Weinstock 2004). It remains the case, in other words, that however arbitrary boundaries of a state are, membership in particular states holds genuine value for its members.

So, while some normative philosophers prefer to imagine a post-national world in which citizenship status is irrelevant, recognizing its importance in protecting the rights of individuals is important for my objective here, which is to think seriously about how to improve the rules and regulations that govern inclusion and exclusion in our contemporary global world. The shape of global space is not likely to change rapidly, even if it does eventually move towards a more post-national or cosmopolitan vision, and so there are good reasons to focus on improving the justice of the rules governing inclusion and exclusion in the present. These proposals can have real impact on the lives of those who are struggling presently.

Conclusion

Through an examination of the deportation of non-citizens and its myriad harms, the purpose of this chapter has been to continue building my account of citizenship. Part of what this chapter has attempted to demonstrate is that, although deportation may seem like a way to resolve the problem of subjection without inclusion, in fact in many situations it is an *unjust* solution, because of the harms that it generates. I have argued that citizenship operates to protect its holders from exclusion from territory, as demonstrated in the discussion of the deportation of long-term regular and irregular migrants, and from membership, as demonstrated in the discussion of statelessness and its harms. The brief foray into the challenges faced by stateless peoples highlights the two dimensions of exclusion from which citizenship offers protection and also shows that they are intimately connected: residential security is not entirely valuable if it does not travel with the rights of full membership. Subjecting long-term residents to state power without granting them full inclusion in the form of citizenship is wrong. In the chapters that follow, I will flesh out these dimensions of citizenship by examining specific challenges posed by movement across borders, starting in the next chapter with an assessment of the rights of citizens who are abroad temporarily or on a long-term basis.

3
Citizens Abroad: In or Out, of What?

This chapter considers a state's obligations to its citizens who are abroad, sometimes for a short time and sometimes for long periods of time. It is widely agreed that states of origin retain some duties towards their citizens, but how broad they are, and how long they extend in time, is not so clear, and they are not in any obvious way connected to subjection. So long as citizens retain citizenship status, the state of citizenship will retain some duties towards them; over time, the bulk of the duties shift towards the state in which individuals reside (if it is not their state of citizenship), that is, towards the state to which they are, primarily, subjected.

Some rights must be protected by the host state, for all those who are on their territory regardless of their status, including tourists, international students, migrant laborers, irregularly present residents, and so on. States of residence acquire the obligation to protect a wider range of rights for migrants on their territory over time; the obligation stems from the ongoing subjection of long-term residents to state power, as discussed in Chapter 1. Correspondingly, as I have articulated over the course of this book, I am proposing that *subjection* grounds an individual's right to full protection by a state, and citizens who are not subjected to the power of their state of citizenship are owed *less* by that state, even if they remain citizens. The process of shifting the state that bears the responsibility to protect the rights of individuals, both basic and more broadly, is not a neat one, and it is never fully complete in the sense that so long as an individual retains citizenship of a state, that state will owe some duties to her, regardless of whether she is residing there.

Crucially, however, some is not nothing, and the central claim I attempt to make persuasive in this chapter is that the state of citizenship retains the obligation to protect the basic human rights of their citizens, as they travel and even as they reside abroad. However, the obligation to do so is a secondary or remedial right only, that kicks in when a state of residence is not able to protect these rights. I will begin with an account of the two rights that most obviously require protection by states of citizenship: the right to consular assistance and the right to return. I will suggest, in fact, that these are largely connected rights. Consular assistance is nearly always required in support of the right to move in general, and the right to return more particularly. I shall illustrate this latter observation with respect to the role that states of citizenship are asked to play, and ought to play, in cases where emergency evacuation is required, for example, in cases of environmental or humanitarian disaster, or unexpected and sudden military conflicts. In most such cases, the host state is either not able to provide protection effectively or benefits substantially from outside support in offering protection. What the case illustrates is that states of citizenship can sometimes have a passive duty to support the ability of their citizens to travel, in particular to exercise their right of return, and also that states sometimes have an active duty to repatriate citizens in need. I illustrate this latter point via a consideration of the appropriate way to respond to the challenges posed by the children of foreign fighters, which I argue require that states of citizenship repatriate citizen-children born abroad. (I leave to the next chapter the appropriate treatment of their parents and foreign fighters in general.) I then consider whether states can permissibly intervene to protect the rights of their citizens in other, non-emergency, cases, and consider the strategies that sending states have taken with respect to protecting their citizens, when they travel abroad to take up temporary foreign labor migration contracts.

I conclude the chapter with a consideration of whether states of citizenship have the obligation to enable citizens abroad to vote—I argue they do not—and how states ought to divide up rights protection for dual citizens when dual citizens have legitimate, sustained ties to two countries. What this analysis demonstrates ultimately is that (a) so long as an individual is a citizen of a state, the state retains at least some duties towards her; (b) that states are obligated to protect at least some rights for all of those who are present on their territory, including non-citizens; and (c) the process of transitioning the state that holds the majority of the responsibility to protect an individual's basic human rights takes time, as subjection to a new state extends in time.

The Right to Consular Assistance and the Right to Return

Article 13 of the Universal Declaration of Human Rights protects freedom of movement, including the right of citizens to leave their state and, crucially, to return to it: "Everyone has the right to leave any country, including his own, and to return to his country" (United Nations 1948). The plain meaning of this right is that any citizen who arrives at the border of her country must be permitted to enter it. She may be subject to identity checks of various kinds, especially if she arrives without appropriate documentation; however, once identity and citizenship are confirmed, she must be admitted. In principle, moreover, it does not matter how long the citizen has been away; her right to return is meant to guarantee that she can return in perpetuity, so long as she has not renounced her citizenship.

The right to consular assistance is under-theorized in political theory, and in legal theory—where it is more frequently discussed—there is no widespread agreement on the roles that consulates and embassies should play with respect to citizens abroad. In most countries, visitors and temporary residents can ask their own state for various forms of support by visiting their state of citizenship's consulate or embassy (Haynal et al. 2013). For example, the US embassy in Edinburgh issued my partner an emergency passport after his then-current passport was damaged during travel. Consulates can help their citizens with other services as well. When I was in Rome with my partner, he contracted what appeared to be chicken pox, and the American embassy was able to recommend an English-speaking doctor (who did house calls) for him. These are basic services that are offered to citizens who are traveling or residing abroad.

Certainly, one major role that consulates play, in support of citizens' right to move freely, including their right to return, is to issue up-to-date travel documentation. These duties, to provide travel support and to enable the right of return, come together when citizens request consular help in exiting a state experiencing a humanitarian disaster or unexpected military conflict. In general terms, the consulate or embassy offers "assistance to a state's own citizens in distress abroad and, when necessary, their family or other designated contacts at home" (Haynal et al. 2013, 1–3). For example, citizens abroad of many countries were evacuated from Lebanon during the Israel–Hezbollah war in 2006; from Indonesia following the 2004 tsunami; from Syria after the onset and worsening of its ongoing civil war; from Haiti after the 2010 earthquake; from Fukushima, Japan after the nuclear disaster resulting from an earthquake and tsunami in 2011; from the floods in New Orleans following Hurricane Katrina in 2005; and so on.

Non-citizens, especially short-term visitors, may be at special risk during moments of crisis. They may be less connected to the channels by which the government communicates to its citizens, or they may not speak the language in which communications are issued (Weerasinghe and Taylor 2015, 30–31). They may suffer especially where disasters result in damage to various communication technologies because they are less likely to have access to alternative robust information networks than resident citizens, and because these may be the mechanisms by which they are gaining information about the dangers they face, and where to seek help, for example in the form of food and shelter. Finally, states may implicitly or explicitly deny support to non-citizens in times of disaster (Weerasinghe and Taylor 2015, 38). Typically, in response to such situations, states coordinate evacuation efforts for their citizens abroad, which includes identifying citizens in need of evacuation, identifying safe travel routes for them, and communicating with the range of organizations that collaborate to offer transport to those seeking exit, including other states engaged in the same effort.

In these kinds of cases, those with citizenship elsewhere and seeking evacuation are not (at least not obviously) responsible for the emergency situation they hope to escape with their own state's support. Additionally, it is often the case that the countries facing the disaster, or the conflict, are not able to offer sufficient protection to those impacted, and so it is appropriate that states of citizenship re-assume their duties to protect their citizens' rights. In this way, states of citizenship reduce the protection burden for states under stress. As I said earlier in this chapter, states are always responsible for protecting those on their territory in some ways, including with respect to basic human rights protection. But the point here is that, in situations of disaster, home states have an obligation to step in for two reasons: to protect the basic human rights of their citizens abroad when their state of residence (or visit) is not able or willing to do so, first and foremost, and because doing so reduces the protection burden on the state experiencing the disaster. Usually, in such cases, host states welcome the support from abroad when they arrive to coordinate the evacuation of their own citizens.

What this discussion has so far suggested is that the requirement that states allow their citizens to return has both a passive and an active dimension. In the vast majority of cases, the duty is a passive one, to admit citizens who arrive at a border intending to return home. The duty to allow for return is, as a practical matter, tied to an obligation to provide valid travel documents (including at embassies or consulates abroad). The legal crossing of borders requires them, and so the refusal to issue such documents to citizens abroad amounts in most cases to a profound failure to respect the right of citizens to return to their own country. However, as the case of state support in evacuating citizens from humanitarian or military disasters suggests, a citizen's right to return to their state of citizenship can require that home states take on a more active role. The obligation to do more than merely allow for citizens to return, to proactively ensure that they can do so, emerges when citizens abroad find themselves unexpectedly in the midst of a disaster from which they cannot easily exit, and where host states are struggling to offer the appropriate support for them to do so. That is, the positive obligation to enable return emerges because the state that has the job of protecting the basic human rights of those on its territory cannot do so.[1] The state of citizenship's positive duty, when it is required, is in that sense a remedial one.

Children of Foreign Fighters

The account above also explains how states ought to respond to what seems like quite a different kind of case, namely, the treatment of citizen-children born abroad to foreign fighters. Let me begin by explaining the context for this issue. There is nothing new about citizens traveling to join wars in foreign countries, which they may do for all kinds of reasons. Famously, George Orwell traveled to Spain to (he said) fight against fascism and wrote *Homage to Catalonia* to document his experiences upon his return to England. Orwell reportedly struggled to get the book published, and then it did not sell very well, but no one seriously suggested that Orwell should be prosecuted for having participated in a foreign military conflict, although the British Government did apparently threaten to expel people who left to fight in the Spanish Civil War, under a piece of 1870 legislation called the Foreign Enlistment Act (Monbiot 2014).

Currently, the most well-known of foreign fighters are those who traveled to Iraq and Syria to fight alongside the now largely defeated Islamic State (ISIS), and who are believed in many cases to have committed horrific crimes in doing so. In the following chapter, I will consider in some detail how they ought to be treated—what protections, if any, their states of citizenship owe them now—but I want to begin by considering how their children should be treated. Over the course of the active conflict with ISIS, an estimated forty thousand foreigners traveled to Iraq or Syria to join the fight with ISIS, of whom thousands remain, mostly residing in detention camps secured by the Kurds (UN Press Release 2017; "ISIS Foreign Fighters after the Fall of the Caliphate" 2020). As of 2019, roughly twelve thousand foreigners are living in northern Syria in detention camps, of whom four thousand are children, many of whom were born there (France 24 2019a). Because many states possess citizenship rules that automatically transfer the citizenship of parents to their children, these children are citizens of states in which they have never lived.

International organizations have warned that the conditions in these camps are dire and worsening daily. A United Nations report from 2021 describes them as follows: "Thousands of people held in the camps are exposed to violence, exploitation, abuse and deprivation in conditions and treatment that may well amount to torture or other cruel, inhuman or degrading treatment or punishment under international law, with no effective remedy at their disposal. An unknown number have already died because of their conditions of detention" (OHCHR 2021). A recent *New York Times* article highlighting, in particular, the plight of children effectively imprisoned abroad described the over-crowded detainment camps as "fetid" and "disease-ridden." Children living there "lack education and adequate health care, and there are often shortages of food and clean water. Infectious diseases are rampant, killing dozens of people a month" (Hubbard and Méheut 2020). Of the deaths at these two camps in 2019, an estimated nearly seventy-five percent were children (Ibrahim and François 2020).

The Kurds, who govern these particular camps, have been asking countries of origin to repatriate their citizens. Countries have been reasonably (although I will argue in the next section, impermissibly) reluctant to support their citizens to return home, even when their citizens have requested it (Hubbard and Méheut 2020). The reluctance stems from worries that foreign fighters have been radicalized abroad and, correspondingly, that they would, if they returned, pose dangers to fellow citizens. The reluctance to repatriate children stems from related, but not identical, worries. While one concern is that children have been radicalized, or at least traumatized, by the circumstances of their early years, another is that repatriating children without their adult caregivers may not be possible or fair to children. Thus, the reluctance to repatriate children stems, at least in part, from an attempt to avoid the repatriation of their caregivers, mainly but not only mothers, many of whom are believed to be so-called jihadi brides. Jihadi brides are women who have traveled abroad to marry foreign fighters, and who are understood therefore to be sympathetic to, or complicit in, terrorist violence abroad. Because of the latter, their states of citizenship are reluctant to enable their return.

Some countries have responded more robustly to the challenge posed by citizen-children abroad. Russia and Kosovo have made the most progress in repatriating child–citizens, as part of a general repatriation effort (MEE 2020). France and Belgium have been proceeding on a case-by-case basis. Comparatively an easy case (because not infused with many of the complicating factors described above), France recently enabled the return of several orphaned children. Belgium has stated its intent to repatriate children under ten years of age, so long as there is proof of a link to a Belgian parent, and although it has attempted to deny re-entry to their parents, courts have required them to do so nevertheless in some cases (Coolsaet and Renard 2020). Other countries have refused to repatriate children, including Tunisia, stating explicitly that they want to avoid pressures to repatriate (or encourage the return of) their foreign fighting parents (France 24 2019a). On the other hand, Denmark initially refused to permit the return of children, moving to deny them Danish citizenship, but then modified its position and agreed to admit children but not their parents. Now it appears Denmark is willing to receive children with their *mothers* but not their fathers (Carlson 2021).

Why do states remain reluctant to repatriate citizen-children, even as they languish in dire conditions? One objection to repatriating children is fundamentally utilitarian—it points to the risk, however limited, that children themselves will have been radicalized in ways that are irreversible and suggests that the costs of supporting their repatriation are therefore not worth it. However, even taking for granted the importance that a state must place on protecting the security of its citizens (Lenard 2020b), there is little evidence that children abroad are likely to pose threats upon return. A second objection is that if children are repatriated *without* family members (whether or not these family members are also citizens and so, in principle, entitled to return), children will be worse off as a result of the separation; even where their conditions abroad are so poor as to be human rights violating, the importance of protecting family unity—but abroad—is more important than repatriating children so that they can escape those conditions. The general thought that children ought not to be separated from their primary caregivers, where this separation is avoidable, is generally widely accepted.[2] The natural response is to propose that children be repatriated *with* their parents, in particular their mothers, but as I indicated above, this response runs into the objection that parents who are suspected or guilty of terrorist crimes abroad are sometimes not welcome back or, at least, that their parents can be justly excluded. As I said, I will consider the proper treatment of adult foreign fighters (including jihadi brides) in the following chapter. For now, my focus is only on the reasons to believe that a state may be obligated to proactively enable children to exercise their right of return.

In the first part of this chapter, I suggested that states have duties to citizens abroad, where the host state is unable to protect their basic human rights. This remedial duty explains why states of citizenship have an obligation to enable the return of their citizens who require support in the case of humanitarian disaster or unexpected military conflict. The remedial duty appears especially strong in these cases because those who are inadvertently caught in such events are not obviously responsible for the danger they face, although it also exists where citizens have intentionally entered dangerous environments, and even in cases where citizens do so *against* the explicit advice of their governments.[3]

This logic also applies to the case of children of foreign fighters: they are not in any way responsible for the situation they are in, and the conditions of detention camps are such that their basic human rights cannot be met. As with all citizens, they have the right of return, and as with citizens who are inadvertently caught up in humanitarian disasters, they cannot exercise that right without support. The human rights of children are, moreover, acknowledged in the 1989 United Nations Convention on the Rights of the Child to be of particular importance in light of their extreme vulnerability, and dependence on the adults around them to provide for their needs (OHCHR 1989). In response to pressure to repatriate Canadian children, the Canadian government has repeatedly argued that Canadians abroad who are able to arrive at embassies on their own can access help in exiting, something which children in detention camps are, of course, not able to do on their own (Evans 2021). As well, the government has insisted that the conditions in Syria are too dangerous for its representatives to travel there to negotiate the return of (at least some) foreign fighters or their children. In making these arguments, it has proven willing to act only on its passive to duty to allow for the return of its citizens, not on the active one that applies to children, who are especially vulnerable to the choices that adults make on their behalf. In the case of these children, the state of citizenship has the duty to support their return in a proactive way, even when that requires the state to take on some risk, as there is no other state that can help and the need is clear.[4]

Protecting Citizen Labor Migrants Abroad

Consider a different case in which a host state is not so much unable to protect the rights of non-citizens, but rather is unwilling to do so. Many citizens of Asian states, including the Philippines, Indonesia, Thailand, and Nepal, migrate to Gulf States as "temporary labor migrants" in a range of industries, including manufacturing, construction, and caregiving. The economies of Gulf States rely on a steady inflow of temporary labor migrants, and although in principle the Gulf States are responsible for protecting the rights of those who take up work in their states, in practice there is ample evidence that such migrants are subject to significant rights violations (Shah 2006). Yet, migrants continue to arrive because the employment opportunities are better than those available at home. And so, the trade is perceived to be worth it from their perspective. Sending state governments, however, worry about the persistent violations of their citizens' rights as they labor abroad, and have little apparent capacity to ensure their protection. A major reason for this worry is that sending states themselves have an interest in encouraging at least some of their citizens to take up such opportunities. In some sending states, there are insufficient quality employment opportunities, and so the migration of some citizens eases the pressure on the sending state to provide them. As well, migrants return remittances, and the value of these remittances to individual families, and the sending state as a whole, is substantial (ILO 2016; Lim and Basnet 2017).

Sending state options in these cases are limited, as I have said, both by the voluntariness of the migration and by the sovereignty of host states, who may resist interference in the rights protection they offer (or in this case, do not offer) to those on their territory. One strategy that sending states have taken in an attempt to secure better protection for their citizens laboring abroad in rights-violating contexts, is to adopt temporary migration bans (Shivakoti 2020; Shivakoti, Henderson, and Withers 2021). These bans operate to restrict citizens from migrating, usually to specific countries and in specific industries; as such, these bans operate to restrict the exit of citizens, which might be understood as a violation of their rights (in general, see Napier-Moore 2017). However, the purpose of travel bans is to pressure host states to adopt legislation that better protects the rights of migrant workers, in exchange for re-opening the flow of such workers. The evidence that such bans are effective in achieving benefits for migrant workers is mixed. The Philippines has had the most success with adopting this kind of strategy, in large part because their citizens are highly valued as foreign workers across a range of domains by host states, for their education and facility with English. Across multiple bilateral negotiations with countries that receive Filipino migrants, the Philippines has been able to secure robust promises from host states to protect the rights of their citizens (Lenard 2021b).[5]

This example illustrates that home states are often concerned about the rights of their citizens; that concern lies mostly dormant when host states are fulfilling their duties. But in cases such as exploited guest workers, home states may sometimes express their strong interest in the rights of their citizens by fashioning mechanisms to proactively secure their protection. The behavior of sending states in this case can be well-understood as an instance of a more general phenomenon observed by Rainer Bauböck, that sending states are increasingly focused on sustaining relations with expatriate citizens, often, though not always, as a part of a political or economic development strategy, for example, to ensure the persistent return of remittances by those laboring abroad (Bauböck 2015, 2009). In the case described just above, at issue are temporary migrants, where the firm expectation is that such migrants will retain strong ties to the sending country *and* therefore will ultimately return home. In other cases of expatriates, sending states may well attempt to retain strong connections even among those who clearly intend to reside abroad on a long-term basis, if not forever.

To summarize where I have arrived, so far: The obligation to protect the rights of citizens abroad applies when, for any reason, their human rights are being violated and the host state is unable (as in the cases of humanitarian disaster) or unwilling (as in the cases of temporary labor migrants) to protect them. Ordinarily, host states are obligated to protect the human rights of all those on their territories—and the duty to protect the basic rights, and then even a more robust set of rights, grows as does the time that migrants spend in the host state. Over time, visitors turn into residents, for all intents and purposes (even where the appropriate legal status does not change), and residents, as I have argued in the first chapter, are *subjected* to the power of the host state. In virtue of this subjection, they become entitled not only to have their basic rights, but also a more robust set of rights, protected by that state, eventually including political rights, and the right to stay on a permanent basis. Correspondingly, the duties that the sending state has towards its citizens abroad can fairly (from the sending state's perspective) be understood as weaker over time. For tourists caught in humanitarian disasters, the obligations of the state of citizenship remain robust; they are less robust for temporary labor migrants; and less so for long-term residents abroad.

The Right to Vote from Abroad

Earlier in this book, I proposed that the best way to understand who is entitled to full inclusion is to consider who is *subjected* by a particular state's rules and regulations; those who are subjected, I argued, are entitled to full inclusion, including the right to vote. However, I did not suggest that the main benefit of full inclusion was the right to vote. Rather, I said, it was the right to stay or, put differently, the right to be protected against forced exclusion in the form of deportation. The right to vote, I suggested, can permissibly be granted on the basis of residence alone. I argued, fundamentally, that the mere fact of residence over the long term entitles one to have a say in the laws that shape the present and future of one's life. In Chapter 1, I defended the expansion of policies that permit non-citizen, long-term residents the right to vote in at least local elections. The fact remains however that voting, especially in national elections, remains a right that is largely reserved for citizens. Yet, for a variety of reasons, millions of citizens live outside of their country of citizenship, and often for extended periods of time. The proportion of the global population that lives outside of their own state's borders has increased from 2.8 percent in 1995 to 3.5 percent in 2019 (Edmond 2020). Should they be permitted to vote in elections in their states of citizenship? Are states of citizenship required to protect the ability of citizens abroad to access this right? The main reason to believe that states are obligated to find ways to enable their citizens abroad to vote is that the right to vote is a key democratic right that ought to be protected for all citizens. Among those who defend the view that states must protect this right for all citizens, many also believe that this is so regardless of where such citizens reside (for discussion see Baubӧck 2015; Owen 2011). The right to vote is often seen as intimately connected to citizenship itself. But, as I already hinted in Chapter 1, this reasoning is mistaken.

In the last several decades, many states have moved to recognize the status of what Rainer Baubӧck has called "external citizenship"; that is, they have moved to identify rights and privileges they wish to offer and protect for citizens who have, for whatever reason, chosen to live abroad either temporarily or permanently (Baubӧck 2009). In some ways, the rights of external citizenship are less robust than are the rights of residential citizenship—as I said, many rights flow with residence in particular—but they remain meaningful, and as Bauböck says, there may well be cases where protecting them is "indispensable . . . for securing individual liberty and well-being" (Bauböck 2009, 477). The right to vote, even while abroad, is proposed to be among these indispensable rights.

One estimate is that nearly three-quarters of all states have moved to make some form of expatriate voting both legally possible and accessible, and many have also adopted strategies to *encourage* expatriate voting in a range of ways (Goldberg and Lanz 2019). This precise question has been litigated in Canada, where in 2019 the Supreme Court ruled that denying non-resident citizens the right to vote (after they had been non-resident for five years) constituted a violation of their constitutionally protected right to vote (Supreme Court of Canada 2019). Before that ruling, Canadian citizens, who were also long-term non-residents, were denied the right to vote from abroad after five years. Their right to vote was reinstated if they returned to reside in Canada for some time. Litigants argued that the removal of the right to vote was unconstitutional and, ultimately, the Canadian Supreme Court agreed that non-residency was not sufficient to extinguish the right to vote, even temporarily.

I think, however, that this decision failed to reckon with the normative priority that ought to be given to residence. In what follows, I shall suggest that it is permissible to deny the right to vote for non-resident citizens, and (as I suggested in Chapter 1 already) obligatory to extend the vote to non-citizen, long-term, residents. States that grant voting rights to long-term expatriates are not behaving unjustly, I should add. Yet, residence entails a specific relationship between a resident and state: residents are *subjected* to the laws of the state and thereby are entitled to have a say in what they are. Long-term non-residents of a state, even if citizens, are not subjected to most laws in their country of citizenship, and in fact if they are genuinely long-term, then they are instead subjected by the laws, institutions, and public culture where they reside. As dual-citizens of the United States and Canada, my partner and I—who reside in Ottawa and have done for over ten years—are required to abide by American tax laws, but beyond that our lives are shaped by the Canadian, and not American, institutional and cultural environment.

In the judgment that I cited above, the Supreme Court of Canada did note that "[r]esidence is significant because it establishes a connection to a particular electoral district and to the concerns of persons living there. While this aspect of Canada's representative democracy is not constitutionally entrenched, residence has been historically and remains today more than just an organizing mechanism. It is foundational to Canada's electoral system" (Supreme Court of Canada 2019). In particular, in democracies that operate on the basis of jurisdictional representation, one is voting for a representative whom one believes has a strong sense of the issues that a local community faces; the representative's job is to speak for her constituents about the jurisdiction in which they both live.[6] Their shared *residential space* is, at least in part, grounds for thinking that a representative can do a good job—they understand the best interests of that jurisdiction (Espejo 2020). Non-residents will, over time, inevitably become disconnected from the pressures and preferences of those who share the space on a daily basis, and their physical separation from that space makes their votes less likely to be taken from a position of insight into the conditions that face that jurisdiction.

As well, it is reasonable to believe that laws—because they subject residents—have a greater impact on the lives of residents, and so it is likewise reasonable to restrict the right to vote to those who will be most impacted by the decisions that are thereby made. There is at least some evidence, moreover, that expatriates support different political parties and hold substantially different political positions than median resident voters (Lafleur and Sánchez-Domínguez 2015; Mencütek 2015); this difference suggests that giving non-residents the right to vote, even though they do not live with the impact of their choices, is unfair to the residents who must live with the laws (Goldberg and Lanz 2019). Of course, domestic political decisions can have an impact on those who live abroad, and those who live abroad may have strong opinions on the politics of their country of citizenship; changes in tax law, as it pertains to those who reside abroad, for example, can have a significant impact on the lives of citizens who reside abroad. The all-affected principle that I rejected in Chapter 1 might well recommend that the *impact* of domestic law on the lives of citizens abroad is in general sufficient to warrant protecting their right to vote while residing abroad. Yet, these impacts are to my mind insufficient to ground the claim that non-resident citizens are required by justice to be able to vote and that states of citizenship are thereby obligated to facilitate their vote. Residence is at the core of subjection and thus at the core of the entitlement to vote.

I do not wish to deny that there are long-term residents who retain a sufficiently robust connection to their country of citizenship that they may rightly be entitled to vote there. And the presence of such individuals raises the question of, if it is permissible do to so, as I have argued, when is it permissible to deny citizen non-residents the right to vote in home state elections? As I have been describing, when citizens visit and then reside abroad, there is a gradual shift of rights-protection duties from the home to host state. I will argue in later chapters that the relatively substantial rights restrictions to which temporary labor migrants are subject are permissible for approximately six months, after which the host state must be willing to expand them on the idea that such workers are, in effect, residents.

There is an asymmetry, here, which is that while extending the rights associated with inclusion ought to begin relatively quickly, the (temporary) extinguishing of rights for citizens abroad ought to happen over a longer-time frame. The justification for this asymmetry is in the harm of unwarranted (and undesired) exclusion, which, in the case of temporary foreign workers, presses in favor of the rapid access to inclusion and, in the case of citizen non-residents, presses in favor of excluding them formally from citizenship rights relatively slowly. Moreover, as I said just above, it is of course true that many non-resident citizens retain deep connections to their home country or move between two countries over an extended period of time. As a result, an exception clause must be added to any policy that extinguishes the right of non-resident citizens to vote: while non-resident citizens can permissibly be denied the right to vote after a period of time (five years seems appropriate), they ought to be permitted to make the case that they retain a sufficiently genuine link to their state of citizenship that their right to vote ought not to be constrained (for a discussion of the notion of genuine link, see Bauböck and Paskalev 2015). For example, international students or military personnel stationed abroad who, largely, have the intention of returning home once they have finished their studies or service, may retain the right to vote from abroad, even as those studies or service take many years.

Who Must Protect Dual Citizens?

In this chapter, I have so far considered how best to identify which state is responsible for protecting the rights of citizens as they travel abroad, and more particularly as they transition to long-term residence, if not citizenship, abroad. I have noted that the transition between duty holders is not a neat one; the duty holder follows the experience of subjection, but the transition from subjection to the power of one state to the power of another happens over time, rather than at a particular moment. So, there will inevitably be disputes over which state holds the responsibility to protect the rights of particular individuals, whether citizens or long-term residents. Such disputes are even more likely as more and more people take on second citizenships. Historically, many states did not allow for dual citizenship—if a national naturalized into another citizenship, the first citizenship was automatically cancelled. Increasingly states permit dual citizenship, and the possession of dual citizenship can seem to make ambiguous *which* state is responsible for protecting a person's basic, and broader, rights (M. M. Howard 2005).

Consider the way in which the status of dual citizenship can complicate the right of return, as well as states' role in permitting it and/or making return proactively possible. This question preoccupied commentators in Canada in 2006, when Canadian–Lebanese dual citizens residing in Lebanon asked for pro-active support in returning to Canada to flee the Hezbollah–Israel conflict. Many argued such individuals were mere "citizens of convenience"; that is, Lebanese citizens with insufficient loyalty to Canada, who resided in Canada just long enough to naturalize into Canadian citizenship, and who used that citizenship as a kind of "insurance policy" (Macklin and Crépeau 2010, 21). When the conflict erupted, some such individuals allegedly sought safe-haven in Canada—and asked the Canadian government to support their evacuation—only to return to residing in Lebanon once the active conflict ended. As Macklin and Crépeau observe, "no reliable evidence was ever proffered in support of this narrative," although it is reasonable to assume that some such individuals did indeed behave in this way (Macklin and Crépeau 2010, 21).

Following the argument developed earlier, these dual nationals were entitled to Canadian support to evacuate during the conflict. Where states of residence are unable to protect the basic rights of citizens, states of citizenship retain the remedial obligation to step in to protect them. What appears different in the case of Lebanese–Canadians is merely that there are two possible states of citizenship with the duty to protect basic rights; just as Canada evacuated its single-national citizens from Lebanon when Lebanon was unable to protect their rights, it properly evacuated its dual-national citizens facing the same circumstances. The only place where dual nationality could cloud this issue would be, for example, a Canada–Ghanaian dual citizen who wants evacuation from Lebanon; in that case, Canada and Ghana could in principle be unsure about which state has the obligation to help their citizen, but in practice they should work together to make sure all of their citizens are properly protected. Again, citizens abroad retain the right of return, even if they are abroad over the longer-term, and the state of citizenship is duty-bound to protect it passively in general; in emergency situations, the duty is an active one.[7]

Conclusion

This chapter has had multiple objectives. One objective has been to defend the claim that states of citizenship retain obligations towards citizens who are resident abroad and, more particularly, to say something about the content of such obligations. The obligations include the duty to provide consular assistance and the duty to allow for, and in some cases facilitate, the return of citizens traveling or residing abroad. The duty to enable rather than merely allow for the return of citizens is often activated in emergency situations, where host states become unable to protect the basic human rights of those in their territory; states of citizenship ought in these cases to step in, to protect their citizens, usually in the form of enabling their return home.

As well, States often taken an interest in protecting the rights of citizens laboring abroad when their rights are violated by their host states, and they adopt policies of various kinds in an attempt to protect them. I considered, as an example here, the way in which Asian sending states act to protect the basic human rights of their citizens laboring temporarily in Gulf States. The goal of that discussion was to highlight the ongoing responsibility that sending states have to citizens abroad. I then turned to two questions that emerged from the discussion, with respect to whether home states must protect the right to vote for non-resident citizens abroad and, where individuals are dual citizens, how best to identify which state is responsible for protecting their rights when they are abroad. I argued that because subjection flows from residence rather than citizenship, the right to vote can permissibly be denied to long-term non-resident citizens (although it need not be), and should be extended to non-citizen, long-term residents. And, I suggested, both states of citizenship are responsible to protect dual citizens abroad, and that circumstances will dictate which state should act to do so. These arguments, over the course of these multiple situations, have set me up to consider a very tricky issue in the next chapter, namely, whether and when states can revoke citizenship status.

4
Revoking Citizenship Status

In the previous chapter, I offered an account of the rights (of citizenship) that citizens maintain even while they reside abroad. States' duties to citizens abroad are much reduced, on my account, especially in the case of long-term residence abroad, when the relevant individuals are *subjected* to a state in which they do not hold citizenship. Thus it is the state in which people reside that holds most of the duties of rights protection. States of citizenship retain the obligation to permit (but not always enable) the return of citizens who desire to return, and in cases of humanitarian or other disasters, they owe their citizens remedial rights protection when the state in which they reside is not able to protect their rights. This way of articulating the duties suggests that citizenship is a stable and irrevocable status, even if the rights the status carries are fewer for those who are abroad on a long-term basis; as well, the rights that states of citizenship are obligated to protect for their territorially based citizens are returned to citizens who return home after long stints abroad.

In this chapter, I defend the claim that citizenship status cannot be revoked by a state without the consent of the affected citizen herself. Note here the difference between waiving a right, which can be permissible in some cases ("I waive my right to a trial," for example), and the state's unilateral choice to revoke a right without the consent of the concerned individual. The thought that citizenship status can permissibly be revoked is central to many states' responses to citizen-terrorists, who are increasingly subject to denationalization procedures. I begin with an account of the right to citizenship, to argue that the right is inalienable, unconditional, and non-forfeitable. I then consider in some detail the claims made by those who argue that terrorist crimes are such that they warrant denationalization, and I do so by assessing the appropriate state response to foreign fighters residing in detention camps abroad. I will argue for the state's obligation to protect their right to citizenship, although I will leave open the possibility that states are not thereby obligated to "go get" their foreign fighters to proactively enable their return home. I will then consider two alleged exceptions to the claim the denationalization is impermissible, namely, that (at least according to some) it is permissible where wrongdoers are dual nationals and where citizens have acquired their citizenship fraudulently. Ultimately, I will argue that neither of these claimed exceptions holds much normative weight, and will conclude that the human right to citizenship is robust.

The Right to Citizenship is Inalienable, Unconditional, and Non-forfeitable

The first thing to say about the right to citizenship *status* is that it is inalienable; that is to say, it cannot be given away by its holder. This statement may seem counter-intuitive because of course citizens are generally permitted to give up one citizenship status and take on another. Historically, citizenship had been understood to mean *perpetual allegiance* to a state, that is, (especially European) citizens were treated as permanently attached to their state of citizenship.[1] However, the idea of citizenship as permanent and non-renounceable was largely abandoned by the end of the nineteenth century, and the right of individuals to shed their citizenship was codified in Article 15 the Universal Declaration of Human Rights, as "no one shall be arbitrarily ... denied the right to change his nationality" (United Nations 1948). States may not "keep citizens" against their will, for example, by refusing to release them from citizenship. Increasingly, states that do not permit dual citizenship are being accused of forcing citizens to "choose" between two states toward which they have loyalty, and in so doing are forcing citizens to keep citizenship status against their will.[2] One might read this to say that citizenship itself is alienable, but this is a mistake, and to see why one must also notice that the right that is protected is the right to *change* one's citizenship, rather than abandon citizenship status altogether. In other words, the right to alienate citizenship is the right to alienate one *particular* citizenship status, but not to alienate citizenship status altogether. States rarely permit citizens to adopt the status of "voluntary statelessness," although the United States is a notable exception here. The right to citizenship status itself is inalienable.

One implication of treating the right to citizenship status as inalienable, while treating the right to a particular citizenship status as alienable, is that citizens are not permitted to choose statelessness. Why should citizens be denied the right to voluntarily accept statelessness, as for example, anarchists may believe?[3] As I noted in Chapter 2, Mathew Gibney gives a partial answer in his argument rejecting denationalization, in particular when it would render someone stateless (Gibney 2013). He notes that forcing an individual into stateless status is tantamount to cruel and unusual punishment. But this response does not explain why someone should not be permitted to *choose* statelessness; it only explains why it is not legitimate for a state to impose it on someone as a form of punishment. Another partial answer is found in the American response to citizens who desire to shed their citizenship and adopt stateless status (Weil 2012), which warns individuals who desire to become stateless that they may as a result face "severe hardship," for lack of a state designated to protect their rights (Foreign Affairs Manual 2018). Without a state, the basic rights of individuals—to work, to move, to vote, and so on—are not protected. The moral reason to deny the right of individuals to become stateless—in other words, to require that individuals possess citizenship status in a state—is that, given how profoundly important states are in protecting rights of individuals, the desire to opt out of this protection is so unreasonable as to be impermissible.

So, justice does not permit the voluntary relinquishing of citizenship status. As well, the right to citizenship must be understood as unconditional, that is, sustaining the status of citizen is not, and should not be, dependent on the fulfillment of certain conditions, nor is the status weakened in the face of failure to meet other conditions. There is an obvious exception here—naturalizing individuals can be asked to fulfill certain conditions to attain citizenship status, although I happen to believe that only minimalist conditions can be justified; I will elaborate on fair and appropriate naturalizing conditions in Chapters 7 and 8.

The claim that citizenship *is* conditional is familiar, however, from social contract theories of the state. Speaking very generally, according to social contract theorizing, citizens are equal parties to a contract with a state, or they join as equal parties to form a state, with authority vested in a central representative, which delineates the conditions of the association; where one party believes the conditions are no longer met, the contract is dissolved. The thought is that, as with marriage or other forms of intimate human relations, where one party is no longer interested in sustaining the relationship or contract, it is dissolvable by that party. In the social contract tradition, there are usually understood to be obligations—conditions, we might say—on both sides of the contract, so that the contract is not dissolved merely because one party desires it, but because one party is no longer fulfilling the conditions of the contract. The point is, in this tradition, the contract is seen as between two more or less equal parties, who both benefit from the contract, and who must fulfill their end of the bargain to sustain it over time. This way of understanding citizenship will be familiar to many from recent political discourse, much of which treats citizenship as a privilege that is granted to people who fulfill the right kinds of conditions and can be withdrawn from those who do not. On this view of the state, the desire of the state to sever the contract (let's assume for a plausible cause) can be legitimate, at least in egregious cases like the commission of terrorism, even where the citizen who is thereby cast out does not consent to, or desire, the severing.

However, this way of understanding citizenship, as a relationship in which states and citizens must meet certain conditions for the contract binding them to persist, is misguided: it implies a kind of equivalence between the rights of states and the rights of citizens. Rather, citizens in general should be understood to have a package of rights, the goal of which is to protect them *from* the state. The right to citizenship status ought to be treated as among the rights that are immune from undermining by the state because of the role it plays in protecting citizens from that state's coercive power. In particular, without a protected right to citizenship status, the state can use its subjecting power to exclude members against their will, and in doing so disconnect them from the relations they value and the community they know.

So far, so good. And yet, a critical reader might nevertheless return to the way in which I conceived the social contract tradition and propose the following: perhaps, such a reader might say, the right to citizenship is not conditional per se, but perhaps the contract is nevertheless dependent on the fulfillment of pre-specified duties. Where citizens' actions can be understood as duty violations, they render the contract invalid. Correspondingly the state is absolved of its responsibilities to protect the rights of that citizen, including the right to citizenship status itself. On this view, certain actions are treated as evidence that the citizen has in fact acted in such a way as to *forfeit* the rights she possesses as a party to the contract.

This view is attractive to those who hold the forfeiture view of punishment to be partially or wholly persuasive (Wellman 2012). The forfeiture view of punishment is an attempt to make sense of what looks like a tension in rights-respecting democratic states. If a democratic state is, as a matter of principle, required to protect the rights of citizens, then it seems like a tension to argue that it may also restrict their rights: in particular, if citizens in democratic states have a wide range of "liberty rights," then it seems like the state cannot permissibly restrict them. But, say advocates of the forfeiture view, the protection of these liberty rights rests on their holder's willingness to abide by the rules and refusing wrongdoing. This view can explain why it is appropriate, for example, to jail criminals: they have forfeited a subset of their rights by committing crimes.

In cases where citizenship status is proposed to be available for forfeiture, the thought is that certain crimes are so grievous that they constitute a forfeiture of the right to citizenship status itself. As with all crimes, so long as the punishment is known in advance, the forfeiture view can make sense of retracting citizenship status as punishment for particular crimes. From this perspective, the commission of certain crimes signals an abandonment of the contract that binds citizens and state; the intent to abandon citizenship status can be inferred by certain actions a citizen takes, and therefore in these cases the withdrawal of citizenship status does not count as having been done unilaterally by a state. It is rather the formalization of a decision the citizen has made to abandon citizenship status. Christian Joppke expresses this kind of view, with respect to terrorist actions: it "is implausible," he writes, that "terrorists should not be able to lose the citizenship that they have repudiated through their own action" (Joppke 2016, 728). And so, a citizen who violates the contract can be understood as *forfeiting* her right to citizenship, and thereby as absolving the state from the requirement that it protect her citizenship rights.

However, it is dangerous to infer from *behaviors* what people intend, and in recognition of that the US Supreme Court ruled—in a well-known case, in which Beys Afroyim, a naturalized-American (from Poland) contested the decision to revoke his citizenship after he had cast a vote in an Israeli election—that the revocation was a violation of Afroyim's right to retain his US citizenship. This decision protects naturalized Americans convicted of terrorist crimes, as well, and the logic of the argument is more generally consistent with the fair and equal treatment of citizens in democratic states. As I articulated above, citizenship should not be treated as conditional on the performance or non-performance of specific behaviors or expressions of value commitments.

But say some advocates of revocation, perhaps it is correct that in *general* individuals can be dual citizens and sustain loyalty to two states, but *terrorists* by their very actions demonstrate a lack of loyalty. By their anti-state violence, focused as it is on undermining the democratic institutions that operate to protect them, they act to sever the relationship with their state of citizenship. They have, in effect, forfeited their right to citizenship and the state of citizenship has merely formalized that forfeiture by revoking citizenship. For those who make this argument, and who are persuaded by the imperative to avoid statelessness, it is *lucky* that some terrorists are dual nationals and so can be denationalized. For them, single nationality citizens have also forfeited their right to citizenship, but states of citizenship in this case are prevented from operationalizing the forfeiture by the imperative to avoid statelessness.

However, in my view, several indeterminacies inherent in the forfeiture account leave it unable to justify the forfeiture of the right to citizenship, without relying on additional material that prejudges the question, in favor of treating the right to citizenship as forfeitable in the first place.[4]

Although the forfeiture view is a kind of framework for understanding where and when rights can be treated as forfeited, it requires an independent account of "which rights they [a potential wrongdoer] forfeit and which they do not ... we still have to explain how, by acting in a certain way, one can lose certain rights but still retain others" (Miller 2012, 13). Many scholars believe, for example, that murderers do not forfeit their own right to life, and that the appropriate punishment for rapists is *not* to subject them to rape themselves. Moreover, very basic democratic rights, which "preclude cruel and unusual punishment, torture, penal servitude, and extrajudicial execution as well as rendition of subjects to rights-abusing countries" cannot ever be forfeited (Ignatieff 2004, 24). It does not do to say, simply, that rights can be forfeited by the commission of crimes; one must also explain why a particular right is, or is not, subject to forfeiture, and for those that are forfeitable, under what conditions they can reasonably be taken to be forfeited. The constraints on available punishments stem from a commitment to respecting the basic rights of wrongdoers, which cannot be extinguished, even where they are liable to punishment.

So, a forfeiture view must explain which rights can be subject to forfeiture. Having identified which rights can be forfeited, it must also explain how long the forfeiture can permissibly extend in time. To help clarify these details, forfeiture theorists typically rely on a proportionality principle.

In most cases, wrongdoers are punished via fines or incarceration, suggesting agreement that the proper rights that are subject to forfeiture in the case of punishment for wrongdoing are, usually, liberty rights and property rights. Yet, as Miller notes in his discussion of the challenge of identifying proportional rights forfeitures in punishment cases, although it may be possible to identify certain rights-restrictions that constitute a wildly disproportional response to a rights-violation, there remains "considerable indeterminacy over which particular rights have been lost as a result of a rights-violating action" (Miller 2012, 18). There is a similar indeterminacy with respect to assessing the appropriate *duration* of lost rights, that is, in assessing how long one should suffer from rights-loss as a punishment for wrongdoing. As above, the way forward is via a proportionality assessment with respect to the length of time a right should be subject to forfeiture, and although this assessment is inevitably subject to some arbitrariness, it is plausible to think that identifying reasonable boundaries is at least possible, that is, some lengths of time are problematically long, and others are problematically short.

It is not immediately clear whether forfeiture views can and do, or even should, permit the forfeiture of rights in perpetuity. In his defense of the forfeiture view, Miller hesitates to defend such a position: "we do not want to say that a person who at one time shows himself unwilling to respect the rights of others is to be placed outside the realm of reciprocity in *perpetuity*" (Miller 2012, 18). So, if an offender, who by her actions has signaled a failure to respect and recognize the rights of others over time, comes to regret her actions and, following a suitable punishment, is willing and able to recognize the rights of others, she must reasonably be able to rejoin the community of individuals bound by reciprocal rights recognition. Thus, Miller proposes, "mandatory whole-life sentences" must be rejected because they "deny those who are given them the opportunity to re-enter the human community as a reciprocal respecter of the rights of others" (Miller 2012, 19). Casting someone out of the community in perpetuity represents a denial of the underlying premise that motivates Miller's analysis, namely, that all individuals must be respected as rights-holders, who are also able to respect the rights of others on a reciprocal basis. This reason emphasizes the importance of respecting the basic rights of all individuals, even wrongdoers, as individuals who are in principle able to return to the community under appropriate circumstances.

One might respond that because returning from expulsion from citizenship is not impossible, it is not permanent in the way that capital punishment is. It is at least in theory possible for someone whose citizenship has been revoked to reapply for, and regain, citizenship. Drawing on the practice of ostracism in Ancient Athens, for example, revocation of citizenship might be treated as *temporary*, from which an individual might reasonably return after some number of years (Malkopoulou 2017). This response is disingenuous, however, given contemporary naturalization procedures, which in most countries deny the right of those convicted of serious crimes to attain citizenship. While it is in principle possible to imagine giving those whose status is revoked an opportunity to re-enter, in practice the likely success of this re-application is so low as to render it inadequate as a fair alternative to what I am arguing for here.

Maybe, though, it is possible that there are individuals who are simply unable to recognize the humanity in others on a reciprocal basis, and these individuals at least may be fairly punished by having their rights restricted in perpetuity, either by permanent incarceration, or by casting them out of the community entirely. Those who advocate in favor of denationalization make this accusation against those who commit, or intend to commit, crimes that undermine the national security of a state; as I wrote above, they are said to have shown by their actions that they are unable to recognize the rights of others in a particular community, and in perpetuity can be excluded from it. Perhaps evidence could be garnered in defense of this claim, but it seems to me to be wildly implausible that such evidence could reveal the *impossibility* of an individual's capacity to return to reciprocal rights recognition.[5]

As a result, the reason to reject the proposal that rights, including the right to citizenship status, can be retracted in perpetuity is simply that this response is disproportionate; denationalization means that the expelled cannot, and are treated as though they could not, return to the community of rights-respecting individuals. In summary: treating the right to citizenship status as forfeitable would mean treating wrong-doing individuals as though they could be cast away from the community of rights-respecting individuals in perpetuity; but permanent exclusion is impermissible in a democratic state, and the right to citizenship must be understood as protecting them from this exclusion and therefore as non-forfeitable.

Denationalizing Wrongdoing Dual Nationals

One challenge to the arguments I have developed above is that they do not apply as clearly to wrongdoers who are also dual nationals. In particular, dual nationals will not be rendered stateless, if one of their states of citizenship denationalizes them; and so, the denationalizing state would not in that case be denying them access to at least *a* state that will protect their rights, even if it is not the state they would prefer to rely on. Additionally, say some, dual nationals may reasonably be treated as having suspect loyalties (and historically they have been treated as suspect in just this way), where they are engaged in military actions abroad.

There are several reasons to resist the claim that the possession of dual nationality can render one liable to denationalization. One reason is that, as a matter of democratic principle, which is founded on a deep commitment to equality of all citizens, the permission to treat dual nationals differently from other nationals along any dimension is a violation of that commitment. Dual nationals are *citizens*, full-stop; they are not partial citizens (Blatter 2011). Liability to denationalization is an undermining of the security of residence to which they are entitled as citizens, and thus constitutes a quite severe undermining of a democratic state's commitment to equality; it treats dual nationals as "less than" full citizens and is thereby objectionable (as, for example, in Herzog 2010). Moreover, if a state permits the denationalization of convicted wrongdoers only if they are dual nationals, then such individuals are subject to a heftier punishment than single nationals; this inequality of treatment, for the same crime, is likewise a violation of democratic equality (Lenard 2016a). One could respond, I suppose, that the possession of dual nationality itself is a kind of inequality—a dual national has more options for residence and can enjoy the various benefits that each citizenship provides, in a way that single nationals cannot—for which "liability to denationalization" might seem to be an appropriate remedy. But here, it is important to notice that such benefits while real, are relatively minor, compared to the grave harm that is the persistent refusal to protect a citizen's residential security.

The proposal that dual citizens can permissibly be entitled to differential treatment—that is to say, reduced protection of their right to residential security—stems from a long history of treating immigrants as having suspect loyalties. Most famously, immigrant-citizens from "enemy" nations have been rounded up and interned during military conflicts, citing the worry that they may be dangers to their states of naturalized citizenship. The interning of immigrant-citizens from states with which "we" are at war, or who are at war with "us," is no longer considered permissible, but the increase in violence by citizens against fellow citizens of Middle Eastern (appearing) background in western states, and state-sanctioned discrimination against them, suggests that the loyalty worry persists, even if it is only implicit. This loyalty concern emerges for example in cases where suspected or actual terrorists of immigrant background engage in military/terrorist violence, in particular where they are dual nationals; in such cases, some suggest that by their actions dual national terrorists demonstrate a lack of loyalty to one of their states of citizenship and correspondingly intend to sever their connection with that state of citizenship (and retain the other, to which they sustain loyalty).

There has historically been resistance to recognizing the legitimacy of dual nationality (the decision in *Afroyim v. Rusk* moved the United States towards tolerating it, for example), but that resistance is falling and continues to do so, as I suggested in Chapter 3: many states have moved from rejecting it to tolerating it to permitting it (M. M. Howard 2005; Spiro 2019). The availability and permissibility of dual citizenship has traveled with increases in movement across borders and the concomitant growing awareness that many individuals are genuinely committed to two separate countries, and that loyalty can be extended to them both without meriting being described as "divided." But, some propose, while there may well be cases in which individuals are genuinely committed to two states, there are many others where dual citizens are not in fact so committed. In some cases, individuals may possess a second citizenship in virtue of their parents, or in a country they have never lived in or with which they have no "genuine link" (Bauböck and Paskalev 2015). In such cases, dual citizens are not in any obvious way loyal to two states, and so it may seem permissible to sever that link by revoking citizenship without violating the relevant individual's right to citizenship. There is a bureaucratic argument in favor of allowing states to formally sever a legal relationship in these cases. *But*, even were such an argument to operate so as to allow states to "clear the books," this sort of permission to revoke citizenship does not apply when an individual has engaged in wrongdoing. The danger, here, is that states will deny the existence of links that persist, and thereby wrongfully revoke the citizenship of someone who is entitled to it, as punishment for suspected or actual criminal activity. So, while "cleaning the books" may not amount to violating the right to citizenship, severing the citizenship link in the context of suspected or alleged wrongdoing does.

The Problem of Returning Foreign Fighters

In most political theoretic examinations of the right to withdraw citizenship, the prototypical character is either a war criminal (as in the cases of Nazis), or a lone or small group of terrorists, generally operating within the territorial boundaries of a democratic state, sometimes with connections to terrorist organizations abroad (Barry and Ferracioli 2015; Ferracioli 2017). Think, for example, of those who carried out coordinated attacks in France, killing over one hundred individuals in November 2015, for which ISIS claimed responsibility (France 24 2019b). More recently, many terrorist attacks have been carried out by far-right extremists whose targets of attack are racial, religious, and sexual minorities (Lenard 2020b). What distinguishes these kinds of cases from foreign-fighter cases is that the wrongdoers are present in their state of citizenship when they commit the crime. So, the focus is largely on whether the removal of citizenship, and then deportation to a second state of citizenship, can be part of a fair punishment for such crimes. In the case of foreign fighters, however, the would-be denationalized citizen is *outside* of the relevant state which, in denationalizing, would remove the foreign fighter's ability to return to that state as well.

As I noted in Chapter 3, there is nothing new about foreign fighters, individuals who travel abroad to join a military conflict (de Roy van Zuijdewijn and Bakker 2004). Historically, many states adopted laws outlining that citizens who join military conflicts abroad can be denationalized, although the frequency with which states availed themselves of this power is not clear. As I outlined earlier in some detail, the largest recent group of would-be returning foreign fighters traveled to join ISIS in their (now failed) bid to create a caliphate; ISIS combatants have been especially gruesome and violent in their attempt to achieve this objective. Now that the conflict is more or less over and ISIS has been largely defeated, many foreign fighters want to return to their countries of citizenship. Although the United Nations, along with many other organizations, has been calling on states to repatriate their fighters, states have shown considerable reluctance to do so (for example, see Landström 2021). Home states have worried openly that returning fighters might have been (further) radicalized abroad to believe that liberal democratic values are anathema and must be defeated, and that they will return home with the intention of undermining these values and the institutions they support, using the violent tactics they learned abroad.[6]

In response, states have sought to adopt or revive denationalization laws, which had mostly been abandoned or fallen into disuse (Lenard 2016a; Gibney 2017; Andrey Macklin 2015). There is considerable variation among the laws that have been adopted, and the circumstances in which they have been deployed. The United Kingdom has been the most aggressive of nations to denationalize foreign fighters, or others believed to be "threats to the public good" (Lenard 2018a). Perhaps most famously, the United Kingdom has denationalized Shamima Begum, who traveled to Syria as a fifteen-year-old, citing not the security risk that her return would pose, but rather that by carrying out terrorist actions abroad, she has forfeited any right to UK citizenship she may have previously possessed. The UK government claims the impact has not been to render her stateless because she has access to Bangladeshi citizenship, a claim that Bangladesh denies. Denmark, too, has denationalized many of its foreign fighting citizens—it appears, as it largely does in the UK, that those who are denationalized are dual citizens, so no one has been rendered stateless by its actions (Carlson 2021; The Local 2019).

However, this strategy is nevertheless a straightforward violation of the right to citizenship status, for several reasons. First, in Begum's case, the alleged connection to a second state that could, in principle, give her citizenship is insufficient to fulfill the requirement that statelessness is avoided. Second, in denationalizing Begum and thereby denying her the ability to return, she was punished without an opportunity to defend her actions in a criminal trial; in punishing her without giving her access to a fair trial, the UK violated her rights of due process. Third, the choice to exclude Begum on a permanent basis obviously fails to treat her as someone who can, at least in principle, be reintegrated into society at least under some conditions. Contrast Begum's treatment with how Norway's criminal justice system has treated Anders Breivik, who killed seventy-eight people (eight via a bomb attack, and the others by shooting them), and who was given Norway's maximum sentence of twenty-one years in prison; although from outside of Norway, this punishment seemed insufficient, the Norwegian system is underpinned by the assumption that even the worst criminals can be reintegrated into society.[7] Fourth and finally, as I have already explained, it is impermissible to interpret actions, however gruesome, as forfeiting a right as basic as citizenship.

Having established that states cannot denationalize their foreign fighters, the question remains whether they must facilitate those fighters' return. There are three further considerations to add to the moral evaluation of this slightly distinct question. One consideration is that, as I outlined in Chapter 3, the conditions in detention camps abroad are extraordinarily dangerous for those detained there, and reports suggest they are deteriorating. An additional complication is that they are not safe spaces for individuals to renounce commitment to ISIS values and objectives; such individuals can face reprisals for their renunciation and by doing so place themselves in extreme danger. Of course, the *preference* is that foreign fighters renounce their past commitments to ISIS—one criticism that was made of Begum was that she did not immediately renounce her commitment to ISIS—but one incentive they have to do so is erased if the possibility of returning home is denied to them (Kennedy 2019).

Foreign fighters whose states will not repatriate them are in effect subjecting them to a form of statelessness, even if they do not formally withdraw citizenship. As a result of their home state's response, the result is that no state is responsible for protecting the rights of the individual affected. When the UK denationalized Begum, citing her connection to Bangladesh, they denied she was rendered stateless; rather, as I said above, she was alleged to be entitled to Bangladeshi citizenship, an entitlement the British government claimed was going unrecognized. From the British perspective, the state that was failing to protect Begum's rights, therefore, was Bangladesh first and foremost. Of course, its reasoning was disingenuous in the sense that Begum's social connections rest entirely in the UK, where her friends and family live. She has never visited Bangladesh and does not speak the language. So even if there is a technical truth to the claim that Bangladesh ought to have recognized Begum's citizenship,[8] it is the UK to which Begum aimed to return because that is where she was born, grew up, and where her familial and broader connections remain. The duty failure is on the side of the British government, for rendering her stateless, and in so doing retracting its or any state's duty to protect her rights fulsomely.

In Begum's case, the UK revoked her citizenship, rendering her effectively stateless (for more discussion, see Lenard 2020b). In other cases, states are simply refusing to enable the return of their citizens, whether or not they are dual citizens. The language of "enabling" is critical here because, as I described in Chapter 3, states are required to permit the entry of their citizens, when they appear at the border. Canadian representatives therefore acknowledged that would-be foreign fighter returnees would be permitted to enter Canada if they arrived at a Canadian border. But, as I said earlier, Canada and many other states are claiming that it is too dangerous for their officials to visit detention camps to assess the status of those claiming citizenship and who, on that basis, want to return home. The refusal to enable their citizens' return, whether or not they are dual citizens, is a failure by states to recognize the duties they have towards their citizens, even when they are abroad. In this case, the failure is not simply to refuse to enable return when support for return is requested, but to do so when the conditions in which citizens remain are such that their human rights are persistently undermined—it is the same duty that explains, as I articulated in Chapter 3, why it is that states are obligated to step in when citizens abroad unexpectedly find themselves in the midst of a humanitarian or military conflict, and the host state is unable to protect their basic human rights. There, I also defended the duty to enable return in the context of the children of foreign fighters, arguing that their entitlement to repatriation—in the face of the abuse of their rights—was sufficiently like the case of citizens in humanitarian disasters, because their rights are not being protected and they bear no responsibility for the situation in which they find themselves.

Here, a critic might return to that argument and suggest that the "no responsibility" condition does not apply to foreign fighters themselves. Foreign fighters made a choice, to join a foreign conflict, and they can be held responsible for having done so; this responsibility, a critic might say, justifies a state's refusal to actively repatriate foreign fighters, even if the lack-of-responsibility argument was sufficient to justify the obligation to repatriate children. Earlier I argued that citizenship was unconditional, that is, there are no behaviors that warrant the revocation of citizenship; so, it is no surprise that I do not believe that foreign fighters can be denationalized on the basis of their actions. There are additional, practical reasons to avoid denationalizing foreign fighters, and to enable their return instead, as a general policy. For one thing, when states refuse to repatriate and prosecute their citizens, in some cases foreign fighters are left at the mercy of a criminal justice system that is well-known to be unfair. For example, Iraq has prosecuted many foreign fighters for their crimes in trials that have failed to meet even the most basic standards for fair criminal trials in democratic countries, and then sentenced them to prison terms in jails that fail to respect the basic human rights of inmates (R. L. Phillips 2021).[9] Another danger is that, if states refuse to repatriate their citizen foreign fighters, the result may be that at least some of them will in fact avoid punishment for their crimes.[10] Perhaps consigning foreign fighters to dangerous and violent detention camps is thought to *stand in* for punishment, but the choice to treat it that way is inconsistent with how democracies treat the issuing of punishment for crime, after an airing of alleged criminal activity, and possible mitigating factors, and the non-arbitrary identification of proportionate punishment. Ultimately, both moral and practical reasons together suggest that foreign fighters are entitled to repatriation-with-trial, so that the question of responsibility can be dealt with at trial, once the relevant citizen has been removed from the situation in which their rights are being violated.[11]

Finally, let me return to the question of the relevance of dual nationality. Can home states evade the charge of rendering citizens stateless where the relevant citizen is evidently a dual citizen, rather than merely putatively so? I believe no. In cases of dual citizenship, as I argued earlier, both states of citizenship are responsible for protecting their citizens' basic human rights. It so happens that in many cases, the state of ordinary residence will have greater responsibility, and the source of this greater responsibility is the ongoing subjection of the relevant citizen to its power. That greater responsibility is heightened by the existing relations, that may be stronger, between a would-be returning foreign fighter and others in their country of residence, that is, the country in which the foreign fighter resided prior to traveling.

For example, the strength of connection to the UK matters to the moral evaluation of Begum's case, even if it were true that she was a dual citizen of the UK and Bangladesh. Remember that the remedial duty to protect the basic human rights of citizens abroad, where the state in which they are present cannot do so, travels with citizenship and *automatically* applies to those who are abroad, regardless of how long they are abroad and for what reason. It may be the case that, for those who are abroad, their connections to one state are stronger than to another; but, the strength of the connections is not for the state of citizenship to determine. It is permissible in cases of dual citizenship that both states of citizenship negotiate for which one possesses the responsibility for a particular would-be returning foreign fighter; after considering the evidence, the state with which the would-be returning foreign fighter has the strongest connection is the one that is responsible for her.

Conclusion

The fundamental claim in this book is that there is a strong relation between the power that a state has to subject citizens and residents and the obligation that that state possesses to grant such individuals full inclusion. As I have argued so far, the purpose of full inclusion—in the form of the status of citizenship—is to protect the residential security of those whose lives are shaped by the subjecting power of a state, thereby enabling them to participate in politics without fear of reprisal in the form of deportation. Denationalization is impermissible precisely because it undermines the residential security to which citizens and many residents are entitled in virtue of that subjection. A state may not permissibly respond by withdrawing, unilaterally, the protection it offered, saying that it prefers to exclude a given citizen rather than persist in granting them the inclusion that is demanded by subjection. Why? Because doing so is unjustified coercion in cases where citizens do not consent to the revocation.

This chapter's objective has therefore been to defend a right to citizenship that is robust against claims, by states, that there are cases where denationalization is permissible and, indeed, justified. Relying on my earlier arguments focused on understanding the right to citizenship status as protecting the very strong interests that individuals have in access to secure residence, I argued that states do not have the unilateral right to withdraw citizenship. Citizenship is inalienable, unconditional, and non-forfeitable. When applied to the case of foreign fighters abroad, who desire to return home, my account explains why states have the duty not simply to permit would-be returning foreign fighters to enter, if they arrive at the border of their country of citizenship, but also the duty to repatriate them so that they face the consequences of their actions in a fair and open trial. That some would-be foreign fighters are dual nationals does not entitle either state to revoke citizenship unilaterally, so as to disclaim responsibility for protecting their basic human rights; rather, it assigns the duty to repatriate to two states, who are permitted to negotiate and agree which of them will carry it out. The right to repatriation does not require that returning foreign fighters escape punishment for their crimes; on the contrary, it means that citizen foreign fighters will be fairly assessed and punished for their crimes, as is appropriate in democratic states that presume that all wrongdoers can, in time and with appropriate recompense, return to society as full and equal members.

The arguments I have made thus far conclude the first half of the book. Its overarching goal has been to explain who is entitled to citizenship status, what the status protects for resident and non-resident citizens, and its robustness in the face of claims that it can permissibly be withdrawn without the consent of its holders. It is the fact of subjection, I suggested, that identifies who is entitled to citizenship status and the rights that flow from this status, and these early chapters have aimed collectively to make it clear that full inclusion in a political society depends on granting citizenship to those who are subjected to a state's power over an extended period of time. I turn next to the procedures by which non-citizens can access territory and, in time, citizenship, including the fair demands that can be placed on would-be citizens as they join a new political community.

5
Visa Issuance and Denial in an Unequal World

Over the course of this book, I have not questioned the fact of borders between states, or the permissibility of excluding would-be entrants in at least some cases. I have presumed the permissibility of border control rather than engage in the rich and thoughtful literature that questions both the fact of borders and the legitimacy of states' claimed right to control them. Largely, this choice stems from a desire to evaluate real policies in the broad space of migration, and to offer proposals that press in favor of more justice in the context that states, especially democratic ones, face. In this chapter and over the course of the rest of the book, I examine the permissibility of strategies that states use to include and exclude migrants from their territory and from membership. I start with an assessment of the visa-issuing regime.

Before any person can migrate to a new state, on a temporary or a permanent basis, they must acquire permission from the host state to do so. Typically, this permission is granted in the form of issuing a would-be traveler a visa. In some small number of cases, migrants are exempted from the requirement to acquire a visa before they enter, and as I described in Chapter 2, some would-be migrants cannot get visas or believe they would not, and so opt to enter states in irregular ways, and with the help of smugglers. In many other cases, and these are the subject of my analysis in this chapter, visas must be acquired pre-travel, and acquiring these visas requires fulfilling a substantial set of visa requirements in advance of travel. These "eligibility conditions," which must be met to access visas vary in their justifiability, as I will articulate over the course of the chapter.

I will begin, just below, by placing the visa system in the broader context of strategies that states use to externalize their borders and note along the way that such a system persists in privileging citizens in relatively wealthier countries by giving them access to a wide range of easily accessible travel options. Over the course of this discussion, I will make the case that the distinction between permanent and temporary migration is muddy, in ways that states recognize and respond to, often unjustly. Then, I will move to a consideration of the specific visa requirements that are attached to gaining the necessary travel documentation, to consider their justifiability. These conditions, as I label them, are "proof that you aren't" conditions; "proof that you are" conditions; and "an acceptance of rights restrictions" conditions. That is to say, to gain access to visas, applicants must often prove that they are *not* criminals, or dangerous in other ways; they must prove that they *are* financially solvent, and often that they really do intend to return to their home countries when their visa expires; and they must consent to the restriction of certain rights, as a condition of accepting the visa for travel. As I will argue, several of these conditions cannot be justified because they undermine a state's claim to meet the minimum criteria of immigration justice. To remind readers, these criteria are that an immigration policy, and its mode of implementation, must (a) not be discriminatory, (b) support the fulfilment of obligations to asylum seekers and refugees, (c) enable the reunification of families, and (d) include a mechanism to transition long-term non-citizens to citizens. Ultimately, I will argue, visas that permit the subjection of residents on a long-term basis, and without permitting access to full inclusion via the granting of citizenship, are unjustified.

Visa Eligibility Requirements in an Unequal World

Let me begin by providing a picture of the general operation of visas in the global mobility regime. Any would-be traveler requires a passport to gain legitimate entry; this requirement has been in force, globally, for nearly a century. As well, *some* travelers, but crucially not all of them, require visas to gain entry to a destination state. Each country identifies a subset of other countries whose citizens may visit *without* requiring a visa in advance; that is to say, without subjecting themselves to pre-screening in advance of travel. For them, the visa requirement is waived, and for others, a range of conditions must be met to get the visas needed for travel. Countries make determinations, using a range of criteria, to issue visa waivers to the citizens of other countries.

There is a well-established literature documenting when visa waivers are extended—sometimes visa waivers are the product of bilateral agreements between two countries, and other times they are the result of a desire to cultivate or dissuade travel from specific countries. In general, however, visa requirements to gain access to travel are unequally applied. Although there are exceptions, there are some notable trends in who has access to visa-free travel and who does not. In general, citizens from relatively wealthier countries can travel to many more countries without applying for visas in advance of travel than can citizens of relatively poorer countries. To give an example, in 2010, citizens of Denmark, Finland, and the United States could travel to 130 other countries without attaining a visa in advance, whereas citizens of Iran and Somalia could access only fourteen, and citizens of Afghanistan only twelve (Luedtke, Byrd, and Alexander 2010, 149).

Most visas are *short-term* visas, rather than visas issued for those who wish to migrate permanently (Mau et al. 2015, 1193). Tourists, international students, temporary labor migrants, and businesspeople seek short-term visas. Comparatively fewer migrants aim to, or are granted the right to, migrate on a permanent basis. This separation between short-term and permanent visas parallels a distinction between short- and long-term migration that is present in much political theory of migration, but the assumption that there is a clear line between these categories is problematic for two reasons.

First, the distinction does not make sense of many, if not most, actual migration experiences. Consider the behavior of those who are, relatively speaking, freer to move across borders. The bulk of global movement across borders is for tourists, international study, or to take up short-term labor contracts. But permanent migration often begins with short-term visits: "Those who come with a long-term perspective have often visited the destination country previously on a short-term basis and thereby probed into other countries, expanded their networks, visited friends and family, and made themselves familiar with future opportunities related to migration plans" (Mau et al. 2015, 1196). That is, among those who cross borders on a short-term basis, many indeed intend to stay only temporarily at the time they have crossed the border. Many temporary travelers find that they develop reasons over time to migrate on a more permanent basis: they complete education and gain employment in their field; they fall in love; they realize they prefer the climate, or the lifestyle, elsewhere. None of these people *intended* to be permanent, but some among them develop a desire for permanent migration over time.

Second, and more problematically, the assumption that migrants who apply for temporary migration opportunities do so from a desire to remain on a temporary basis only is not warranted. On the contrary, the suggestion that there is a clear line between those who desire temporary or permanent migration opportunities gives rise to the easy conclusion that it is permissible to grant different bundles of rights to migrants based on their supposed intentions.[1] The logic is, if visitors are merely short-term, there is no obligation to offer them a wide range of rights; such rights are required to be offered and protected only for migrants who are admitted with the intention that they stay on a permanent basis. For example, in the political theory literature that assesses the justice of temporary labor migration programs, some argue that because the associated work contracts are only temporary, it is permissible to restrict (sometimes severely) the rights and benefits that are available to migrants who take them up (Stilz 2010; Mayer 2005). Tiziana Torresi and Valeria Ottonelli make a similar claim about temporary labor migrants, insisting that restricting some migrants to temporary visas is respectful of their life plans—they may well *want* to be temporary visitors, only, and we should not assume that they desire to stay (Ottonelli and Torresi 2012). However, it is not possible to know what migrant workers *intend* or *desire*, as their choices are heavily constrained by the visa options available to them.[2]

Rather, in imposing conditions on visa acquisition, states are generally attempting to ensure that only those who genuinely intend to return home are admitted: "when issuing a visa, many destination countries put much effort into scrutinising an applicant's intent to return" (Mau et al. 2015, 1196). Others are prevented by the terms of their initial admission from remaining permanently, regardless of what they intend or desire. In other words, the visa regime operates to shape and restrict the options that some individuals have to gain entry—for example, some people may only be able to fulfill the requirements of temporary visas—and their intention, or desire, cannot thereby be inferred from the visa status they hold. Ultimately, the choice to require would-be travelers to secure visas in advance is part of states' attempts to control their borders from afar: "Requiring a visa allows states to exercise exterritorial control in the sense that the encounter between the control agency and potential border-crossers already takes place in the countries of origin" (Mau et al. 2015, 1194). The visa-granting system thus operates as a "first line of defense" in protecting a state from migrants it prefers not to admit (Czaika and Neumayer 2017, 75). Correspondingly, the requirement that citizens of certain countries submit to pre-travel assessment and get "cleared" of suspicion via the issuing of visa is an obstacle in the way of some would-be travelers, and in other cases operates to deny travel altogether.

The Ethics of Visa Requirements

In Chapter 2, I distinguished between admission policies and their enforcement mechanisms. In considering the visa-issuing system, the intersection between policy and enforcement emerges clearly. The visa system just *is*, one might say, one key mechanism by which immigration policies are implemented and enforced, and so do not require separate moral evaluation. Assuming a simple connection between the adoption of immigration policies and their enforcement is not always warranted, however. Rather, as much recent scholarship demonstrates, the enforcement of immigration policies requires separate moral evaluation from the policies themselves, as the enforcement is too often brutal and inhumane (Cabrera 2010; Hidalgo 2015; Mendoza 2015). Correspondingly, the near impossibility of fair enforcement of immigration policies presses at least some scholars in favor of abandoning border control altogether, in favor of borders that are maximally fluid (Sager 2017). This conclusion is too strong, however. Instead, I propose that the enforcement mechanisms deployed in support of immigration policies must, like the policies themselves, meet minimal standards of migration justice. They must be applied in a non-discriminatory way, they must not interrupt the asylum-seeking and asylum-granting system, they must enable reasonable family reunification opportunities, they must not contribute to the creation of a class of long-term non-citizen residents with sub-standard rights protection, and they must permit the return of citizens, regardless of the reason or length of their absence. I will rely on these five criteria to assess the most common clusters of visa requirements.

In what follows, I focus specifically on the requirements for short-term travel visas because, as I indicated above, the bulk of international travel is ostensibly intended to be short-term. Short-term visas range dramatically in form and target, and include the visas issued to international students, temporary workers, tourists, and those escaping humanitarian disasters, among many others. Although it is consistent with my view that democratic states can, at least in some cases, permissibly exclude, as I will show, questions of permissible exclusion become harder to evaluate if and when states desire to include some migrants, but only on a temporary basis. There are three general clusters of requirements, which would-be migrants must typically meet in order to be issued a visa, and which I will consider in what follows: (1) "prove that you are not excludable" criteria, which require for example that applicants prove that they are not security or health risks; (2) "prove that you are includable" criteria, which require for example that applicants prove that they possess the means of subsistence during their stay; and (3) a "a consent to rights restrictions" criterion, which requires applicants to agree to abide by the visa conditions associated with their visa. When I consider the third criterion, I will disaggregate the analysis into a consideration of the rights that temporary visa holders are often denied, including: (a) the right to access social services, (b) the right to travel with family, (c) the right to work, and (d) the right to apply for permanent status.

Visa requirements operate to make travel more difficult for those who are subject to them. And, obviously, the tougher the visa requirements, the harder it is for applicants to be successful in getting a visa. The processing time for visas can also be significant, requiring many weeks or months of advance planning to be able to travel at the desired time, for example, to participate in a wedding or other family scheduled event (Czaika and Neumayer 2017, 76). There are three factors that I will not consider that influence the ease with which visas can be accessed. One factor is the mechanism by which a visa application is filed. In some cases, visa applications can be submitted entirely online, and in others, visa applicants must prepare physical copies of relevant documents and deliver them to appropriate consulates or embassies for consideration. To the extent that visa applications can be made entirely online, they are generally more accessible (although an application procedure that was only accessible online would be restrictive in a problematic way as well). A second factor is the fees associated with visa applications, which can be steep and which operate effectively as a tax on travel (their justification is typically that would-be travelers should be asked to pay the cost that the destination state incurs to assess their claim); their impact is to render visa application less accessible for those with limited financial means. A third factor is the need for in-person interviews as part of the application to gain a visa. This last factor highlights the tremendous discretion given to visa officers in assessing the credibility of a visa applicant, and research suggests that visa officers often behave in discriminatory and racist ways (or operate with discriminatory and racist biases) that result in unfair visa denials (Salter 2006, 182). To the extent that these features are deployed and make the application procedure unnecessarily difficult, they are not permissible; I do not intend to consider them further. I am here focused instead on whether the documentary evidence requested of some but not all applicants can be justified, in light of my accepting that it is permissible for a state to limit some visitors to short-term stays.

"Prove that you are not excludable" Criteria

Migrants often need to prove that they are "medically admissible." In many cases, in advance of travel, temporary movers must undergo a medical exam, by a designated doctor, to prove that they are not carrying infectious diseases, including usually tuberculosis and syphilis, which the destination state believes constitute a threat to public health. As well, visa applicants are often asked to provide proof of vaccination for a range of diseases, including any diseases that are endemic in the destination state. Visitors to many sub-Saharan African countries may be required to get yellow fever vaccinations before gaining admission, for example, or prove that they are carrying anti-malarial drugs on entry. The designation of medically "inadmissible" may also be attached to individuals who have chronic medical conditions, which may (in the view of the destination state) result in the would-be traveler requiring expensive medical care, especially if providing this medical care would undermine the state's capacity to provide similar care to its own citizens (IRCC 2018; Australian Government 2021). Alternatively, visitors may be asked to prove that they possess health insurance to cover the costs of any medical visits during their temporary stay (this latter condition is connected to the set of services to which visitors are not entitled, as I will discuss below).

Migrants must also often prove that they are not dangerous; that is to say, that they do not pose a threat to the security of the destination state. In some cases, would-be migrants must provide police checks; in others, they must answer questions focused on past involvement in military activities; in some, they must answer a set of questions, including whether they have participated in genocide or human trafficking; in yet others, they must confirm that they do not possess nefarious intent upon arrival in the proposed destination state. All these requirements are imposed to protect the security of the destination state. The security threat that a would-be migrant might pose can be difficult to assess—many would-be migrants have been forced to participate in military action against their will, for example, and others have committed crimes, and have been convicted of them, which are not recognized as crimes in the destination state, including homosexuality or political protest.

A state is typically understood to be obligated to protect the health and safety of citizens, and ensuring that both are robust is "in the collective interest of the political community, and the state should act in defense of the public interest" (Song 2018, 160). Exclusion on the basis of either public health or security threats has generally been treated as defensible, on the grounds that a state ought to be able to exclude travelers and migrants who pose threats to important public goods. Yet, as Song observes, as a matter of historical practice, both criteria, which are in principle the basis of morally defensible exclusion, have been used in discriminatory ways. A familiar example is the exclusion of HIV positive individuals, an exclusion that persisted in many countries well after the mechanisms for keeping viral load suppressed were both identified and put into widespread use; their continued exclusion after this point was indefensible from a public health standpoint, and almost certainly stemmed from a combination of persistent homophobia and ongoing racism against sub-Saharan Africans. A key factor with respect to health-based exclusions is that they must treated as reversible, if the relevant basis for exclusion changes. It may be legitimate, for example, to exclude an individual with active tuberculosis, but after the tuberculosis is under control, exclusion on that basis is no longer justified.

The requirement that would-be travelers prove that they do not pose a threat to national security is similarly defensible at the level of principle, and similarly subject to discriminatory application in practice. Especially since 9/11, states have been focused on denying would-be terrorists opportunities to travel across borders, using a variety of tools including "no-fly" lists, where terrorism suspects are denied the right to board airplanes, and the non-issuance or non-renewal of passports to those who are suspected of desiring to travel for nefarious purposes.[3] It is reasonable to focus on protecting a state's security, of course, but the over-representation of individuals with Middle Eastern background on national no-fly lists suggests that at least some racial profiling is at work, at least historically (Lenard 2020b).

Similarly, the challenge of avoiding the discriminatory application of visa regulations is substantial—and the costs of errors are high. Recall the non-discrimination requirement of a minimally just immigration policy. A commitment to non-discrimination in general underpins the view that immigration policies cannot exclude people based on characteristics which are, as John Rawls has explained, arbitrary from a moral point of view (for a discussion, see Brock 2020, ch. 4). So, immigration admission policies that specifically exclude migrants based on religious, racial, or ethnic characteristics cannot be justified under any circumstances. The result is that it is rare (or at least, it should be rare) for a liberal, democratic state to explicitly exclude individuals on the basis of religious and racial characteristics.[4]

Historically, of course, this sort of discriminatory policy was common. For example, Asians were for many years excluded wholly or in part from both the United States and Canada. The American "Chinese Exclusion Act," adopted in 1882, prohibited migration from China (and was repealed in part in 1943, and then fully in 1952); similarly, in Canada a 1923 law called the Chinese Immigration Act, banned most forms of migration from China to Canada.[5] More recently, former US President Donald Trump issued immigration regulations that came colloquially to be known as the "Muslim ban," which formally banned citizens from multiple Muslim-majority countries from entering the United States. The Trump administration never admitted its intention to ban Muslims in particular, citing rather national security imperatives, and noting that Muslims live in many countries that were not subject to the restriction, but multiple courts refused to let the regulation go into practice as it was originally written, forcing modifications to the policy to remove at least its overtly discriminatory elements (Song 2018, 160–161).

What is a fair way to proceed, then? The proper strategy is to persist in requiring that would-be travelers prove that they do not present a danger to national security, and at the same time to adopt transparent and efficient appeals mechanisms so that individuals who are denied entry on national security grounds, which they believe are unfounded, can contest the decision quickly. For such a strategy to be adopted, travelers whose visa applications are denied on national security grounds must of course be informed of that reason with some specificity. In Canada, for example, would-be travelers are sometimes informed merely that they do not meet the requirements as outlined in the Immigration and Refugee Protection Act, but not how they fail to meet them.[6] This lack of information prevents would-be travelers from knowing how to contest the designation, and the result is that legitimate migrants may be denied the opportunity to be with friends and family on important occasions, to travel as a tourist, and so on.

"Prove that you are includable" Criteria

The criteria that I considered above are "negative" criteria, in the sense that they require would-be travelers to prove that they do not possess certain characteristics that render them justifiably excludable. Would-be travelers frequently must do more than meet these requirements to gain entry. Often, they must also meet what I have termed "prove that you are includable" criteria, at least on a short-term basis. Let me consider several of them in turn.

Visa applicants must often prove that they are truly just *visiting* on a temporary basis. In some cases, this proof comes in the form of an invitation letter, for example from a family member or friend in the destination country, from an organization that has invited the visitor to speak (for example at a conference), and in others as admission to a university program or time-limited job contract. In many cases, temporary labor market contracts can only be issued where the destination country has pre-designated an acute labor market need (via a labor market assessment procedure). The format of letters of invitation is typically designated in advance by the destination state and requires the inviters to confirm their connection to the visitor and to specify travel plans for that time period, including (where relevant) who is responsible for materially supporting the visitor during their stay.[7]

Alongside evidence of an invitation, which specifies the reason for a visit and attests to its temporariness, visitors must often also provide evidence of sufficient resources to cover the costs of their stay. Sometimes visitors are asked to provide a bank statement with a sufficiently high balance, or to show evidence of continued employment in their home state or other regular source of income (Mau et al. 2015, 1196). Visitors can also be asked to acquire insurance—travel and/or health—that can cover unexpected travel-related costs, including especially the unexpected use of health services in the destination state. Some travelers must, additionally, show proof of having purchased (or in some cases reserved) a return ticket.

All these requirements are intended to allow visa-issuing officers to assess whether a visa applicant intends, in fact, to visit temporarily only. Visa-officers assess the evidence provided, seeking signals that a would-be visitor intends to stay beyond the short-term. In some cases, the objective of rooting out would-be visa-overstayers is subtle; in others, it is explicit. In Norway, for example, visa refusal letters sometimes indicate that a visa has been denied on the grounds that officials have reason to believe, on the basis of the information provided and on the basis of characteristics of the applicant, which are shared with past visa-overstayers, that the applicant does not intend to leave once admission to the state is granted (Bo 1998, 197).[8] States explicitly recognize, in other words, that a short-term visit can be a "central entry channel for irregular immigration . . . people may arrive legally but then stay on after their visa has expired, so that the states' reluctance to grant a visa is often a form of precaution" (Mau et al. 2015, 1196) against admitting individuals who will transition, in time, to irregular migrant status.

Earlier, I implied that it is permissible to restrict some travelers to short stays only, at least in principle. Is it fair, though, that citizens of some counties are required to attain pre-travel clearance whereas others can simply show up at the border? Notice that if one does not agree that limiting some travelers to short visits is okay—if one believes that states must simply admit all visitors (who do not pose health or security risks)—then this question is moot. The question I am posing here has two parts: (a) is there a violation of equality when some but not all travelers are subject to additional pre-travel screening requirements? And, (b) if the answer is no, what can permissibly be required as proof that visitors intend to stay for a short period only?

Why might there be a violation of equal treatment, in requiring some travelers to provide proof of their intentions to gain access to a state? Of course, it is important in democratic states to treat people equally—even those who are outsiders—and one signal that this commitment to equality is not being respected is when people in similar situations are treated differently in what appear to be normatively irrelevant ways. Of course, not all differential treatment is objectionable from a normative perspective, and on the contrary, there are many cases where it is appropriate and preferable to treat apparently similarly situated people differently (for a discussion of the principle, see Nagel 1973; Kamm 1985; Shin 2009). For example, it is not generally understood to be a violation of the commitment to equal treatment to extend parental leave to new parents, even though such leave is not available to others. Similarly, it is not generally understood to be a violation of equal treatment to accommodate religious requirements in multiple spaces, including with respect to the provision of halal or kosher food in cafeterias or, as I will consider later, by permitting women who cover their faces to take citizenship oaths when, normally, the requirement is that one is not permitted to do so. These are accommodations made to reduce the burden of certain rules or regulations on minority citizens.

But it is also sometimes acceptable to increase the burdens on some people without obviously violating the conditions imposed by an equal treatment requirement. So, with respect to visa requirements, is imposing additional requirements on some but not all travelers a violation of the commitment to equal treatment? Can we offer a persuasive answer to a would-be traveler who asks, "Why do I have to fill in all of these documents, when she does not have to? It isn't fair!"?

What looks problematic in the case of visa requirements is that those who are subject to them are citizens of relatively poorer states, who (from the perspective of many destination states) are often racially, ethnically, or religiously distinct. So, the worry is either that visa restrictions are imposed in a discriminatory way on "minorities," or that they are imposed in ways that operate to protect and perpetuate wealth inequalities by denying citizens of poor countries access to labor markets (and other goods available) in wealthier ones. Indeed, in general, in assessing the trends in access to global mobility, it is hard to avoid the worry that the application of visa requirements on some countries is the result of explicit, or at least implicit, racism: as one scholar observes, citizens from every African country, and most Asian countries, require visas to travel to Europe, whereas nearly all of those who can access visa-free travel in Europe not only live in countries with comparatively higher GDP per capita, they are historically white and Christian (Heijer 2018, 472).[9] So, the choice to adopt visa requirements in these cases may look uncomfortably similar to racial profiling. Defenders of at least some forms of racial profiling argue there are cases where efficiency reasons justify its use (Risse and Zeckhauser 2004). However, the analogy should be resisted.

It should be resisted, at least in part, because (if I have persuaded you so far) the state is entitled to ask some visitors to stay for short visits only, and also in part because the data about who overstays visas are available. States engage in an assessment of what proportion of visitors from particular states typically over-stay their visas and, on the basis of that historical pattern of visa-rule violations, require that citizens from those countries undergo additional assessment of their intentions. Perhaps it can be agreed that an individual who herself violated the conditions of an earlier visa can be subjected to additional scrutiny in advance of attaining another one; in this case, an individual is held responsible for her own past rule-violating behaviors. And while I agree that the claim is more contentious, it seems in principle acceptable to subject citizens from states that have produced visa-overstayers to undergo additional assessment of their intentions in visiting; that is, to impose additional burdens on them on the basis of others who share their national origin. Just as it may be reasonable to ask young men to pay more in car insurance than young women on the basis of data collected about which group is more likely to get into traffic accidents, it may be reasonable to ask some would-be visitors (from states that disproportionately produce overstayers) to meet additional requirements to gain access to valuable travel opportunities.

However, it is *not* acceptable for a state to base the assessment of visa applicants (and their intent to stay short periods only) on their fellow-citizens' record in claiming asylum; such an assessment is a violation of that state's commitment to international refugee law. An attempt to exclude individuals on the basis that, historically, some fraction of candidates with their national characteristics claimed asylum upon arrival in the destination state is evidence that cannot justly be used to deny a visa applicant access to the state's territory. One reason that states adopt rigorous visa requirements, as I outlined just above, is to ensure that temporary visitors remain temporary. Their main objective is to identify likely visa-overstayers—people who intend to stay after their visa expires. This goal is explicit. Its impact, however, can be particularly ruinous for asylum seekers, who according to international law are permitted to seek asylum where they have arrived on a state's territory. But to seek asylum they must *gain access* to the relevant territory, and visas that are granted only to those who appear to be serious about returning home, prevent that access, *on purpose*. There is a strong correlation between robust visa requirements and asylum-producing countries, that is, citizens from countries that produce asylum-seekers also tend to be required to meet robust requirements to gain entry to the territory of other (relatively wealthy) states (Bo 1998, 193). It is well-known that the externalization of border controls, in this case requiring visas in advance of travel, is in part to stem refugee flows, and that the result is that asylum seekers turn to irregular, and dangerous, methods to gain entry to safe states (Shachar 2020; Gibney 2006).

The adoption of robust visa requirements, which is part of this externalization, can undermine a state's claim to be respectful of the obligations imposed by refugee law, and thus undermine its claim to possess a just admissions policy. Technically, international refugee law requires only that asylum claims be considered from those who have reached a state's territory. But the robust efforts that states make to ensure that would-be asylum seekers cannot make this journey, while not necessarily illegal, are certainly immoral, and amount in principle to a violation of the right to seek asylum. As I said earlier, one key condition for a state's justified right to exclude is that it abides by the rules of justice for admitting and protecting asylum seekers. Visa requirements that are targeted at identifying people who will make an asylum claim so as to deny them admission undermine a state's claim that it excludes fairly. Ultimately, then, substantial requirements for the issuance of visas are permissible; but states may not impose them to avoid admitting potential asylum seekers.

Visas and Rights Restrictions

I have outlined the criteria that must be met to gain a visa for travel. I suggested that there were two broad clusters of criteria to consider: criteria that demonstrate an applicant can be excluded fairly and criteria that assess whether an applicant should be admitted. In assessing whether, overall, a visa procedure is defensible, a final consideration is whether the conditions that attach to short-term visas themselves are just. That is to say, the matter is not simply whether one is admitted; the permissibility of the conditions that attach to admission must also be assessed. In this section, I consider four rights restrictions that are often associated with short-term visas, all of which deny particular rights to visitors with short-term visas, and which thereby exclude them from certain goods they might prefer to access.[10] These goods are access to social services on the same terms as citizens and long-term residents, the right to travel with one's family, the right to work, and the opportunity to apply for visas that permit transition to permanent status.

First, it is common, as I have noted above, that visa applicants must prove that they possess the resources to support themselves when they travel on a short-term basis, sometimes including the requirement to prove that insurance against various possible harms has been purchased in advance of travel. The general purpose and defense of such a requirement is that it is important and reasonable to avoid situations in which visitors impose costs on host state. In some cases, a particular motivation is to avoid visitors taking advantage of services, especially medical services, which are largely supported by tax revenue generated by contributing members of a destination state. Because short-term visitors do not contribute to the taxes that fund these important services, they can permissibly be excluded from these goods; of course, the exclusion is not total, which is to say that a visitor in need of urgent medical support must be able to access it, but they can be required to pay for the services they use. As long as short-term visitors are not denied acute and critical services they need, as medical providers assess whether payment is forthcoming, the general restriction on using medical services free-of-charge is defensible. The contribution argument is not the whole story for residents and citizens of a state of course—members who cannot for various reasons contribute to the taxes that support public services cannot be excluded for that reason. But the argument is reasonably presented as an explanation for why visitors can be permissibly excluded from them.

The exclusion can be more problematic in cases of short-term visitors who are engaging in more than mere travel, for example international students or temporary labor migrants. In these cases, contribution arguments weigh in favor of granting access to key services: in the case of temporary foreign labor migrants for example, as Joseph Carens has well-noted, it may be permissible to exclude them from certain public services that are available to long-term residents and citizens (like pension plans), but not from work-place safety regulations and appropriate compensation for injuries received on the job, especially, but not only, if these safety regulations are violated (Carens 2008).

A second constraint that is often attached to visas is a prohibition on traveling with family members. This prohibition does not typically apply to individuals applying for tourist visas, where a family of tourists can apply collectively for visas for all its members. But it is common to deny temporary foreign labor migrants the right to travel with their families. The often unstated reason for this prohibition is to ensure that migrant workers retain an incentive to leave after the completion of their work contract. The prohibition can be justly applied, however, only if the temporary labor contracts are very short. Why is this so? In general, the reason to insist on a time limit on family separation is that the right to family unity is a basic human right, and recognized as such in national and international law, for the deep importance of families in the lives of individuals (Morris, Lenard, and Haugen 2021). To give just one example, the Universal Declaration of Human Rights states that the family is "the natural and fundamental group unit of society and is entitled to protection by society and the State" (United Nations 1948). The principle that, wherever possible, families should be united, or reunited if they are separated, is central to immigration policies in general, including with respect to refugee admission policies that preferentially admit family members of refugees who have been admitted for resettlement.

These policies—specifically in which family members are prioritized for admission—have rightly faced considerable criticism for their narrow, western understanding of families, usually prioritizing partners and dependent children, rather than parents, grandparents, cousins, aunts, and so on. I do not intend here to discuss whether there are better ways to identify which types of familial connections ought to be prioritized, other than to suggest that whatever type is selected, an accessible exception procedure should be adopted to enable alternative important connections to be prioritized.[11] There is precedent for proceeding in this way. For example, Canada made an exception when admitting Yazidi refugees, permitting "family" to include aunts and cousins (because ISIS had systematically murdered male Yazidis). Similarly, in many western democratic states that welcome LGBTQ+ refugees from countries where marriage between same-sex people is banned, partners are treated as "spouses" (in Canada, which accepts common-law partners as spouses for the purposes of family reunification, the "live-in" requirement for common-law partners can be waived where living together would have been a substantial safety risk).

One might respond here by saying that while *forced* family separation is evidently unjust, would-be migrants are not in fact forced to take up temporary labor migration opportunities or university studies abroad. By analogy, one might say, many people choose jobs that require separation—astronauts working on the international space station and members of the military, for example, all choose occupations that require family separation for extended periods of time, and no one believes that a wrong is done here, or that families should be permitted to travel along as a condition of their permissibility. One might observe more generally that many people do, in fact, choose to migrate away from their families and live entire lives separated by borders from many of those they love the most.[12] What distinguishes these latter cases from the ones under discussion here, however, is the nature of the choice to take up opportunities that require family separation. In all cases, there are multiple considerations at play that shape and constrain the options individuals have, including to be close to their families or otherwise; what distinguishes labor migration opportunities from these others is that, typically, they are one of very few options that those considering them have (whereas someone who is considering whether to be an astronaut can be presumed to have alternatives that are also valuable, and which would not require family separation), and there is nothing about the job that cannot be carried out, or would be done significantly differently, if a migrants' family was permitted to travel along with the migrant. It is worth noting as well that the importance of family is increasingly recognized even in jobs that do require family separation, for example, in the form of extending parental leaves for new military parents.

Note that my claim is not that the family separation required by short-term labor migration contracts is impermissible if it is reasonably short. Rather, my claim is that so-called chosen family separation—chosen, in the sense that these opportunities can be selected only if would-be migrants agree to leave their families behind—becomes forced over time. There is evidently vagueness in this claim because how long "short" is, is not determinate (Carens 2013, 114).[13] The point, however, is to recognize the harm of extended family separation, even if it is merely temporary, and even if it is in some sense chosen. In this case, I propose that the absolute limit on permissible forced family separation—forced in the sense that would-be migrant workers can take up labor contracts only if they agree to leave family behind—is six months. The limit is important because many "temporary" labor market contracts are longer than six months, or can be repeatedly renewed. Where extensions or renewals are permissible, but where the conditions disallowing family travel persist, the prohibition is indefensible.

A third and related constraint that is often applied to temporary visa holders is the prohibition against taking up paid employment in the host country during the visit. This prohibition of course does not apply to those who enter the destination state expressly for the purpose of working. But it often does apply to international students and visitors, who are either not permitted to work or are restricted to some work opportunities only (for example, international students at the University of Ottawa may work *at* the university but may not enter the wider labor market). This prohibition is connected to the prohibition against family travel because there are cases where temporary migrants are permitted to travel with their families (for example, to study or to take up temporary labor market contracts), but where the prohibition against work applies to family members. So, a woman traveling to take on a temporary labor market contract may be permitted to travel with her partner and children, but her partner can be denied access to the labor market. Here, a state is acknowledging the importance of family, but is imposing constraints on the family's options in the destination state (the accompanying family members may also be denied access to various social services).

The reason states impose either the prohibition on family travel or the prohibition on work in general, and especially the prohibition on work by accompanying family is, as I indicated above, to reduce the likelihood that such families desire to remain in the destination state over the longer term; that is, to ensure that incentives to leave persist. In my view, such restrictions on work opportunities are bad policy in the sense that they raise the likelihood that such families will need financial support from the destination state, costs which could be avoided if work were permitted. But to the extent that states are permitted to sustain a distinction between short-term and long-term visitors, they are not necessarily violations of the rights to which short-term visitors are entitled.

I suggested in the introduction to this chapter that the line between short-term visitors and long-term residents is hard to identify. Earlier I also expressed skepticism that migrants who select temporary opportunities, especially labor opportunities, are choosing temporary status only; rather I said, there are instances where these options are the only ones available to them, so they are choosing between them and nothing at all. And, even in cases where migrants genuinely intend to migrate only temporarily, their objectives can change over time; as I said, they can meet someone and fall in love, or they can find that they adore the culture of their host state and wish to remain there. Ultimately, where migrants have spent enough time in a place that, using the language I introduced in Chapter 1, their lives are meaningfully shaped by the formal and informal institutions of that place, they are properly described as subjected to them. They then become entitled to the wide range of political and residential rights that accompany subjection.

So, again although there is vagueness here with which we must contend, *at some point* individuals who are admitted on short-term visas, who are permissibly subject to certain rights restrictions, recognizably become long-term residents who cannot be permissibly subject to these same restrictions. This transition is assumed, often, to occur because short-term visitors choose to overstay visas, but in fact in a great many cases the transition occurs during the course of lawful extensions either as labor contracts are renewed, or as international students continue to pursue educational opportunities. As a result, the prohibition on accessing the labor market, for example for partners of migrant workers, is permissible but, just as with family separation itself, only for approximately six months; after that point, it is reasonable to expect states to open the labor market to partners.

The fact of this transition from short- to long-term residence, and that it is often encouraged by the destination state, raises the question of the justifiability of a final visa condition that I wish to consider: the condition that a temporary visa-holder *not* apply for permanent residence access, usually by applying for a new kind of visa. The best-known case of long-term labor migrants who were denied the opportunity to transition to permanent status, at least until recently, are the Turkish (and Italian and Greek) guest workers who migrated to Germany after the Second World War, to rebuild the German economy (Castles 1985). Nearly one million labor migrants arrived in Germany in a relativley short period of time, and estimates are that roughly half of them—mainly Turkish—remained as their initial two-year contracts were renewed and renewed again. Only in the early 2000s did changes to German immigration law permit some guestworkers to access German citizenship (but only if they gave up Turkish citizenship). The injustice of denying permanent status to laborers who were clearly essential to the German economy has been well-observed (Walzer 1983; Chin 2007; Barbieri 1998). This form of overt and persistent exclusion from permanent residence is no longer common in democratic states (but persists elsewhere, perhaps most egregiously in the Gulf States), but it is not gone, especially in the space of temporary labor migration. For example, the TN visa is available for citizens of Canada and Mexico with certain qualifications to move temporarily into the United States, to take up labor opportunities for a maximum of one year (they can be renewed as well). Officially, they contain the proviso that they are available only for temporary movers, and holders of a TN visa may not apply for any visa that allows long-term stays. Any person who aims to circumvent this rule is liable to be charged with visa fraud. I can attest personally that there are ways around this proviso (they involve expensive lawyers' fees, an admission of "guilt" to the offense of visa fraud, and a request that extenuating circumstances, unforeseen at the time of original application, be considered in order to overcome the prohibition).

Other visas require that holders leave the country after a set amount of time, but do not in principle deny future opportunities to apply for admission on a permanent basis. For example, another American visa, the J-1, contains the requirement that any person who takes it up *must* (unless they apply for a waiver of this requirement from their home country) return to their home country, when the visa expires, for between one to two years before applying for a new visa to the United States.[14] While general prohibitions on transition among visas, in particular from visas that are temporary to visas that permit long-term residence and transition to citizenship, cannot be easily defended, temporary exclusions may be permissible in some cases. J-1 visa holders are typically required to return home, usually after having gained valuable training abroad, to share their skills with their home country. The justification for such mandatory repatriation is similar to the justification offered in the so-called brain drain literature, in which comparatively poorer states justify requiring citizens who have been educated at state expense to remain home for a set period of time, offering benefits to their fellow citizens, before they are permitted to migrate abroad.[15] What distinguishes "mandatory repatriation" from the refusal to permit migrants to transition from temporary to permanent status is that repatriation is typically demanded by the sending state, and any individual who wants that requirement waived must petition the sending state, whereas, the morally problematic cases described above are adopted by host states that refuse to give permanence to temporary migrants, on whom their economies depend.

There are three reasons to think that denying temporary migrants the right to transition to permanent status cannot be defended. One reason is that whereas it is permissible to issue short-term visas, it is not permissible to punish short-term visa holders by denying them the right to apply for alternative, longer-term, options. While short-term visa holders are not guaranteed to qualify for the longer-term visas, the prohibition on seeking them is an unreasonable restriction of a migrant's mobility rights. A second reason is that because many short-term visitors ultimately do remain, lawfully, for the relatively longer-term, as a result of renewed visas, the prohibition on transitioning to permanent status becomes more unjust over time. The injustice is exacerbated where the reasons for extending the visa are connected to the ongoing contribution that a migrant makes to a state's economy by filling acute labor shortages (Lenard and Straehle 2012a; Hanley et al. 2012). A third and related reason is that as migrants reside lawfully over the longer term, contributing to the labor market and gaining education, the *reasons* motivating long-term exclusion diminish. The willing and repeated renewal of short-term visas ought to be understood as a *signal* that the (alleged) reasons to deny long-term status in the first place—that such individuals do not wish to stay or that such individuals would impose large costs on the destination state—no longer apply. The fact of ongoing, life-shaping subjection entitles them to full inclusion in the state to protect them against forced exclusion.

Conclusion

Ultimately, in this book, and more specifically in this chapter, I have accepted the premise that states may sometimes exclude individuals, and I correspondingly defended a corollary of this claim; that is, that the short-term inclusion of some individuals is permissible under some conditions. The analysis is necessarily complicated by the fact that there are substantial, and unjustifiable, wealth inequalities that divide states and which borders sustain, the result of which is that some citizens have more opportunities to travel freely across them than others. This inequality in travel access is manifest in many ways, including, as I have considered here, via the system for issuing travel visas. Citizens of many wealthy countries are the lucky recipients of visa waiver programs, by which they are permitted visa-free entry to many more countries than are citizens of relatively poorer countries. But, citizens from poorer countries are typically required to apply for visas, which are difficult to access and which often contain substantial rights restrictions, as I have described above.

Even if the legitimacy of a state's allowing temporary entry only is accepted, the conditions attached to obtaining temporary visas must be separately assessed. States have unfortunately demonstrated themselves to be over-zealous in restricting access to their territory when they believe applicants intend to stay, even when they have applied for temporary visas only; of particular worry is that such zealousness may be infused by racism in white majority countries against would-be travelers who hail from African and Asian states. As well, I have demonstrated over the course of the chapter that some of the conditions that attach to acquiring visas are more defensible than others.

I have argued that public health and public safety conditions are justifiable, as protecting both security and public health are central to a legitimate state's job. I argued, however, that the additional, positive conditions cannot be justified where they are discriminatory, where they operate to deny access to asylum, and where they refuse opportunities for long-term residents to transition to citizenship. And while limited conditions—that is, rights restrictions—can permissibly be imposed on temporary visitors, it is not justified for states to impose conditions on temporary visa holders that persist even as it becomes clear that the visitors are in fact residents, as their visas are extended or renewed repeatedly. So, I argued, states ought to grant *all* temporary visa holders the right to apply for permanent status or longer-term visas, in time. As well, where states prove willing to renew temporary visas, they must be prepared to remove the prohibitions—including bans on traveling with family and accessing publicly provided services on the same terms as residents—on the grounds that the visa-holder is no longer, really, a temporary visitor, but is rather a long-term resident who is entitled to transition to citizenship and to access the associated package of rights.

6
Deserving Citizenship?

Typically, as I said in Chapter 5, acquiring a visa is the first step towards gaining entry to a state's territory, and in many cases, towards gaining entry into full membership in time. Not all admitted migrants are legally permitted to transition to citizenship, however, as I outlined there. The process of acquiring citizenship is termed naturalization, and it marks the transition from resident to citizen, with the full inclusion that citizenship status provides. In the process of determining who can be included via naturalization, states also exclude those who do not meet the standards. In the next three chapters, I will consider the justifications for some of the choices states make about whom to include and, as a result, whom to exclude. As I explained in Chapter 1, citizenship is first and foremost warranted simply on the basis of long-term residence. There, I noted as well that long-term residence often travels with features that scholars have argued are central to the granting of citizenship, including the experience of subjection (with which I agree), contribution to the state itself in multiple forms, and connections to fellow citizens and residents, which hold immense personal value. Here, I consider whether there are cases where it is permissible to elevate "contribution," as a reason to extend citizenship to migrants who might not otherwise be able to access it or to those who have not yet met residency requirements.

As COVID-19 spread through Canadian long-term care homes for the elderly, Quebec premier François Legault publicly thanked the front-line workers who offered "essential" support, calling them "guardian angels." These guardian angels were, in substantial numbers, asylum seekers from around the world who were waiting for their claims to be adjudicated by Canadian immigration authorities. Legault proposed that such workers be rewarded with citizenship for their service; it seemed only fitting to reward individuals who had risked their lives to support the Canadian elderly during such a dangerous time with the safety that Canadian citizenship can offer. This case, however, raises difficult questions about whether some individuals can, rightfully, be treated as more deserving of citizenship than others based on their contributions; in other words, is there a case to be made that some migrants can *earn* citizenship as a result of the actions they take?

In general, states retain for themselves the discretion to extend citizenship on an individual basis in exceptional cases. For example, when then-asylum-seeker Mamoudou Gassamma climbed four floors of a Parisian apartment building to rescue a toddler, he was rewarded *exceptionally* with citizenship in France. Here, his contribution was a daring and fantastic physical feat, and President Emmanuel Macron used his government's discretion to grant him citizenship on that basis (Vandoorne, Beech, and Westcott 2018). In what follows, I will not consider these kinds of one-off choices to grant citizenship. Instead, I will begin with a consideration of temporary labor migration programs to argue that, in general terms, they must permit those who participate in them to access citizenship in time. This argument is consistent with the claims I have made already in Chapters 1 and 5, that denying the right of long-term residents to transition to citizenship is unjust. Then, I consider two examples of programs that formalize the idea that citizenship can be earned; both program types contain elements of considerable discretion around whether and when to treat specific contributions as meriting citizenship. One cluster of programs treats specific types of labor as deserving of citizenship. A second cluster offers citizenship on an exceptional basis to migrants who have made a particularly important contribution to the society in which they live. Each cluster of cases presents moral challenges that I will assess over the course of the chapter: risks of exploitation in the first and claims of unfairness in the second. I will, ultimately, defend both types of exceptions to the general rule that residence should be the main determinant of citizenship access. But my account stipulates that they are defensible only because the global migration management system is unjust—these programs or exceptions are made available because of persistent immigration injustice, defined according to the minimalist account I described in the Introduction, and refusing to grant citizenship in these cases would perpetuate it.

Labor Migration and Access to Citizenship

The thought that immigrants ought to show their worthiness for citizenship by demonstrating the value of the contributions they can and do make to their host society is commonly expressed in public discourse and manifest in many immigration admission policies (Monforte, Bassel, and Khan 2019;

Dhaliwal and Forkert 2015). Targets for numbers of immigration admissions are often evaluated in economic terms: in historically immigrant-receiving states, it is common to hear that X number of migrants is essential to support ongoing economic vitality, for example. Point-based systems for selecting among migrants to admit, as operate in Canada and Australia, encourage the idea that migrants are first and foremost economic contributors to their new state. Global competition to recruit high-skilled migrants in particular, and even investment-for-citizenship programs, likewise encourage the thought that immigrants can be fairly evaluated for admission to territory, and especially to membership, based on the economic value that they can be expected to contribute (Shachar 2011; Shachar and Hirschl 2014).

Similarly, where states recruit temporary workers but deny them access to a wide range of rights, including the right to apply for permanent status, they do so for allegedly economic reasons. In very general terms, international labor migration is a major source of global migration, and increasingly so. The International Labour Organization (ILO) estimated recently that there were 169 million labor migrants in 2021, up from 150 million in 2015, making up nearly five percent of the global labor workforce (ILO 2021). Most of these migrants are low- rather than high-skilled, and they are selected to fill acute and sometimes even chronic labor shortages.[1] Often low-skilled migrants are subject to substantial rights constraints, on the grounds that such constraints are key to the economic benefits generated by temporary labor migration (Ruhs 2013). There is an alleged trade-off here, between "numbers and rights." According to Martin Ruhs and Philip Martin, "more employment rights for workers generally mean increased labor costs, generating a numbers–rights trade-off" (Ruhs and Martin 2008, 254). This trade-off is said to be as follows, in other words: the more rights that employers and host states are required by law to protect, the fewer the number of migrants who will be admitted to fill acute labor needs. I will return to this alleged trade-off shortly.

As I argued in Chapter 1, subjection-based residence grounds a claim for inclusion, protected by the status of citizenship. In my view, a focus on a migrant's economic contribution to a host society is problematic. Many migrants who ought to be entitled to citizenship because they are subject to laws and norms of the host society over extended periods of time or because they contribute to their society, but in ways that are not explicitly economic, would be excluded if a strict "economic contribution" view were adopted. But also, as in the case of temporary foreign labor migrants, a focus on economic benefit seems to lend legitimacy to the choice to restrict migrants' rights in an attempt to optimize their contribution. In what follows, I consider two forms of exceptional cases: one that, as a matter of contract, offers citizenship in exchange for contributions, and another that highlights the exceptional contributions that certain migrants have made, with respect to the personal dangers they accepted for themselves and to the benefit they thereby provided, for example in times of national emergency.

The Canadian Live-in Caregiver Program, which operated from 1992 until 2014, was structured as a contract that invited migrants to take up a range of caregiving jobs—mostly as nannies to young children, but also as caregivers to the elderly—in exchange for citizenship (Carens 2008; Macklin 1994; Bakan and Stasiulis 1994).[2] The mainly women who accepted this work were initially asked to live in the homes of their employers and were subject to a range of additional conditions. The program's requirements shifted over time to remedy some of the injustices and abuses to which its participants were often subject, but in general it required that women take up caregiving in a specific home, and access to permanent residence and then citizenship was not granted until the caregiver fulfilled the terms of her contract—approximately twenty-four months of care work in a three-year period. Once the migrants fulfilled these conditions, they were permitted to apply for permanent residence and then, after a period of residence, and so long as no crimes were committed or were revealed to have been committed in the past, attain citizenship (Brickner and Straehle 2010).

Two programs in the United States are structured similarly. One is the Naturalization for Military Service program (NMS). This program offers expedited processing of citizenship applications to migrants who have served one year of peace time military service and less than that if they have served during designated periods of hostility (USCIS 2021). Although historically this was not always the case, only those migrants who are lawfully resident of the United States may presently take part in this program. The main benefit of the NMS program is accelerated access to citizenship—any migrant who is admitted to the United States legally, and who possesses permanent residency status (called landed immigrant status in the United States) may enroll in the military and, once they complete their service, apply immediately for citizenship, bypassing the residency requirement that must typically be met by landed immigrants (Sullivan 2019). Expedited access to citizenship is valuable, in particular, for the opportunities for family sponsorship that citizenship offers; if only citizens are permitted to access family reunification immigration programs or if citizens are able to do so more easily than are permanent residents, then those who have left family behind to migrate have an incentive to access citizenship as quickly as possible. From 2009 until 2016, the Military Accessions Vital to National Interest (MAVNI) program was also in operation and it permitted US residents on valid temporary visas to join the military in certain key roles, in exchange for which (and assuming the successful completion of the role) they became entitled to citizenship (Rosenberg 2018). MAVNI opened options for legally present immigrants who did not (before joining the military) have the right to stay permanently in the United States.[3]

These kinds of programs—and there are others like them—share some key features. One is that the conditions that are attached to them are defined in advance. Migrants can assess the conditions, and the benefits, and make a choice about whether to apply to participate in them. No one is coerced into taking up the opportunities. They are, effectively, contracts in which migrants commit to carrying out specific tasks which, if performed well, give them access to citizenship. These two cases share, as well, that the contract is between two parties—the migrant and the employer[4]—and the state acts as the arbiter of the contract between them; moreover, it is ultimately the state that proffers the benefit once the employer–employee contractually defined obligations are complete. They differ in one key way with respect to their status in advance of the signed contract. Caregivers must have completed their service before they were entitled to permanent residence. Moreover, they signed a contact in advance of arriving on Canadian soil; their legal entry to Canada was dependent on their signing the contract and thereby agreeing to its terms. Military recruits participating in NMS must already be present on American soil and possess the status of landed immigrant before they are permitted to enroll in the military; neither their admission, nor in principle their access to US citizenship, is dependent on their willingness to enlist.

One objection to programs constructed in these ways is that they are fundamentally exploitative, as some have claimed is true of temporary foreign labor migration programs in general (Lenard and Straehle 2010). It is key to recall that the interest in temporary labor migration programs among relatively wealthy countries emerges in a context of global inequality. This context, as I described in the Introduction, shapes the choices that states make with respect to whom to admit and when, and it also shapes the interest that migrants have in crossing borders. The best defense of temporary labor migration programs in general is that migrants, especially from relatively poorer states, want to take them up even where the opportunities travel with rights constraints that are relatively severe. As well, these programs appear to have salutary effects on global wealth inequalities through skills transfer when migrants return home, reduced pressure on home-state labor markets with high unemployment, and the sending of remittances (Lenard and Straehle 2010; Deonanan and Ramkissoon 2018; Lim and Basnet 2017). In light of these obvious goods, why are such programs accused of being exploitative?

There are multiple sources of exploitation that threaten to render a standard labor migration contract problematic, if not straightforwardly unjust. In some cases, the contract itself can be exploitative in the sense that the benefits received by the host community can far outweigh the benefits received by the migrant, suggesting that the contractual exchange is unfair. In others, the work may be very poorly remunerated. Another source of exploitation stems from the limited alternative migration pathways available to low-skilled migrants from developing states, and so while migrants may *choose* to participate in labor migration programs, the choice is made under conditions that offer few, if any, *good* choices to would-be migrants. Finally, labor market contracts may formalize conditions that make exploitation and abuse likely over the course of the work, even if they do not themselves formalize an exploitative relationship. This objection is frequently made of domestic care-giving work, which happens in the homes of employers, thereby allowing more opportunity for exploitation, against which workers have little power to resist. For some scholars, the benefits that migrant workers gain from voluntary participation in such programs is sufficient to justify their continued use, even if they are exploitative (Stilz 2010; Mayer 2005). For others, including me, the presence of exploitation and other harms translates into the recommendation to abandon purely temporary labor migration entirely (Lenard and Straehle 2011).

Some of the opportunities for exploitation of temporary labor migrants can be mitigated, at least in principle, by better monitoring. These are contractual exchanges, where conditions for both parties are set out in advance, and where both parties to the contract are entitled to some protection from authorities. Both employees and employers can be criticized for failing to meet their responsibilities as a result. Furthermore, because the contractual obligations are known, it is possible for advocacy groups to mobilize against conditions that are especially exploitative or lend themselves too easily to the abuse of migrant workers (Tungohan 2012).

The crucial difference between most temporary labor migration programs and those under consideration here is that *some* of the sources of exploitation are eased, if not erased, by the access to citizenship that is gained at the conclusion of the contract. That is to say, the benefit of access to citizenship may be sufficient to undermine the claim that the contractual obligations themselves are exploitative. Why might this be the case? In earlier work, I outlined three proposed mechanisms by which the accessibility of citizenship can serve to mitigate the exploitation that often travels with temporary labor migration programs. First, the availability of citizenship, following the completion of the contract, renders the benefits for both parties more equal than contracts which are judged exploitative for benefiting one party (in this case, the employer) more significantly than another (the foreign worker) (Lenard and Straehle 2011). A second is that employers may be less likely to abuse or exploit workers they know will join the state as citizens; their status as presumptive citizens may, in other words, offer some protection against otherwise ill-meaning employers. A third, and related, mechanism is that the interest of the state in monitoring the conditions of work may be heightened if such migrants are on the path to citizenship. Together, these three reasons offer support to my claim that temporary labor migration programs must allow for the eventual transition to citizenship for migrant workers (Lenard and Straehle 2011, 2010; Lenard 2012b).

The justification for the view that citizenship must be accessible to all labor migrants is fundamentally democratic. To borrow from Michael Walzer, it is a matter of democratic justice that labor migrants do not occupy a systematic second-class status in host states (Walzer 1983). His analysis of "guest worker" programs focused primarily on the harms generated by the German guest worker program I described in Chapter 5, which permitted and encouraged the migration of Turkish (and other) citizens to work in Germany on a "temporary basis." The German state proceeded by repeatedly renewing their temporary visas, on the grounds of the importance of their labor, rather than offering them access to citizenship. In the German case, the exclusion from membership in German society over the long-term was extraordinarily harmful, and it has continued to impact the success of Turkish origin citizens and residents of Germany; even as German immigration policy has liberalized to permit the naturalization of Turkish guest workers and their families under some conditions, they remain disadvantaged across multiple dimensions of Germany society. A recent report suggested that across Europe, Germany has the worst record of "minority" representation in its national parliament, for example, and that only thirty percent of residents of Germany with Turkish origin have the right to vote (Leistner 2021). As well, educational outcomes and employment income for residents of Germany with Turkish origin lag significantly behind those who are natively German (Hartmann 2016).

In the political theory literature on temporary labor migration programs, it is agreed that the German strategy must be avoided; the injustice of permitting Turks to remain in Germany, laboring, while refusing to support their integration (and indeed encouraging their separation), is agreed. To put the point slightly differently, no matter where one stands with respect to the permissibility of temporary labor migration, and the prospects for making it fair, there is widespread criticism of the German model as undemocratic and otherwise unjust. Having agreed that what happened in Germany cannot be defended, political theorists assessing the fairness of temporary labor migration programs respond in two ways to the conclusion that Walzer drew from his analysis. Walzer concluded that the appropriate response to temporary labor migration was to secure democratic equality, in the form of citizenship, for all of those who reside on a territory for a sufficiently long period of time. This view, the democratic justice view, is one that I too have defended, and it underpins the defense I offer here for the position that temporary labor migration programs must, as a matter of justice, permit the transition to citizenship after some appropriate period of time. Temporary labor migration programs are permissible if and only if, after a short period of subjection without inclusion, full and complete inclusion is made available. This commitment derives from the more general version of the commitment I described in Chapter 1, namely, that any form of long-term subjection without inclusion is impermissible.

Others, however, conclude differently that the main harms of temporary labor migration programs can be mitigated short of full inclusion. As I indicated earlier, one reason to want to rescue temporary labor migration programs is that they generate substantial wealth for low-income countries through remittances sent by their citizens abroad. So, a concern with global distributive inequality tells in favor of these programs, as a kind of second-best way to ensure wealth redistribution, in light of the global north's unwillingness to seriously consider the structural changes that would make wealth equality among states more achievable (Lenard 2016c). A second reason has to do with the "numbers versus rights" trade-off I described earlier, which alleges that where employers are required to protect a wide range of rights for labor migrants, fewer labor migration opportunities will be made available. And because labor migrants are so desperate for these options, and because welcoming states are so unwilling to admit them with expansive rights, the proposal that citizenship be granted to them in time is dismissed as a death-knell for temporary labor migration programs. Here is Sarah Song expressing this worry: requiring citizenship as a condition of just temporary labor migration "may drastically curtail opportunities for impoverished foreign workers to improve their lives. If migrants could only be admitted on a permanent basis, wealthy countries may well decide to admit far fewer migrants. This would mean many potential migrants would never have the chance to gain legal admission in the first place" (Song 2018).

Instead, those who wish to protect labor migration opportunities emphasize that significant improvements can be made to them without granting citizenship. For example, rather than advocating for citizenship access for temporary labor migrants, both Song and Gillian Brock respond instead by proposing that the main harms of presently operating temporary labor migration programs can be eliminated by adopting regulations that include robust workplace protection regulations, conditions that ensure "fair contracting" between employers, and rights for workers to exit harmful work environments without facing immediate deportation (Brock 2020, 159). Here is Song's account of which rights must be protected to ensure the above: "labor rights, including health and safety standards, the right to collective bargaining, and access to legal remedies for wage theft and other abuses," as well as "certain social rights, including rights to housing and medical care" (Song 2018, 157). Genuine enforcement of these protections must also be in place. Song writes, summarizing her proposed strategy: "We should instead insist on more robust rights protections for temporary workers and much greater government oversight and enforcement of the terms of their contracts" (Song 2018, 158).

Song and Brock highlight several benefits of this strategy over one that insists that citizenship be made available to temporary labor migrants. One main benefit, says Song, is that not all labor migrants desire to stay over the long-term (as I noted in Chapter 5), and this kind of strategy—to improve the quality of the conditions under which migrants labor—does better at responding to their needs and preferences, including with respect to the dangers of exploitation (Ottonelli and Torresi 2012). A second benefit is that it manages to protect the redistributive benefits of labor migration, by ensuring that host states are willing to employ large numbers of migrants, whose remittances and skills-development are ultimately of benefit to their home country (Brock 2020, 140).

In my view, none of these benefits is sufficient to outweigh the importance of democracy's commitment to inclusion and of ensuring that longer-term labor migrants have access to legal and genuinely accessible permanence in their host states. Of course, I am in firm agreement that improved workplace protections for temporary labor migrants are key to protecting them from exploitation. Protecting access to citizenship in time adds to the protective mechanisms available for migrants. In the short-term, denying access to citizenship is not exploitative, certainly. But over the long term, this restriction denies the right of subjected migrants to access the decision-making institutions that most affect their lives.

There is nothing problematic about insisting simultaneously on improved workplace protections *and* citizenship access for migrants who remain in a host country for more than a short period of time, of course. Brock and Song present these strategies as though a choice must be made between them, suggesting that *if* host states believe that temporary labor migrants will *eventually* be permitted to gain citizenship, then they will not be willing to admit them for employment in the first place. However, this explanation conflates the preferences and needs of employers with the preferences and needs of the state; employers are seeking laborers and are themselves likely to be indifferent to the question of whether these laborers transition to permanent status. A program that permits employers to access the benefits of temporary labor migration does not obviously require that the state denies admitted migrants access to citizenship in time. More importantly, the supposed reason for which employers desire labor migrants is that they are less expensive than domestic laborers. But protecting the wide range of rights that Song lists above is not evidently less expensive. Song and Brock's proposals do not respond effectively to employer preferences for affordable (and compliant) workers; rather, they expand the set of rights to which temporary labor migrants must have access as a matter of justice so much that, it appears, the supposed redistributive benefits that stem from reduced rights will not apply. Moreover, having accepted this extensive set of expensive rights for labor migrants as required by justice, it is not clear what *additional cost* they believe requiring access to citizenship would impose.[5]

It is not clear, either, that these proposals do better to respond to migrant preference than does offering access to citizenship. This preference, "not to stay," drives the argument in Valeria Ottonelli and Tiziana Torresi's new work, which argues that evidence for how migrants behave suggests a strong desire either for circular migration, that is, to move freely between host and home countries, or simply for extended stints abroad to save money for projects at home (Ottonelli and Torresi forthcoming). Again, this argument is mistaken. As I argued in Chapter 5, temporary labor migrants are constrained by the conditions of their visas, and it is not appropriate to conclude from their behavior under current visa-related constraints that the choices they make are in fact a manifestation of their true preferences. If migrants genuinely prefer "not to stay," then no harm is done by permitting them to stay after an extended period of time; those who do not wish to stay will return home or continue to engage in circular migration patterns. Opening access to citizenship will simply ensure that migrants can make the choices they prefer without constraints.

So far what I have suggested above is that the rights to which migrants should be entitled, according to Brock and Song, are costly to the host state and especially to the employer, and therefore the protection of such rights—which I agree are key to protecting justice in host states—does not resolve the dilemma allegedly posed by the rights versus numbers debate. The demand to protect these work-related rights, as robustly as these authors argue, will not preserve the redistributive benefits they attach to temporary labor migration programs, which in turn is used to justify the exclusion of these migrants from citizenship. Furthermore, the protection of these rights does not respond to the alleged preference ascribed to temporary labor migrants to remain temporary; if citizenship were made available in time, no migrants would be required to take it up unless they desired it. Opening access to citizenship serves only to increase the options for labor migrants. Why then insist on denying citizenship to temporary labor migrants, who contribute in essential ways to an economy, by reducing both acute labor shortages and pressures on the employment market abroad? In my view, the remaining reason is, effectively, a concession to the populist anti-immigrant positions that dominate the newsreels—temporary labor migration finds widespread political support for being temporary in host states that do not wish to welcome migrants on a permanent basis, and arguments citing the redistributive benefits of such policies offer convenient cover for these views.

The position I defend here should, on the contrary, mitigate at least one major source of anti-immigrant animus. Of course, some among those who defend exclusionary policies are racist and anti-immigrant, and therefore cannot be persuaded that it is right to admit labor migrants to citizenship on any terms. But many anti-immigrant views are founded on the worry that migrants are costly to the host state, mainly for their alleged unwillingness to work and therefore for their need to rely on social assistance. Yet, migrants admitted on labor visas to migrate temporarily are not costly in this way; rather they demonstrate a willingness and ability to work in labor areas facing shortages, suggesting not simply that they contribute to the host state's economy by carrying out these jobs but also that they are needed for economic reasons. Protecting access to citizenship, in time, need not change this dynamic in any significant way, *and* it serves to bolster a robust response to those who are anti-immigrant by providing evidence that immigrants are not costly (and are in on the contrary essential) to the host state.

So far, I have suggested that there are no persuasive reasons to insist that temporary labor migrants remain temporary. However, there are at least three additional considerations that must be confronted to assess whether temporary labor migration programs are fair in general. One consideration is about the work that migrants are asked to do, even admitting that the benefit they stand to gain is substantial. It is frequently observed that many jobs that labor migrants are asked to carry out are "dirty, dangerous and demanding," and which citizens and permanent residents are therefore not keen to do (Attas 2000, 74). The jobs' general undesirability along all three of these dimensions is what fuels the interest in temporary labor migration programs, although normatively it is the question of danger that such migrants face that is especially troubling. Of course, the ordinary way in which job contracts are negotiated is that a potential employee applies for a job and is offered a wage to complete it. If a job is perceived to be especially "dirty, dangerous and demanding," such that employees are hard to find, then an employer may respond by offering a higher wage in the hopes of persuading someone to take the job. This behavior is normal in a capitalist system: the employer sets wages in the hopes of attracting employees, who in turn can reject offered jobs if the conditions are not suitable for them in some way. At least in principle, there is nothing problematic about this way of proceeding—the would-be employee is not coerced, nor is her vulnerability taken advantage of—as it permits would-be employees to make choices about whether the potential wages available are worth the risk to them. Whether the risk is worth accepting is a matter of personal evaluation by would-be employees based on their own circumstances which may, it is worth noting, include financially precarious circumstances. It may well be that absent such precarious circumstances, a would-be employee would decline the job on the grounds of the exposure to risk involved.

These comments highlight what is at stake in the case of military participation. Some may fret that asking migrants to serve in the military, with the risks that military service produces—especially during times of hostility—may simply be too dangerous to ask of people who are in positions of substantial vulnerability. Even though the contractual conditions are known in advance, and even though migrants may willingly take up this option if it is offered, the danger to which migrants are exposed must be a relevant consideration with respect to whether the opportunity is made available in the first place. Why might it be reasonable to deny this option to migrants who are willing to do the work? I do not deny that many migrants are willing and keen to join the US military, and to participate in hostilities on behalf of the United States. Many, if not most, of those who would do so would do it from deep loyalty to the US; and among those migrants who do join the military, most are proud of the work they do or have done.[6] As well, in many states, including the United States, the military is held in high regard, and those who join it are viewed with respect and admiration because they are willing, at least in principle, to lay down their lives to defend the state.

However, one reason to be concerned with the choice that migrants make to join the military is that those who do so may be desperate to gain access to wealthy economies—and they are made desperate by a global migration regime that leaves them with very few opportunities to cross borders in search of employment and, even, basic economic and physical safety. While a typical (citizen or resident) employee can find a different job, if needed, and so has the freedom to turn down employment that she deems to be too dangerous and not worth the risk, a migrant seeking citizenship status may not have alternative options.

In the case of the currently operational US program that offers expedited access to citizenship in exchange for military service, the carrot is expedited access to citizenship, not citizenship itself (whereas the now-cancelled MAVNI allowed legally present migrants, who were not otherwise on the path to citizenship, to join the military to gain access to citizenship). So, it may seem that the benefit to be gained from this exchange is reduced in such a way that the exploitative nature of this contract is also reduced. This result is, in a sense, paradoxical, that is, that the exploitation is reduced because the benefit is less valuable to the potential recipient; yet, what this program ensures is that no one agrees to put themselves in physical danger to get US citizenship because doing so is the only way they can access it. Because those who join the military in exchange for expedited access to citizenship would, had they chosen otherwise, remain on the path to citizenship, albeit a slower one, they are not as vulnerable as those whose option is, as it was in the case of the Live-in Caregiver Program, to sign the contract as the *only* (realistic) way to get access to Canadian citizenship. That said, the value of expedited citizenship—and its role in permitting family reunification—is substantial enough to act as a strong incentive to join the military, and thus the question remains of whether migrants can be asked to do especially dangerous work in exchange for substantial benefits that they would not be able to access otherwise at all, or for a very long time.

One might respond that it seems paradoxical to propose that because the benefit (of citizenship or expected access to citizenship) is so valuable, it ought not to be extended as an enticement. One might just say that if people are willing to do the work for the benefit offered, even if the work is dangerous, they ought to be able to make the choice to do so. To see why this response should be resisted, consider an outlandish example in which someone is asked to do a job that carries a fifty percent risk of death on any given day of work, for which they are offered one million dollars a day. The risk of death makes this job impermissibly risky, *even though* the remuneration is substantial. So, careful work will need to be done to assess whether particular jobs are risky enough that they should not be offered to those in vulnerable circumstances (or at all), even where the benefits would be substantial.

The potential danger associated with a particular job is not the only consideration that matters for assessing the fairness of contracts. A second consideration is whether the remuneration is sufficient to count as a "living wage," however that is defined. Minimum wage regulations exist to protect workers, even though some of them might well work for less than minimum wage, by ensuring that the wage is sufficient to enable them to provide for themselves. In general, these considerations do not obviously apply to the case of the American military, as many Americans also join it, suggesting it is not in general impermissibly risky, and that the remuneration is generally believed to be reasonable.

A third consideration, with respect to the fairness of temporary labor migration programs, is that the status of migrants is highly vulnerable to the discretion of the state in matters of immigration in general, as well as to their employers' discretion. In the case of the Live-in Caregiver Program, for example, caregivers had originally been required to live in their employers' home. Multiple studies revealed that the result was frequent abuse and exploitation by employers who took advantage of the vulnerability of their caregivers, knowing they faced deportation in the case of job loss (for an overview, see Banerjee, Kelly, and Tungohan 2017). Even though the contract was signed in advance by parties who understood the conditions and constraints of the contract, migrants too often felt compelled to remain in violent and abusive situations for fear of losing the opportunity to access citizenship. Policy changes over the program's lifetime reduced the likelihood of caregiver exploitation, for example by giving migrants the right to seek alternative employment in cases of job loss, without (immediately) forsaking their opportunity to access Canadian citizenship (Banerjee, Kelly, and Tungohan 2017). As well, participants in the program that has replaced the Live-in Caregiver Program may now take up caregiving opportunities without living in the employer's home.

But the direction of change is not always to reduce opportunities for exploitation and abuse. In the case of the US military, it is crucial that access to expedited citizenship applies only to those who complete their obligations. Those who are discharged prior to completing their service are not only denied expedited access to citizenship, but they can be denied citizenship altogether. This danger was particularly acute with respect to MAVNI, which permitted legal residents of the United States—who were not otherwise on the path to citizenship—to join the military when they possessed especially valuable skills, including medical and language skills. This program allowed residents on student visas, asylum seekers, and (as a result of a change to the original policy, enacted by the Obama Administration) those who were covered by the Deferred Action for Childhood Arrival (DACA) legislation to join the military in exchange for citizenship.[7] These residents, too, were required to successfully complete their service to access citizenship itself rather than merely expedited access to citizenship.

However, once elected, the Trump administration altered the regulations associated with this program, including by increasing the security tests that had to be passed and, in so doing, effectively reneged on the promises made to those who had already enrolled and begun their service. The Administration adopted the view that "immigrants who want to enlist in the U.S. military are potential security threats with questionable loyalties, even if they entered the country lawfully and have already passed immigration-related background checks" (Sullivan 2019, 75). One result of these increased regulations was the discharging of many military recruits who had, in effect, been promised access to the permanent right to stay in the United States, in exchange for their service. A US District Court Judge, commenting on the policy change when its legality and permissibility were considered in court, noted the harm generated by the policy changes, citing the risk of deportation for those who are discharged, followed by harsh punishment in a home country for participating in a foreign military (Sullivan 2019, 76). For example, one recruit, discharged for alleged security risks (which were not explained to him) stated, "It's terrible because I put my life in the line [sic] for this country, but I feel like I'm being treated like trash," and refused to offer his full name because he feared reprisals if deported to Iran (Baynes 2018). What these changes demonstrate is that the vulnerability of those who participate in these programs remains high, even where contracts are delineated in advance, because host countries retain the right at any moment to unilaterally change the conditions of those contracts. Because they are not citizens, participants have relatively little recourse to mobilize against these sorts of discretionary political decisions.

Migrant workers do not need to be protected from all risk; as I said earlier, some risk is permissible and, even, inevitable. Some risks are endemic to the choice to take up employment in general and across borders; one can always be fired and, if abroad on a visa that requires legal employment, be asked to return home. But these choices are reasonable in general, so long as they are freely made and the remuneration is fair. Many if not employment contracts are permissible, even if the employee is fired, and is therefore worse off than she would have been had she refused the contract. What distinguishes this standard situation from the one faced by MAVNI recruits is that (a) the conditions to which they were subject changed after they had signed the contract and had begun to fulfill their side of the contract, and (b) the impact of the discharge was not simply unemployment. Rather such recruits, where they were returned to the temporary legal status they occupied before they joined the military, were not necessarily permitted to stay permanently; they were thus put at unfair risk, as the quote from the discharged soldier suggested, of having to return to countries that treat participation in a foreign army as a criminal offense.

However, the question I am mainly focused on is not whether temporary labor migration programs ought to be protected and supported but rather whether connecting specific work—some of which is difficult and dangerous—to accessing citizenship can be justified. In the first section of this chapter, I suggested that labor migrant programs are permissible only if they leave open the opportunity for such migrants to transition to citizenship. Just above, I have noted three concerns even with such programs, where the willingness to take on specific jobs travels with citizenship access: first, they remain exploitative because migrants are offered the benefit only if they take on dangerous work; second, they may not offer a living wage; and third, such programs remain highly discretionary, such that migrants can do their part and find that the host state retracts its promise, resulting in sometimes harsh outcomes for those who lose their jobs as a result. These conditions mean that migrants enter situations in which they remain highly vulnerable and in which they do not have much control over the conditions in which they labor, even if the future promises their full inclusion on equal terms.

A strict commitment to the subjection-based view that I defend might appear to recommend against these programs absolutely: temporary labor migrants accept long-term subjection without a sufficiently firm commitment from the host state that citizenship will be available in time, and that may seem to be sufficient to denounce them. But, as I said in the Introduction to this book, a contextualist approach sometimes allows for deviations from the strict application of normative principles if there are reasons to believe that progress towards justice in general will be made.

Moreover, a commitment to the view that subjection requires political inclusion in the form of citizenship does not necessarily preclude accepting additional routes to citizenship. In this case, there is room for permitting these programs to operate because they do seem to generate incremental improvements towards achieving global migration justice, and better alternatives are not available. Moreover, as Song and Brock do observe, many of the negative features of these programs can be addressed by more careful attention to program design and with better oversight. Ultimately, the obligation rests on the host state to adopt policies that minimize the conditions that render participants vulnerable (a point that is emphasized in Ottonelli and Torresi forthcoming). To remind, such policies include robust workplace protection, non-punitive mechanisms by which migrants can access support if their employers are not fulfilling their end of the contracts, and a strong commitment by host states to shield existing contracts from discretionary political choices that might appear to grant states the right to renege on their promises. These conditions together render temporary labor migration programs permissible in general, so long as they allow for transition to citizenship over time; they apply, as well, to programs that permit expedited access to citizenship in exchange for certain labor market contributions. In this way, the programs ensure that employers can access valuable labor migrants; labor migrants can, in time, transition to permanent status; and their workplace rights are protected as they await the transition.

What About Exceptional Contributions?

The cases above consider the permissibility of programs that invite migrants to take up employment in certain sectors, for a specified time, after the completion of which they are invited to take up citizenship or to access expedited citizenship. As demonstrated above, however, thinking about such programs from within a contractual logic does not entirely work; it is only in principle that these programs operate like contracts, where each party to the contract agrees to carry out its own role. In practice, not only does the state retain the right to alter the conditions of the contract, migrants remain in a position of substantial vulnerability, both to unscrupulous employers and to the political tides of the state, against which migrants cannot easily mobilize. In this section, I consider a different kind of case, in which exceptions are requested for certain categories of migrants, including those who would not otherwise have legal entitlement to access citizenship, on the basis of their having offered exceptional contributions to society. Consider the following two examples.

In several countries, migrants were at the forefront of delivering essential services during the height of the COVID-19 pandemic, and in thanks for their contributions, several states moved to offer them citizenship.[8] Near the end of 2020, for example, France announced that migrant front-line workers were eligible for expedited naturalization procedures (Brunnersum 2020). The program allowed migrant workers to apply for naturalization after two years of residence rather than five; as of January 2021, nearly three thousand workers had taken advantage of the program, including "health care workers, childcare professionals, cleaners and retail staff" (The Local 2021).

Similarly, in August 2020, the province of Quebec announced the adoption of a temporary program called the Special Program for Asylum Seekers during COVID-19 (El-Assal and Miekus 2020). The program was adopted in the wake of Quebec premier François Legault's recognition of the province's "guardian angels" as I noted in the introduction to this chapter, referring to asylum seekers delivering health care to Quebec's most vulnerable citizens and residents during the first wave of COVID-19, which wreaked havoc on the province's long-term care homes. The Canadian government announced subsequently a national program that would do the same, and in announcing the program then-Minister of Immigration, Refugees and Citizenship, Marco Mendocino, said, "We really wanted to place an emphasis on the exceptional contributions of the asylum-seekers who put themselves at the greatest risk" (Jacobs 2020). As general practice, asylum seekers in Canada are permitted to work while their applications for refugee status (and thus the right to stay permanently in Canada) are being assessed. The rate at which asylum seekers' claims are accepted, permitting applicants to stay in Canada, varies by year, but the success rate is rarely over fifty percent (Statistics Canada 2019); that is to say, of those asylum seekers who became eligible to apply for citizenship on the basis of their work in long-term care homes, one would expect that approximately one-half would not otherwise have been permitted to stay. So, the opportunity to forego the asylum assessment system to access certain Canadian citizenship was especially valuable to these individuals.

Asylum seekers are individuals who believe their lives are in danger in their home countries, usually from persecution or war, and who migrate in search of safety and security. Following international law, states are required to admit asylum seekers and consider their claims seriously; if they meet the conditions of refugee status, usually as outlined by domestic interpretations of the 1951 Refugee Convention relating to the Status of Refugees, they are permitted to stay. Those who are not found to meet these conditions are eligible for deportation to their country of origin. There is no shortage of scholarship demonstrating that the global refugee and asylum-seeking system is unjust in various ways, including with respect to whether the criteria that must be met to access safety are fair and consistently applied (Parekh 2020; Owen 2020; Saunders 2017). What does appear to be true, however, is that those claiming asylum have assessed their own situation as critical and believe that there are strong reasons to cross borders in search of safety and security.[9] Those who apply for asylum believe they would be in danger if they were required to return home and thus are tremendously vulnerable to the host state's decision-making procedures. Opportunities to apply for permanent status that obviate the need to have one's claims assessed are, in other words, tremendously valuable.

I am certain that among advocates for refugees, asylum seekers, and irregular migrants, there is no objection to the adoption of policies that permit them to more easily access citizenship. But the reason that objections are unlikely to be substantial stems not from a moral evaluation of schemes like the one adopted in Canada but rather from the general conviction that there are so few opportunities for any asylum seeker to gain security and safety that any option that opens them more widely ought to be celebrated. The same is true in the case of mobilizing around selected irregular migrants; no advocate of irregular migrants' rights objects to the exceptional granting of citizenship (or other secure status) to those around whom a community mobilizes. But these pragmatic responses to specific cases do not explain how to respond morally to the more general question of whether to grant citizenship to those who have made an exceptional contribution, as a one-time event rather than as part of an ongoing immigration stream.

There are several reasons to be wary of celebrating "exceptional" programs like the ones I am considering here. Just as with the formal programs discussed in the last section, one challenge is the evident discretionary nature of such policies in the case of granting citizenship to asylum seekers. They depend on vulnerable migrants being seen and appreciated by those around them, that is, policy makers or neighbors, who are then moved to support them. Usually, when exceptional cases garner action by officials, they are associated with raising the work of vulnerable migrants to a position of uncommon visibility: in the case of asylum seekers, the COVID-19 pandemic highlighted the ways in which Quebec's health care sector relied on asylum seekers to do mostly low-paid but nevertheless extraordinarily important work. While that work in the health care system was unseen, the same set of migrants did not benefit from the willingness of a community to recognize their contributions. Is granting extra benefit, in this case access to citizenship, on the basis of who can best command attention in the news or social media a good way to exercise discretion?

The worry about discretion can be understood as a worry about fairness with respect to who becomes visible for their exceptional contributions. Megelere Dor, an asylum seeker in Quebec who worked in a factory making frozen pizza during the early months of the COVID-19 pandemic, expressed the view in this way, when he learned that only health care workers would be eligible to have their status converted: "It hurts us because we're workers, too... We went to work so people at home could still eat during the pandemic"

(Stevenson 2020). His question is a personally expressed version of a more general question that many communities have been asking themselves: how should essential work during a pandemic be identified, if the community's objective is to reward those who do it? For example, in deliberations around who ought to be entitled to early access to COVID-19 vaccines, there were calls for prioritizing so-called essential workers so that they could keep doing the work that communities depend on, and which required greater risk of exposure to the virus. Hospital admissions showed that workers like Dor were highly vulnerable to SARS-CoV-2 exposure in their workspaces. These observations force the question: was it fair that health care workers were prioritized for citizenship access when those who worked in the food industry were just as important to sustaining the community throughout the worst months of the COVID-19 pandemic? This special selection of certain workers, but not others who also put themselves at risk, seemed arbitrary and thus unfair.[10]

A second potential danger of exceptional programs like these is that they can create a moral hazard: if asylum seekers or other migrants know that exceptions are made in some circumstances to grant citizenship, they might migrate in hopes that they will be the recipient of such benefits. This sort of moral hazard worry is launched against more general arguments for amnesty for long-term irregular migrants. According to some critics, semi-regular amnesties simply act to encourage others to migrate in the hopes of benefiting from a later amnesty (for discussion see Carens 2009; Bosniak 2013; Blake 2010). However, these moments are sufficiently rare that they do not seem to offer an obvious attraction to those who might like to try their luck in taking advantage of such a policy.

In my view, although the reasons above suggest it is important to be attentive to the conditions under which citizenship is granted on an exceptional basis in unusual circumstances, none of them leads to the conclusion that such exceptional actions ought to be abandoned. The simplest reason to defend them is, as I said above, that any opportunity that vulnerable migrants have, as a matter of policy, to remain in safety ought to be taken. That is to say, the context of the unjust migration and asylum system, which produces conditions under which it is difficult for many to gain entry to relatively wealthy states, are such that most opportunities for migrants to gain economic and physical security ought to be embraced. Even opportunities that occur rarely (or even only once) are, at least, small steps towards greater justice in migration.

Ultimately, I think it is permissible to preserve a space for exceptional contributors to merit citizenship access. Avoiding doing so, on the grounds of the objections I have raised, would amount to a leveling down that ought to be rejected. I offer this conclusion with some trepidation, however, as a widespread acceptance of exceptional contribution-based access to citizenship may seem to encourage the thought that immigration ought to be treated primarily in terms of contribution. In turn, this acceptance could allow policymakers to make powerful symbolic gestures that benefit a relatively small group of people, distracting attention from more fundamental problems with asylum and migration policy.[11] On balance, however, the reasons above tell in favor of the permissibility, and indeed value, of programs that allow for the recognition of individuals who make exceptional contributions to a political community, where they are not citizens of that community. Essential to any such program is that its implementation responds to the frustration that Dor expressed about who is eligible to benefit from it and who is not. The identification of criteria for what counts as an exceptional contribution is perhaps not possible in advance of adopting such programs (since they are adopted in an ad hoc way, in response to specific emergencies), but once a program is adopted, a fair and transparent assessment of which contributions are judged meritorious is critically important. In the case of rewarding health care workers in Quebec, and Canada, for their exceptional service, it seems reasonable to extend the reward to all those who contributed to sustaining essential services during the pandemic, rather than singling out those who became especially visible.

Conclusion

The danger of admitting the permissibility of recognizing exceptional contributions is that it suggests that, perhaps, *contribution* to a community ought to be a more general measure of whether one is deserving of citizenship. Such a conclusion is the one that Michael Sullivan draws, after an analysis of the role that immigrants have played in the US military. His view is that irregular migrants ought to be permitted to join the US military and that in exchange for honorable service therein, they should be eligible for US citizenship. And, he says, the *reasons* for this view stem from the important contribution such individuals would make to the US military, and American society more generally.[12] He argues further that these reasons—these valuable contributions—can and should be extended more broadly to recognize both the role that irregular status parents make, where their children are citizens, to raising American children, and the role that irregular immigrants play more generally by filling low-paid caregiving roles in US society. While I agree that all of these represent valuable contributions to society, my view remains that those contributions should not be the primary means of determining who is permitted to stay.

Rather, the contribution-based view for accessing citizenship produces the conditions for exploitation that I highlighted earlier, associated with programs that formalize the exchange of citizenship for contributions, and is therefore one that should be avoided in general. However, as I have said, *if* states persist in creating and encouraging the use of temporary labor migration programs, then they ought to create the conditions under which such migrants can transition to citizenship in time. In other words, a system that permits migrant workers to transition to citizenship, citing their ongoing contribution to the economy or some other social good, is better than one that persistently renews temporary visas for labor migrants without giving them access to permanent status, thereby subjecting them without granting them full access to the political spaces in which decisions are made, in the form of citizenship status. Where such programs are adopted, the host state's job is to create fair conditions for accessing citizenship and to ensure that the rights of migrants remain robustly protected throughout the process of carrying out their end of the bargain, and while they remain acutely vulnerable to political whims, especially, of anti-immigrant leaders and political parties. Otherwise, as demonstrated by migrant military recruits who were discharged from the US military without explanation, labor migrants remain without adequate recourse in the face of unscrupulous employers and state power.

The additional conclusion that exceptional contributions may justify gaining access to citizenship for those who might not otherwise qualify does not undermine my starting contention, namely that residence ought to be and remain the central criterion by which entitlement to citizenship is evaluated. The granting of citizenship can be contingent on meeting certain criteria—for example the demonstration of language competence and knowledge of the state one is joining—and I will consider these in later chapters in more detail. Any move towards prioritizing contributions creates the conditions for injustice and unfairness in the distribution of a valuable good (i.e., membership), which can be avoided by protecting residence as the central criterion for granting citizenship. So, while I am willing to support the adoption of temporary foreign labor migration programs that offer access to citizenship, and one-off grants of citizenship in exchange for exceptional contributions, both such programs have notable flaws. My view therefore remains that residence ought to be the central criterion for citizenship, and deviations from this commitment should be treated as exceptions that are permissible only because they support more rather than less migration justice.

7
Resettling (LGBTQ+) Refugees

Where migrants are admitted on the idea that they will reside permanently in the new state, they begin the sometimes-long process of naturalizing to citizenship; the length of time from admission to naturalization varies across democratic states, ranging from four to twelve years (Hampshire 2011). As well, states ask would-be citizens to provide evidence on a range of fronts, including competence in language, basic knowledge of the host society, and sometimes financially stability over an extended period, in order to naturalize. In nearly all cases, there are also residency requirements, during which it is assumed that immigrants begin and make substantial progress towards integrating. Integration is challenging for many, and host states make choices about how much effort to expend in supporting it. The reason to think seriously about the imperatives the process of naturalization imposes is that, as residence extends in time, residents are subjected to power, but they do not (until they naturalize) possess the full set of rights to which such subjection entitles them. The worry about subjection to power and the importance of permitting naturalization to proceed fairly quickly as one key element of integration together motivate arguments in favor of fewer rather than more substantial requirements for naturalization (Hampshire 2011; Carens 2010b; 2013, ch. 3). Effective and efficient integration, including rapid access to naturalization, serves to avoid the creation of two classes of citizens in a democratic society.[1]

This chapter begins with an account of integration and the duties it imposes, both on states and immigrants, in part with the purpose of distinguishing a separate category of duties—duties of resettlement—that are owed to resettling refugees; that is, refugees who are admitted with the intention that they remain permanently. In most states, refugees are admitted as a distinct migration stream, often as part of a state's humanitarian obligations. Some individuals are admitted on a temporary basis, with the legal permission to reside until they can safely return home; some individuals are admitted to states as refugees, with the intention that they resettle permanently; and some individuals are admitted as asylum seekers (for example, the so-called guardian angels I considered in Chapter 6), who are individuals seeking refugee status, whose case is adjudicated after entry by a host state. In what follows my focus is primarily on immigrants and refugees who intend to, and are permitted to, reside permanently—that is, to transition to citizenship status, if they desire—in the host state. All migrants who settle in a new state must integrate, but refugees' path to the host state is in significant ways distinct from the path taken by voluntary migrants. Refugees face different sets of challenges and, correspondingly, states have distinct duties towards them. In this chapter, I aim to articulate what these duties are in relation to the more general integration duties that states and immigrants possess. I then consider how integration programs should confront the persistence of ongoing injustice in host societies, especially injustice that shares a resemblance with the form of persecution resettled refugees may have escaped.

I begin by considering how the political theory of refugees has treated the duties owed to refugees and how the duties associated with resettlement in particular fit in that discussion; I argue that, so far, they have not been adequately considered. I then offer an account of integration to highlight that the assumptions underpinning the appropriate duties of states and migrants with respect to integration do not hold in quite the same way with respect to refugees. I argue, as a result, for treating the duties of resettlement as a subcategory of the duties of integration more generally, which I elaborate. The goal of integration is contested among scholars, but in what follows I treat its goal as avoiding persistent social exclusion.[2] More specifically, the objective of integration is to create the conditions under which newcomers are *not* excluded from the central goods offered in and by democratic societies. Both integration and resettlement should aim at the same objective, namely, generating the conditions under which immigrants are not excluded, or put slightly differently, under which they can protect themselves from exclusion. One key element of non-exclusion is self-sufficiency, which is often conflated with labor market integration. But self-sufficiency has a broader meaning in the case of refugees, which in part shapes how duties of resettlement must be conceived. Finally, I confront a difficult question, namely, how a generally welcoming society should, nevertheless, inform immigrants, and in particular, refugees, of the injustices that persist within it. I examine this question through the lens of the duties owed to specifically LGBTQ+ refugees who escape persecution on the basis of their sexual/gender identity and who resettle into spaces that nevertheless suffer from homophobia and transphobia. The basic claim of the final section is that there is a special duty owed to refugees who have escaped persecution to protect them especially from that form of persecution in their country of resettlement. How to offer this protection requires some conversation, in which I engage in the conclusion to the chapter.

Political Theory of Refugees and Asylum Seeking

To give a robust account of what is owed to resettled refugees, I will first take a step back to situate this duty in the broader discussion of the political theory of refugees. As a matter of international law, refugees are defined as individuals who have escaped their countries of origin as a result of persecution on the basis of membership in key social groups, including ethnic, cultural, religious, and political groups. Many scholars consider this definition too narrow and suggest that the category "refugee" ought to be expanded to include those who flee civil conflict (an expansion largely accepted as a matter of practice, and codified as such in many regional refugee documents including the Organization for African Unity's) as well as those who are severely economically deprived (Song 2018; Miller 2016c; Shacknove 1985). Asylum seekers are people who have sought safety outside of their country of citizenship and whose claims for refugee status have not yet been processed.

Among political theorists of refugees, it is generally agreed that states owe something to refugees (Gibney 2004). As many scholars explain, it is a condition of the legitimacy of the state system in general that states are willing to admit refugees; equally, a particular state's legitimacy stems in part from its willingness to admit refugees (Brock 2020; Owen 2020). In principle, at least, support for refugees ought to be distributed equally among states, but describing what counts as equal distribution in this space is difficult (Schuck 1997; Bauböck 2018a). One difficulty is that refugees are not spread evenly around the world. Rather, refugees typically seek refuge in states that neighbor their own, and these are often relatively poor states; as well, many refugees prefer to remain near their home countries, anticipating their return when conditions permit. A second difficulty is widespread disagreement about what precisely receiving states owe to refugees within their borders, once they arrive. For some theorists, what is owed is temporary safety; for others, permanent homes (for discussion see Owen 2020; Carens 1992; Gibney 2004; Brock 2020).[3] Correspondingly, for some, refugees are entitled only to have a small subset of their rights protected in their country of refuge; for others, refugees are entitled to have a full range of rights protected. A third difficulty is that receiving states themselves differ in terms of what they are capable of offering to refugees. So, while political theorists of migration typically agree states should share responsibility for refugees, to preserve the legitimacy of individual states and the state system in general, they disagree about what this responsibility is and how it should be distributed. And having determined that a responsibility-sharing regime of some kind is critical to establish, a fourth complication emerges, which is that merely stating that states are obligated to support refugees in some way is not necessarily sufficient to persuade them to carry out these obligations in practice; some states will shirk their duties towards refugees, leaving open questions about whether other states ought to take on more responsibility towards them (Owen 2016; Stemplowska 2016).

This sketch of the challenges of establishing a fair international refugee regime has not included an account of whether states are required to resettle refugees on a permanent basis, leaving open the possibility that offering temporary and permanent refuge are both permissible state responses to refugees and asylum seekers. That said, according to the 1951 Refugee Convention, there are three pathways to resolve permanently the situation of refugees: (1) they may return home, once the persecution or conflict that drove them to flee is no longer a threat; (2) they may be "locally integrated" into their country of refuge, often one that is next door to the state they have fled; and (3) a small proportion of refugees may be resettled permanently in a third state (United Nations High Commissioner for Refugees 2019). This resettlement option is made available to only a small proportion of refugees, usually among those designated by the United Nations High Commissioner for Refugees (UNHCR) as especially vulnerable in their state of refuge, for example because they are ill, have chronic medical conditions, or are elderly (UNHCR 2019).

Although it is not the subject of the discussion that follows, it is worth noting that the willingness of states, especially neighboring states, to offer temporary refuge is an essential element of refugee protection. Would-be refugees must be able to cross borders into neighboring states if they are in danger, and while neighboring states are bound by the duty of non-refoulement to offer immediate refuge, they are not as obviously required to permit refugees to remain on a permanent basis. The reality of refugee protection is that many refugees remain in situations that are supposedly temporary for years, if not decades, waiting for a permanent solution to their precarity that does not come (Parekh 2016). Some states offer temporary visas to refugees as well, requiring that, when possible, refugees return home. There are many problems with temporary visas, which I leave aside here, to focus on cases where refugees intend to remain on a permanent basis, and are treated as such (for discussion, see O'Sullivan 2019; Ilcan, Rygiel, and Baban 2018).

Because there will always be some refugees who simply cannot return to their home country, or whose country of refuge is unsafe, resettlement is an essential element of a just global refugee regime. Most political theorists agree that states ought to engage in the resettlement of refugees—sometimes citing the importance of a duty to rescue and other times citing the importance of sustaining the legitimacy of the state system—and many also agree that even among those that do admit refugees for resettlement, they ought to admit more. However, most states do not admit refugees for the purposes of resettlement, preferring to exclude them entirely or grant them only temporary status, and the result is that of the world's roughly twenty-five million refugees, only about 150,000 are permanently resettled every year to a handful of states. So while states may have a duty to resettle, the small number of resettled refugees indicates that the duty is going largely unmet (Lenard 2021a; Owen 2016; Parekh 2016).

Most political theorists conclude the discussion here, with the observation that states are failing to carry out the duty to admit and resettle refugees. I am in agreement with this general claim. But the duty to admit refugees, and to accept them on a permanent basis—a duty that I will refer to as the duty to resettle—is distinct from what they are owed, after they are admitted. Like immigrants more generally, resettled refugees must integrate into the receiving community; but, as I will articulate shortly, they sometimes arrive less-equipped to handle the challenges of integration than do voluntary migrants. There is a danger here, which I aim to be attentive to, that accepting that some refugee arrivals as less-equipped for the rigors of integration could appear to devalue their experiences, but that is not what I intend; I will elaborate the differences between being respectful of refugee arrivals' capacities and devaluing the challenges they have inevitably overcome to reach safety.

The role that the state must take in supporting the integration of resettling refugees is different, in some ways, than the role it takes in supporting the integration of voluntary migrants. I will refer to the obligation the state has to support the resettlement of refugees as the duty of resettlement in what follows. Certainly, simple admission of refugees is better than non-admission, even if it comes with only the generalized support offered to immigrants in general, and even if does not come with any support at all. Nevertheless, it is worthwhile to consider more deeply what resettlement is, so that would-be resettlement countries know what they are being asked to do, and why; moreover, philosophical attempts to work out how to share responsibilities will produce fairer outcomes if the tasks associated with resettlement are properly delineated, to include the tasks required by the duty of resettlement.

Political Theory of Integration

The meaning of integration, and what it entails for immigrants to a political society, is contested (see especially the section "The Study of Integration Processes" in Penninx 2019; Harder et al. 2018; Carens 2005), and scholars of integration focus variously on whether newcomers participate in politics, in the labor market, in civil society, and so on. For many, the most relevant form of integration is labor market integration, and so at issue is whether immigrants can successfully find employment and what conditions need to be in place so they can do so. Much discourse around the arrival and welcoming of immigrants highlights their economic contributions, citing their importance to growing the tax base and correspondingly to economic growth; this observation was central to the analysis in Chapter 6, where I examined the relevance of contribution in accessing citizenship. Others expand integration to include social and political dimensions, considering whether immigrants are easily able to find adequate housing, or whether they live in ethnically segregated neighborhoods, for example, or whether immigrants vote or participate in political life in other ways. Still others focus on the sense of *belonging* experienced by immigrants, wondering whether immigrants feel themselves to be members of the larger community to which they have migrated or whether their attention is in some way directed back "home" (Banting, Keith, Courchene, and Seidle 2007).

The importance—for both newcomers and the host state—of integrating newcomers into a new state's political, economic, and social spheres is largely accepted. Even among broadly liberal, democratic, states, "the way we do things" differs significantly, and newcomers must learn those ways to be successful in their new homes. Yet, there remain several key disputes. One dispute focuses on what requirements immigrants can be permissibly asked to meet to access both territory and membership in host states and correspondingly on the extent to which welcoming states are obligated to respect newly arrived and unfamiliar ethnic and religious practices. Here, a key question is whether immigrants can be asked to conform to the way host states operate, even when doing so requires them to abandon norms, values, and practices that they hold dear. I consider this dispute in more detail in Chapter 8. As well, there is much disagreement about what counts as successful integration, and scholars have typically distinguished between assimilation, which requires newcomers to adopt, fully, the values and norms that define a new state and shed those with which they traveled, and integration, which emphasizes instead quality employment, educational success, and linguistic competence alongside political participation. These elements of integration are measurable, and where newcomers are able to access employment and education, and where they learn the host state's language, and where they participate in political life, they are understood to be integrated (Harles 1997). On this latter view, of course, newcomers are not required to shed the values with which they traveled, although many do over time nevertheless.

For the integrationist, welcoming states are obligated to provide at least some resources so that immigrants can be successful in their new societies, such as access to language lessons, support in finding housing and employment, and a basic orientation to the structure of the host society. But many assimilationists will also endorse policies that provide support for these basic services. The main distinction between these two views is one of emphasis: for those who favor assimilative practices, the burdens fall largely to immigrants to reformulate themselves and their lives in conformity with the priorities of the welcoming state, whereas for those who favor integrative practices, the burdens fall jointly on immigrants and states to devise fair terms of integration, which specify the accommodations that welcoming states and immigrants must both make.

In particular, the assimilationist objective does not typically allow for much accommodation of cultural or religious differences; rather, the goal is to incorporate immigrants into the existing society and for them to leave behind any parts of their culture that appear to conflict with the host state's culture. Unlike assimilation, integration does not require unquestioning conformity by migrants, although they are certainly expected to learn about and understand the practices of their new home (Harles 1997; Schneider and Crul 2014; Joppke and Morawska 2002). The integrationist recognizes that the host state can and ought where possible to bend to accommodate the desires or cultural needs of newcomers, so they can have access, for example, to a state's educational and employment opportunities without needing to leave their culture behind or abandon meaningful cultural or religious practices, including wearing a turban or a hijab, or abiding by particular dietary requirements. Ultimately, then, those who defend integration over assimilation are generally willing to recognize the importance of key cultural and religious accommodations, especially where the failure to grant them slows or halts integration along the metrics I identified above. So, as I have explained it, integration is a two-way street, and both parties, the state and newcomers, have duties to facilitate that integration (Kymlicka 1998). States are required to generate the conditions under which immigrants can and do feel welcome, and immigrants are required to put their efforts towards adapting to their new home's way of doing things, even if these efforts can be substantial.

The precise duties that states have to facilitate and support the integration of immigrants are the subject of considerable dispute. Nevertheless, there is significant agreement that states are required to create employment conditions that are hospitable to newcomers (for example, by facilitating the recognition of foreign credentials and protecting immigrants against employment discrimination), to make sure that they can access high quality and affordable educational options including with respect to language, and to ensure that requirements for gaining citizenship status itself are reasonable. In most of the political theory debate around the precise duties of integration possessed by states, a few assumptions are typically made. One assumption is that immigrants have moved voluntarily, with the expectation of integrating into a new society, and correspondingly that they have arrived prepared to adopt at least some new ways of going about their lives. A second assumption is that, especially as developed states move towards stronger prioritization of high-skilled migrants, many migrants arrive with a relatively robust set of skills that they can direct towards integration (Shachar 2011). These assumptions, that migrants are relatively skilled, voluntary movers who arrive with the expectation that they will need to learn how their new home works in order to thrive there, underpin discussions of what can reasonably be asked of migrants and of what they are owed by their host states.

I outline this picture of how integration works and the duties that a commitment to integration imposes, especially, on welcoming states, so that I can better situate the related but not identical duties of resettlement that apply when migrants are not voluntary migrants, but rather are resettling refugees.[4] Notice that the first assumption, that migrants are voluntary movers who in some sense pre-accepted the challenges of integration, does not hold in this case. In particular, immigrants have typically weighed the benefits and burdens of immigration and made a choice to move. Refugees are forced migrants, who have been required by war or persecution to leave their home countries; they merit being treated as forced even if they have chosen to seek refuge elsewhere, having weighed the benefits and burdens of staying home versus migrating in search of safety. Additionally, resettled refugees typically have little say in the country to which they are resettled. So, for refugees, but not for voluntary migrants, the burdens of adaptation to a new place are unchosen, and may weigh more heavily on them as they attempt to move forward. This burden is especially acutely felt for refugees whose families have been forced to separate by the global refugee resettlement regime (for example, if some members of a family are resettled to one country and others to another), or whose families have chosen to remain in unsafe conditions. The second assumption, that integrating migrants have substantial, marketable, skills, holds in some but not all cases; some refugees arrive with skills, including linguistic competence and substantial education, but others do not. Those who arrive with little by way of education and linguistic competence may find the progress of integration slower and more challenging.

How should these differences between refugees and immigrant arrivals in general impact our theorizing about integration? As I shall go on to articulate, in the case of both types of migrants, the state's objective is to reduce their exclusion. But the duties associated with reducing exclusion must be conceived differently in the case of refugees, whose conditions of migration—forced rather than voluntary—distinguish them from more general immigrants. Before I give an account of these duties, however, I will consider more deeply the (so far relatively small) role that resettlement plays in discussions among political theorists who consider what is owed to refugees.

The Duty of Resettlement

Usually, refugee resettlement begins with the journey to a country of resettlement. Refugees who are resettled are typically offered basic orientation to their new home and at least some state financial support after they arrive. During this time, refugees are offered help in finding medical care, education, language lessons, accommodation, and so on. These services are provided by a range of actors, including settlement organizations, private individuals, and schools. Roughly thirty countries globally have refugee resettlement programs, and most resettlement spots are provided by the United States, Canada, and Australia (Selm 2014).

Although resettlement is considered somewhat by political theorists of refugees, there is not yet a full account of what a duty of resettlement might entail. To articulate its content, it will help to think more deeply about the goals of resettlement. One objective of resettlement is to provide the safety that refugees have, by their departure from a country of origin, been seeking. This objective is uncontroversial and is fulfilled simply by admitting refugees to a human-rights respecting environment. Moreover, it is fulfilled by states that admit refugees for temporary or permanent admission. As I said above, temporary refuge is a key dimension of refugee protection taken as a whole. But, as with temporary migration visas, visas that issue temporary protection for refugees, but which do not allow for the transition to permanent status, will eventually violate the obligation to proffer full inclusion to those who are subjected to a state's political power over an extended period of time.[5]

Gaining self-sufficiency is the second objective of resettlement for refugees. The settling state ought to create conditions under which resettled refugees can attain self-sufficiency, at which point the resettlement process is complete from the perspective of the host state. This objective, to enable self-sufficiency, is different from the one that is usually ascribed to integration. As I wrote earlier, integration is generally understood by social scientists to focus mainly on the labor market and ensuring that immigrants can access it fairly. Political theorists often treat integration as a broader term, including the sense of belonging or experiences of membership or identity that immigrants come to have over time. But given the well-documented, deep connection between meaningful employment and individual well-being, including migrants, ensuring free and fair access to employment creates the conditions under which these broader goals of integration can be met (Bevelander and Pendakur 2014; Wilkinson 2017).

It would therefore be reasonable to suggest that, as for immigrants in general, an objective for refugees should be their integration into the labor market as a pathway to securing both their general well-being and enabling them to develop the more affective measures of integration. However, the differences between arriving refugees and general immigrants are such that their efficient labor market integration is far from assured. Settling states cannot rely so heavily on employment to provide resettling refugees with the broader integration that all immigrants need. Because in some cases, refugees arrive with less education or less competence in the national languages of the host state than immigrants in general, labor market integration can prove challenging. Moreover, refugees may occasionally arrive with injuries or medical conditions (physical and mental) as well as substantial trauma associated with surviving war or state persecution, which make employment difficult, if not impossible, at least until such injuries or conditions are well managed. Recognizing these challenges is not equivalent to saying that refugees cannot integrate or that their past experiences are irrelevant to the process of integrating and can be dismissed. The recognition of these challenges is central to ensuring that host states carry out their resettlement duties well and with good effect.

As I explained in Chapter 6, it is common in public discourse around immigration to consider whether immigrants are an economic benefit or a burden on the society they are joining. When pro-immigrant advocates make their case, they often argue that immigrants are net contributors to the economy, that they enlarge the tax base, that they fuel economic growth, that they rely less on welfare services than others, and therefore that admitting more migrants is warranted to secure all these benefits. These benefits are real, and they can serve to persuade those who are nervous about the impacts of immigration to accept the admission of more immigrants. There is a tendency, as well, among refugee advocates to make the same claims, that refugees in the long term are net economic contributors and that their economic value to a host society is a reason to admit more of them (e.g., Barder and Ritchie 2018). So, although refugees are admitted for humanitarian reasons, or for reasons of justice, not for their anticipated contribution to the economic well-being of a state, their advocates are nevertheless keen to highlight the contribution they are ultimately likely to make.

Many philosophers, including me, are uncomfortable with focusing on the economic contributions of refugees, however—although it is critical to notice that, especially among states where the duty to admit refugees has been met, it is not unreasonable for refugee advocates to highlight the economic benefits of refugee admission as a way to encourage the admission of even larger numbers of them. But notice this: whether refugees are able to become economic contributors, given their sometimes disadvantaged starting point compared to other immigrants, is significantly connected to how well resettlement is done.

This observation leads to a second one, about the relationship of resettlement to integration. In discussions about the nature of integration and what supports are owed to migrants as they integrate, integration is largely described in instrumental terms. The focus is on identifying the supports that immigrants need to gain meaningful and appropriate (to their skills) employment because that is why (it is assumed) immigrants have migrated and also because employed immigrants are net economic contributors. The *reason* that states provide integration benefits to such immigrants is, in an important way, self-interested for hosting states: if migration is aimed in part at supporting an economy, then the host state has a strong motivation to ensure that migrants can access it on free and fair terms. I do not want to overstate the instrumental understanding of integration supports. Rather, I mean to highlight again that broader integration typically follows success in the labor market. Where immigrants find that their credentials are recognized and their skills appreciated and fairly remunerated, they also come to believe that they are valued members of society and indeed, over time, that they belong to it.

The same is not true for resettlement, at least not in a straightforward way. Resettlement's objectives are focused first and foremost on meeting the distinct needs of refugees who have been admitted for humanitarian reasons, rather than on getting them efficiently into employment. Resettlement objectives, in other words, are not directed exclusively at creating the conditions under which refugees will generate economic benefits. So, for example, while many immigrants are not able to take advantage of welfare state policies upon arrival (it is expected that they work immediately or be supported by families who have sponsored them), refugees are typically offered state support upon arrival. Some will require this support in perpetuity.

Resettlement aims to secure the capacity of newly arrived refugees to achieve self-sufficiency, and self-sufficiency has a broader meaning than does integration (Lenard 2019). Refugees, again because of the circumstances of their arrival, often do not start in the same place as voluntary migrants, and their objectives in migration differ substantially. In their travels, refugees have lost the conditions under which a whole life can be made; they have been forced to depend on the good will of states other than their home state to survive. Many refugees arrive to resettlement countries with a keen desire to work, but the range of physical and mental health conditions with which they arrive may prevent them from doing so immediately, even for those with strong educational and linguistic skills. Resettlement aims to create the conditions under which they can recreate a meaningful life for themselves.

In the ordinary English language use of the term, those who are self-sufficient can provide for themselves without direct aid from others. No one is truly self-sufficient in that sense, of course, but in general to be self-sufficient means that one has an independent capacity to provide for one's needs. Most refugees to a country will find employment and so be economically self-sufficient. But, in the case of resettlement specifically, self-sufficiency may in some cases be secured for refugees via alternative means, for example by ensuring that financial support is reliably provided, and also that they are able to seek additional help when they need it. Refugees must be *agents* in their own lives, even where they are not able immediately or ever to contribute in a straightforward way to the receiving state's tax base. This sort of approach acknowledges that resettlement can be successful even in cases where refugees are financially supported by their resettled state in perpetuity—although not economic contributors, they are self-sufficient in the way that successful resettlement requires (Lenard 2019).

What Precisely Are Resettlement Duties?

To recall, both integration and resettlement aim to create the conditions under which newcomers will be able to partake in all major spheres of society; that is, to create the conditions under which they will *not* be excluded. In this section, I will be more specific about the content of resettlement duties in particular and then will explain how this objective is met specifically in the case of refugees. In particular, there are three clusters of resettlement duties, which correspond roughly to the stages of welcoming resettled refugees: (1) safe pathway duties, (2) basic arrival duties, and (3) duties to create the conditions of self-sufficiency. I discuss these just below and the duty to avoid social exclusion in the next section. In the following chapter, I move from considering refugee resettlement to considering the way in which naturalization requirements can operate to exclude immigrants in more general terms, even as they are (paradoxically) meant to be processes for including them formally into a political society.

Duty to Ensure Safe Arrival

The first duty is to ensure that refugees can safely arrive at their country of resettlement. The broad context for resettlement is this: the UNHCR recommends refugees for resettlement, who then must travel to resettlement countries. Countries that receive resettled refugees are largely in the Global North and, therefore, far away from most countries of immediate refuge. So, in agreeing to resettle a refugee, the resettlement country takes on the duty to ensure safe passage. Transportation is paid for by the resettling state,[6] typically, but the coordination of travel is often carried out by the International Organization of Migration, which books flights and arranges for refugees to get to their new homes, including with respect to preparing many of the documents that refugees need to gain admission. In some cases, resettling states take responsibility for arranging travel for refugees (Blouin 2022).

Arrival and Basic Orientation Duties

The second set of duties are basic arrival duties. Resettling states must arrange for newcomers to be met at the airport, to be taken to some sort of temporary accommodation, and offered food and drink. These are the kinds of basic provisions that any person needs to survive, and it seems clear enough that the duty of resettlement requires providing them to newly arriving refugees, who do not necessarily arrive with the money or knowledge to arrange their own accommodation. In Canada during the Syrian initiative of 2015, when Canada moved quickly to resettle 25,000 refugees, most of the arrivals landed in the middle of a deep winter, and so initial provisions included warm clothing that was appropriate for the weather. The point is that resettling refugees generally arrive with no foothold in the receiving country and so require that their basic needs are satisfied from the moment of their arrival. These basic arrival duties persist for the first few weeks after arrival, and include the provision of some basic orientation to the way the new state works.

All newcomers to a state, especially those who are coming for extended lengths of time (including but not limited to permanently) require some sort of access to basic orientation. There should be no expectation that newcomers understand how their new society operates—and therefore host states must be expected to take on the duty to orient newcomers to how it works. This orientation duty includes providing information about the operation of the employment system, the transportation system, the health care system, and so on, and is needed for all newcomers, and not simply refugees. But, as I said earlier, refugees who are resettled are moving from insecure and often under-developed states to highly developed states. So, the orientation will, in some cases, take longer than for voluntary migrants, and it may need to be more focused on supporting people as they develop an understanding of the basic skills one needs to live in a developed state.[7] For newly arrived refugees, the many steps of the resettlement process can take a varying amount of time, depending on their specific needs; for those coming from very different home countries, the orientation may take longer. It will often require that those offering resettlement services are trained in the specific cultural context from which refugees arrive so that support can be attentive to their unique situation. One refugee resettlement manual in Canada warns those who work with refugee-arrivals that basic orientation around safety is key: "Explain all hazards in the house. Hot water can burn children. The electric stove is easy to start and leave on accidentally. Electricity and water don't mix" (Anglican Diocese of Canada 2015, 29).

Duties to Support the Development of Self-sufficiency

These observations underpin an important theoretical claim that is central to arriving at an understanding of the duties of resettlement. The duties of resettlement must at least in part be conceived as the duties to create conditions under which refugees are likely to resettle successfully. That is, refugees who arrive for resettlement should be offered conditions under which their ability to integrate, in the sense of achieving self-sufficiency, is real and substantial. As I already noted, resettled refugees are sufficiently different from other types of voluntary migrants, who make choices and can perhaps be expected to bear the costs of their choices to migrate. Because refugees are forced migrants, the duties receiving states hold towards them are typically understood, at least in part, in terms of a collective remedy for the harms they have been caused by their home state. States often make resources available to help voluntary migrants integrate, and those same resources are generally available for refugees, but I use the duty of resettlement to highlight the resources that must be made available in particular to resettling refugees.

(But of course, refugees can take advantage of both integration and resettlement opportunities.)

Let me briefly contrast the duty to create the conditions for refugee-arrival self-sufficiency with the duties owed to refugees in situations of temporary refuge. There is considerable debate around what countries of refuge owe to those who have sought temporary protection on their territory, and also what the global community owes both refugees in states of refuge (as distinct from resettlement) and what it owes to the states that provide this refuge (Parekh 2016). Temporary refuge status is, first, a legal status, protecting refugees from refoulement, so that whatever else they have to worry about, they do not need to worry about being sent home against their will. As well, it includes the provision of basic security, including accommodation, basic sustenance, and access to emergency health care. Although some states of temporary refuge will offer permanent status to refugees (Turkey offered citizenship status to some Syrian refugees, for example), they are not typically required to do so as a matter of international law; the obligation is limited to the protection of refugees' basic rights.[8]

One debate in the literature on the treatment of refugees who are assumed to be temporary residents is whether they have, or ought to have, the right to work.[9] In most cases, refugees in temporary states of refuge would prefer access to the labor market so that they can support themselves and their families while they wait to return home or for permanent resettlement. However, in many receiving states, refugees are denied the legal right to work, and are instead forced to rely on handouts of food, shelter, and medicine from the receiving state and the UNHCR. One reason to deny them the right to work is that, from the perspective of the receiving state, that right would make temporary refugees more likely to stay permanently, something that they may wish to discourage. In many cases, refugees have secured temporary refuge in states with struggling economies, which cannot necessarily or easily handle the entry of additional workers. Resettling states—unlike states of temporary refuge—must give refugees full access to work. In other words, to state the obvious, the duty of resettlement includes the duty to ensure that refugees can enter the labor market, if they are able to do so; refugees in resettlement countries intend to stay permanently, and therefore they must have the right to work. This observation raises two additional questions: Should states of resettlement *expect* refugees to work, and how should refugees who are unable to work be treated? I consider these questions in turn.

On the question of whether resettlement states should expect refugees to work, notice that the term "expectations" has two meanings here, one of which is descriptive and one of which is moral. Refugees who work require fewer state resources, so states want to encourage them to work; evidence that refugees quickly enter the workforce and contribute productively to the economy enables states to gain support for admitting more refugees, as I have already observed. So, states that take seriously the importance of offering refugees support in accessing the labor market not only increase the likelihood that refugees will be an economic boon, they also increase the likelihood of their being widespread public support for additional refugee admission.

It is, however, a reality that not all refugees will be able to enter the labor market—the elderly, for example, or those with physical and mental health challenges. These resettled refugees are also entitled to access meaningful self-sufficiency, even outside of the labor market. While ensuring smooth access to the labor market is one of many resettlement duties possessed by a host state, it is a duty that stems from the more general obligation to ensure that resettled refugees achieve self-sufficiency. So, resettlement states can expect, descriptively, that refugee arrivals will enter the labor market and thereby contribute to the tax base. But, they are not permitted to presume that refugees who are not able to do so have failed in some way. The goal of resettlement is just that, resettlement, and in many but not all cases that will entail integration into the labor market. For those who cannot enter the labor market, host state resettlement duties are to provide material support for them to achieve the self-sufficiency at which resettlement aims.

In summary: resettling states have a duty to enable refugees to achieve self-sufficiency, which generally will mean that refugees join the work force and contribute in productive ways to the economy. States and refugees both, independently, want refugees to find work, for instrumental reasons. States are engaged in a kind of a cost–benefit analysis: the willingness to resettle refugees may well depend on how likely it is that such individuals will contribute to the economy. Resettlement activities that enable resettled refugees to learn about, be introduced to, and even receive specialized mentorship regarding local labor markets are key to ensuring that they can enter the labor market and achieve success therein. This work may be more in depth for refugees than voluntary migrants. Both the duty of resettlement and the instrumental desires to encourage work point in the direction of substantial resettlement supports, which may need to be available for an extended period of time, especially for refugees whose transitions are the most difficult. Because it is well-known that people's overall wellbeing is stronger when they are working, supporting refugees to gain access to meaningful employment is in the best interests of refugees as well; therefore, high quality resettlement support will increase the likelihood that refugees are ultimately economic contributors and that is in the interest of the host state, but it will also support the journey towards self-sufficiency that I have placed at the heart of resettlement obligations. In the end, the duty of resettlement entails a focus on refugee self-sufficiency, only one route to which is via successful labor market integration.[10]

Protection from Social Exclusion

As I said above, one major way to define refugees is as individuals who are fleeing persecution. On this account, refugees flee persecution based on their belonging to specific social groups, traditionally understood to include mainly religious, cultural, and ethnic groups, and expanded to include women and sexual minorities. In this section, I consider the relevance of the grounds of persecution—the dimension along which a refugee was persecuted by her home state, which caused her to seek refuge—to the host state as part of its resettlement obligations, and I do so with a closer look at refugees persecuted for their sexuality or sexual/gender identity, that is, LGBTQ+ refugees.

LGBTQ+ persons become refugees for many reasons, of course, and one reason is when they are persecuted by their state, or by fellow citizens with the complicity of the state, because of their sexuality or gender identity. They are often equally at risk in their states of refuge, for example as are Ugandan refugees in Kenya, or Iraqi refugees in Lebanon, where rates of homophobic violence remain high. As a result, LGBTQ+ persons are often prioritized by the UNHCR for resettlement (Vitikainen 2020). They are resettled to states governed by constitutions that protect liberal democratic values and, correspondingly, where they can reasonably expect that their rights will be protected. But, of course, anti-LGBTQ+ sentiment is far from absent in resettlement countries. So, while resettling states do not typically persecute LGBTQ+ persons for their sexuality, it is wrong to behave as though resettlement states are free of anti-LGBTQ+ violence and discrimination. Why does this matter, aside from the obvious fact that it is a sign that liberal democratic states do not always live up to their ideals?

In resettling refugees who have fled group-membership-based persecution, host states have a duty not only to protect their rights on an equal basis, they additionally have a duty to protect them from the particular forms of danger that they have fled, which have been especially traumatizing for them.[11] There are two reasons for such a duty. One reason is that, as I indicated earlier, the goal is to enable refugees to reach self-sufficiency. There is good reason to believe that experiencing discrimination in their new homes can make reaching self-sufficiency, for example, by discouraging them from taking advantage of resettlement supports if they believe that settlement workers may harbor homophobic views. This example is not theoretical. I co-run a community organization that supports the resettlement of LGBTQ+ refugees in Ottawa, and one trans woman with whom we work stopped going to her English classes because the teacher refused to use "she/her" pronouns. A second reason is that, typically, refugees who are selected for highly scarce resettlement spots are often among the most vulnerable, as with LGBTQ+ refugees, and part of the value of resettlement in these cases lies in undoing the harm they have experienced so that they can live flourishing lives.[12] If they continue to face discrimination based on the status that led them to be refugees in the first place, this goal is undermined.

There are many ways that this danger can be mitigated in the host state. Governments in host states can adopt language and gestures that are inclusive, as a way to reduce discrimination and hostility towards, in this case, LGBTQ+ persons. They can ensure that those who are most directly connected to refugees (i.e., resettlement workers) on arrival understand the specific traumas of LGBTQ+ persons and that they are appropriately trained to offer sensitive support across a range of resettlement areas (Chávez 2011). Because refugees and other immigrants are generally served together by resettlement and integration services, all new immigrants must also be instructed in the importance of tolerating (if not respecting) the diverse ways of life that are welcomed in the host state. In the case of LGBTQ+ refugees, the persecution they experienced in their home countries was often at the hands of homophobic fellow citizens. In some cases, those same fellow citizens will have also arrived in the country of refuge, either as refugees or voluntary migrants. Part of ensuring that LGBTQ+ refugees are comfortable to access settlement supports is ensuring that settlement spaces are not themselves venues of homophobia, which can require instructing all newcomers in the importance of tolerance and respect for others. Here is a statement, for example, from the guidebook that accompanies Canada's cultural orientation course for resettling refugees: "People in Canada are expected to show tolerance and respect towards all people regardless of their age, gender, race, social class, marital/family status, language, religion, nationality, immigration status, sexual orientation and ability or disability" (Canadian Orientation Abroad 2020, 13).

It is also important to be honest with refugees that discrimination can and does persist in the host state; the failure to do so has been linked, by some social science research, to feelings of disillusionment among resettled refugees (Fratzke and Kainz 2019, 12). Host states may also offer immediate connections to LGBTQ+ citizens and allies, who can offer support in identifying and responding to homophobia where it is encountered. I am not arguing that the discrimination and violence that LGBTQ+ persons experience in host states is as harmful as the persecution they endured in their countries of origin. I am arguing, however, that the duty of resettlement includes a commitment, which may be met in a variety of ways, to protecting such refugees from social exclusion on the basis of their LGBTQ+ status.[13] Protections against social exclusion are entitlements for all citizens, of course, including all refugees, but the trauma of persecution on the basis of an identity generates a special duty to focus on adopting strategies to ensure that exclusion on these same bases can be avoided.

Conclusion

This chapter has examined the mechanisms by which refugees are resettled into third states. According to just about all political theorists of refugees, states have a range of duties towards refugees, which ought to be fairly distributed between states. With the exception of the duty of non-refoulement, which falls to all states, the precise duties that are owed to refugees vary by state according to their location, history, and wealth, among other factors; assessing any one state's responsibility includes a consideration of their capacity to support refugees and their preferences with respect to how they do so. For states that accept resettling refugees as one of their ways to support refugees globally, they must accept the corresponding duty of resettlement. This duty is related to the duty of integration that is owed to immigrants in general—both aim at protecting newcomers from exclusion—but because refugees are in crucial ways unlike voluntary, skilled migrants for which integration services are typically designed, special consideration must be given to the supports that refugee arrivals require in order to resettle effectively. The duty of resettlement therefore focuses more directly on how to protect refugee-arrivals from social exclusion, given the specific contextual factors that have pressed them to seek refuge.

The main difference between integration and resettlement is that while both focus on self-sufficiency, and supporting immigrants and refugees to achieve it, the conception of self-sufficiency that underpins resettlement must be understood more broadly than in terms of mere economic labor market integration. Rather, resettlement states must aim for conditions under which refugees can reliably access income, which may be in the form of employment and may also be in the form of shame-free, conditions-free, state-provided income, with which refugees can both recover from trauma and attain self-sufficiency. As a final consideration, I examined the special case of LGBTQ+ refugees, mainly to acknowledge that resettling states do not always live up to the equality commitments that they take to be foundational, and thus where refugees are refugees in virtue of persecution along a particular dimension—in this case, sexuality or gender identity—resettling states have an additional duty to protect refugees from social exclusion along that dimension.

8
Cultural Accommodations and Naturalization Ceremonies

The general objective of this book has been to examine, via specific cases, the ways in which democracies exclude migrants, from territory and from membership, to assess when such exclusion is permissible or justified. I have suggested throughout that *subjection* to power underpins a resident's claim to citizenship status and also that the more one is subjected to power, the more robust that claim is. I have also argued that citizenship status protects residential security first and foremost. The last three chapters, and this one as well, focus on the trajectory of transition, from admission to resident to citizen; as subjection grows—that is, as the life-shaping aspect of a political, economic, and social institutional space extends in time—residents become more and more entitled to the full inclusion that citizenship supports. This chapter tackles the final step in the naturalization process, the oath ceremony, and considers whether *inclusion* requires accommodating cultural practices of would-be citizens or whether a host state can permissibly refuse accommodations at this stage. The sheer length of time that naturalization takes, even at its speediest, means that a denial of citizenship at the final, oath-taking stage, is likely to be deeply harmful; the harm of denial at this late date offers at least a presumptive case for accommodating cultural and religious practices at the oath ceremony. This chapter considers requests for accommodations, and attempts to deny them, in additional depth.

In 2020, a German court ruled that it was permissible to deny citizenship to a long-time resident of Germany on the grounds of his refusal to shake hands with the female official responsible for handing him his citizenship certificate. The justification was, broadly, that his refusal was evidence that he had failed to integrate fully into German norms and values. Muslim residents of Switzerland were denied citizenship on similar grounds, as were two Muslim school girls who refused to take part in co-ed swimming classes (Staufenberg 2016; BBC News 2018). In Canada, Zunera Ishaq was initially denied the right to take the citizenship oath because, for religious reasons, she covers her face and the oath procedures in Canada traditionally require that one's face is uncovered during the ceremony itself. These cases raise multiple questions, including whether these requirements (and others) violate a naturalizing individual's right to freedom of conscience, whether they amount to treating individuals differently on the basis of morally arbitrary characteristics, and whether they make citizenship too difficult to access. More generally, they raise the question of what sorts of requirements can permissibly be asked of naturalizing individuals over the course of the naturalization process.

Some migrants arrive on temporary work-related visas, from which they can in time apply for the right to stay permanently, and others are admitted to states with a kind of pre-approval to apply for citizenship. In these latter cases, so long as they meet the state's naturalization requirements, they are permitted to apply for citizenship in time. Individuals admitted to "permanent resident" or "landed immigrant" status are often high-skilled workers or refugees who have been accepted for permanent admission or resettlement. One of the major requirements that must be met is simply residence—so, in several immigrant-receiving nations, once such migrants have fulfilled a relatively short residency period, of between three and four years, they are permitted to apply for citizenship. Others, admitted on work visas, from which they can apply for naturalization in time, will require a longer period of residence before they can access citizenship.

Applicants for naturalization must complete many additional steps, including sometimes language tests and citizenship tests. As well, sometimes, as for example in Belgium, Denmark, and the Netherlands, they must complete civic integration classes to prepare them for these tests. In several countries applicants must be present for and participate in a citizenship ceremony, which in many cases includes the reciting of an oath. This chapter examines whether—if the residency requirements are met and the relevant tests are passed—it can be justified to refuse religious or cultural accommodations at the oath stage. I ultimately make the case that religious and cultural accommodations ought to be protected at the oath stage, but it is important to be careful about the reasoning here; I will explain why, even if naturalizing individuals can be permissibly asked to complete a rigorous application process in order to attain a status that many others are simply born into, accommodations can and ought to be made at this final, and deeply symbolic, stage.

I begin with the context that has framed recent political theory discussions around the legitimacy of citizenship tests, namely, the claim that many (especially European) states are making access to citizenship harder, citing the importance of ensuring that immigrants are sufficiently integrated before they can be citizens. The contextual considerations help to show that, too often, the adoption of more stringent naturalization requirements is borne from an animosity towards immigrants, especially those from Middle Eastern and Muslim-majority countries. I then consider the permissibility of citizenship tests and agree that they are, at least in principle, defensible; I suggest that they can, in their best versions, support the integration of newcomers into multiple spheres of society. Next, I articulate the purpose of citizenship ceremonies and the oath taking that is at their center: fundamentally, I suggest, the taking of the oath represents the formal acceptance, by naturalizing individuals, of subjection to state power, in exchange for the state's commitment to protecting their full and equal rights as citizens. On this conception of what the citizenship ceremony is, the accommodation of religious and cultural practices does not undermine the purpose of the ceremony and thus should be permitted.

I then respond to three objections. One objection says that accommodation rights are rights of citizens, not residents, and can thereby be denied at the oath stage. A second objection says that the cultural and religious practices that require accommodation are evidence of a severe failure to integrate, and thus citizenship can be denied to those with these practices. A variation of this objection says that citizenship is so valuable that those whose religion or culture would, in practice, require accommodations, should be willing nevertheless to forgo these accommodations as a sign of their commitment to the welcoming state and the benefits that they will gain as a result. A third objection says that these practices are evidence of a desire and willingness to undermine liberal democratic institutions, and so those who require accommodations can be denied citizenship; here I consider, in particular, the claim that democratic states can exclude those whose values are straightforwardly anti-egalitarian. None of these objections is persuasive, however, and so I conclude that such accommodations ought to be granted.

Citizenship Ceremonies and Naturalization

Most countries have a wide range of naturalization requirements in place, including language and citizenship tests or courses and citizenship ceremonies.

To consider the legitimacy of citizenship ceremonies, it is key to understand them in the context of the range of naturalization requirements that states ordinarily impose on would-be citizens.

Naturalization requirements are crucially different from admission requirements. Admission requirements are those that must be met by individuals who aim to gain authorized entry to a specific territory, whether they intend to stay temporarily or hope to stay permanently. These admission requirements vary, as the earlier chapters have demonstrated, according to the stated intention of the migrant—tourists must meet different admission requirements than temporary foreign labor migrants for example. But there are some requirements that all migrants, whether temporary or permanent, must meet to gain entry: in particular, they must meet health and security requirements.[1] I have defended these requirements as legitimate in Chapter 5, at least in principle, on the grounds that there are plausible reasons to exclude individuals who pose health or security risks to a destination state. Naturalization requirements apply *only* to those who desire to access citizenship, that is, to gain the complete set of rights and privileges accorded to full members of the community. As a matter of practice, naturalizing individuals must typically prove that they persist in meeting admission requirements during their period of residence: for example, permanent residents who apply for naturalization, but who during their mandatory residency period commit grievous crimes, can be denied access to citizenship and deported. Here, I focus on the legitimacy of naturalization requirements specifically.

In recent years, in many countries, the list of tasks a would-be citizen must carry out to naturalize has grown longer. The impetus to increase the rigor of naturalization procedures has stemmed from worries about the challenges that low-skilled migrants and refugees, who are often of Middle Eastern or Muslim background, allegedly face in integrating (for discussion, see Joppke 2014; Lenard 2010; Peach 2007). The stated justification for more, and more robust, naturalization requirements is that such migrants struggle to integrate, in particular with respect to the adoption of liberal democratic norms, and so more effort must be made to ensure that naturalizing individuals have learned and can demonstrate the relevant commitments. Some states have pushed some of these requirements back to admission, adopting "mandatory integration from abroad" measures, which ask would-be migrants to complete a variety of tests in advance of admission to a state's territory in the first place (S. W. Goodman 2011,

237). For example, would-be migrants to the Netherlands must complete a pre-arrival test in order to gain access to a temporary residence visa, which examines both linguistic competence and knowledge of Dutch society (S. W. Goodman 2011, 244–245; Government of the Netherlands 2019). A wide range of would-be migrants to the Netherlands are exempt from these tests, including those who are designated highly skilled and those who, in general, come from relatively wealthy countries. The result is that those who are in fact subject to these requirements are largely only those who intend to reunite with families already in the Netherlands, mainly from Morocco and Turkey.

Even where a reasonable case can be made for a particular, plausible naturalization (or admission) requirement, the context of its imposition matters (S. W. Goodman 2011). After all, many historically immigrant-receiving and immigrant-welcoming nations—notably Canada and the United States—have long asked naturalizing individuals to complete citizenship tests, and to participate in oath ceremonies, to gain citizenship; in these cases, the use of tests as one of the final steps in the naturalization procedure has not, by and large, been criticized as exclusionary.[2] By contrast, in the case of pre-arrival linguistic competence for family migrants in the Netherlands, the requirement serves merely to keep families separated and denies family members the opportunity to learn a language *in situ*, as part of the integration process itself.

One way that social scientists assess whether the adoption of more robust naturalization requirements is having an unjust impact is to compare naturalization rates before and after such requirements are toughened or adopted for the first time, as well as to compare pass rates as tests are made longer and, in some cases, more difficult. Such scholarship focuses as well on assessing what counts as a fair pass rate for citizenship and language tests and what counts as a fair naturalization rate. For example, when Randall Hansen defends the adoption of citizenship tests, he proposes that so long as they are acceptably easy ("so that anyone with, say, a high school education could be expected to pass it") and the pass rate is high enough (he proposes 70 percent), they do not unfairly impose roadblocks on attaining citizenship (Hansen 2010, 25). Hansen and others leave room for considering, as well, what kinds of adjustments should be made for those who may experience additional barriers in taking, and passing, both language and citizenship tests. For example, some states, including Canada and the United States, exempt the elderly from language and citizenship tests, acknowledging that language acquisition gets harder with age. Others permit tests to be given orally to applicants who are not literate or who have physical disabilities that otherwise make writing the test challenging or impossible. As Ricky van Oers has demonstrated in a comparative study of Germany and the Netherlands, however, "the obligation to pass knowledge tests is particularly harmful for immigrants in disadvantaged positions, who are experiencing trouble finding their way in society" (van Oers 2020, 11), and it may not be fair *enough* to say that those who have a high school education could pass it, or that they can be done orally in case of literacy difficulties.

Nevertheless the general point is this one: so long as naturalizing immigrants could pass the test easily enough, and so long as adaptations to the regular testing procedure can be accessed where they are needed, the requirement that naturalizing immigrants pass citizenship tests is permissible. They may be permissible even if the choice to adopt such tests is borne from hostility towards immigrants in general or towards immigrants from specific parts of the world. However, where evidence suggests that naturalization rates drop substantially after the imposition of the tests, especially among those who are most vulnerable, it is important to consider whether an injustice has occurred, and therefore where remedy is warranted. For example, it can reasonably be inferred that injustice has occurred in the cases of Germany and the Netherlands, which adopted robust testing requirements between the years 2003–2008, in the context of a generalized hostility towards migrants, especially targeted at racially and religiously distinct migrants, the result of which has been that pass rates, especially among those who are most vulnerable, have declined substantially (van Oers 2020). In summary, then, on the one hand, new and toughened citizenship tests can be permissible as a way to encourage naturalizing citizens to learn about their new home; but they are unlikely to be permissible if they are deliberately or even implicitly serving to screen out certain allegedly undesirable, would-be citizens, and made unreasonabley difficult (as demonstrated by declining pass rates) as a result. More generally, a better strategy is one that requires attendance at a civics class, successful completion of which effectively guarantees a pass on the subsequent test. The importance of gaining deeper knowledge of local history and customs can reasonably be treated as part of the life-shaping aspect of subjection and encouraging the learning of that knowledge can thereby be permissible and even welcome.

The requirement of linguistic competence raises slightly different normative questions. Requiring proof of linguistic competence in advance of travel is not unusual, even in immigrant-welcoming states. In particular, obtaining high-skilled visas often requires demonstration of linguistic competence. It is widely (although not universally) accepted that at least minimal language competence can be asked of naturalizing immigrants. There are many pragmatic reasons to require this: many of the basic tasks of integration, and more general participation in society over the long term, demand some competence in a state's national language(s) (Kymlicka 2001; Kymlicka and Patten 2003). The demand for proof of competence is, in some sense, a protective strategy to ensure that naturalizing migrants can advocate for themselves and attain self-sufficiency across a range of spheres. As with citizenship tests, tests of linguistic competence come in varying levels of difficulty and can be assessed for whether they present unfair obstacles for would-be citizens.

The naturalizing process—which includes the ceremony but also includes the associated language tests and, where relevant, civic integration classes—has as an objective, at least in principle, to instruct newcomers in local practices. On a best understanding of their purpose, they aim to ensure that newcomers gain sufficient awareness of key features of their new society. For example, among those theorists who are prepared to defend such tests, it is typical to defend questions that ask test-takers about contextually specific political and historical information that citizens ought to be familiar with. The thought is that preparation for the citizenship test is essentially educative, intended to ensure that citizens will have the information they need to participate in political and economic society. Whereas natural-born citizens learn this information in school, naturalizing citizens learn this information by preparing for a citizenship test (Hansen 2010, 25). As Hansen observes, it is *reasonable* to ask residents to show evidence of having learned the basics of how their new society works, as this information is key to their successful integration (Hansen 2010, 25). So, at least in principle, and so long as they are constructed properly, such tests are permissible for the contribution they can make to supporting the integration process for newcomers.

To assess whether they are in fact constructed fairly, political theorists focus on the content of the tests themselves, proposing that some kinds of questions are permissible, while others are problematic. Questions that focus on key knowledge about the welcoming state's politics and history are typically defended as permissible, for their connection to the practicalities of integration, whereas value-based questions raise concerns that key basic liberal rights are being undermined.[3] First, some say it may be wrong to demand of newcomers that they demonstrate specific values where these are not necessarily shared among the citizenry already. For example, one scholar writes of the Dutch test, "The Dutch curriculum suggests the general acceptance of social norms such as concubinage or homosexuality among the Dutch population although not all social and religious groups in the Netherlands do accept these norms and although the acceptance of such norms is not necessary for a liberal democracy" (Michalowski 2010, 6). Second, some other proposed and actual citizenship test questions may amount to a violation of the liberal commitment to freedom of conscience. Christian Joppke writes that a "test that is inquisitional about the 'true' values or beliefs of an individual, even if they pertain to the rules of liberal democracy, is pernicious from a liberal point of view" (Joppke 2010, 2). Both these objections, as I shall show below, are relevant to considering the question of whether accommodations ought to be permitted in the course of citizenship ceremonies.

The Permissibility of Citizenship Ceremonies

In states that have citizenship ceremonies, they are typically the final step in the process of naturalization. New citizens are asked to take an oath, marking the moment of their transition into citizenship. In some cases, the ceremonies are merely ceremonial, as, for example, in most Scandinavian countries, where new citizens are invited to participate in the ceremony but are not required to do so as a condition of gaining citizenship status. In others, they are a mandatory step in the process, without which citizenship is not granted (Damsholt 2018, 2704). Some oaths are quite clearly focused on affirming allegiance to a new state (Orgad 2014, 115)—the American oath ceremony requires newcomers to "absolutely and entirely renounce and abjure all allegiance and fidelity to any foreign prince, potentate, state, or sovereignty" and to "bear true faith and allegiance to" the United States (USCIS 2020). Allegiance-based oaths reveal a worry about potentially divided loyalties among newcomers and ask oath-takers to confirm their full and complete loyalty to the new state. Others emphasize obedience to law in addition to loyalty, as, for example, in Norway where the oath reads in its entirety: "As a Norwegian national, I pledge loyalty to my country Norway and to Norwegian society, I support democracy and human rights and I will respect the laws of the country" (Ministry of Children 2014). In both cases, taking the oath has substantial expressive value in recognizing newcomers on equal terms with citizens. In what follows, at issue are ceremonies that are mandatory.[4]

Oaths are a kind of especially weighty promise. They usually have two elements. One is the promise itself, which is at the center of the oath, and another is a symbolic or expressive dimension that attends the oath-taking, signaling that it is being treated as an especially important promise. The particulars of any oath-giving moment may vary but the core of oath-taking as an expressively important promise-making moment remains. For example, health care professionals take the Hippocratic oath to signal their commitment to the well-being of their future patients and their intention to do their best by them. In many countries, those who testify in courts are asked to take an oath signaling their intention to tell the truth to the best of their ability.

In the case of citizenship ceremonies, the purpose of oath-taking as the final step in the naturalization process is at least partly expressive, focused on recognizing the importance of taking on a new citizenship, the rights and privileges that such status grants, and the obligations it imposes. Oaths in this case "serve as a means for an immigrant to subscribe to the tenets of the community" (Orgad 2014, 99) and are aimed at "creating a sense of belonging and loyal citizens" (Damsholt 2018, 2701). Immigrants themselves often appreciate the opportunity to participate in this rite of passage. For many it is a much-anticipated celebratory moment and described as such: "I think the oath was actually beautiful. I didn't think I would be emotional until I started saying the oath" (Damsholt 2018, 2707).

In other words, the citizenship oath operates as a formal acknowledgement of a connection between an incoming citizen and the state. A new citizen is openly and formally accepting her obligation to abide by the rules of the new state and to the best of her ability to participate in sustaining it. In exchange, the state takes on the legal obligation to protect her rights, on an equal basis with all citizens. The oath signals, on the part of incoming citizen, a recognition of her subjection to the laws that regulate a state, in exchange for which she is granted full and formal rights to contest the conditions of that subjection; that is, she gains access to the full range of political rights that, at least in principle, render that subjection legitimate and fair. The citizenship oath is thus different in one key way from the oaths I described earlier—the citizenship oath is effectively an obedience pledge by incoming citizens, with the understood promise that an important exchange is transpiring: the pledged obedience is in exchange for the robust rights protection that is granted by citizenship status.

Gaining state protection is significant; however true it is that some rights attach to people in virtue of their humanity (and I will return to this below), at least some rights do attach to citizenship status itself. In particular, one right that is conventionally understood to travel with citizenship is the right to vote and more generally to participate freely in the political life of one's new state. In many states, voting rights are restricted to citizens, and so the citizenship ceremony marks not only the formal acceptance of subjection to a state's laws, but also the gaining of the full set of political rights required to render than subjection legitimate. As I explained in Chapter 1, my view is that residence, rather than citizenship, grounds the right to vote; residents are subjected in ways that, I argued, give rise to an entitlement to a full say in the shaping of that subjection (Lenard 2014; for an objection to the residence-based argument, see de-Shalit 2019). The main benefit of citizenship status in particular is that it protects those who hold it from expulsion, in addition to guaranteeing robust rights protections more generally (including the right to return home, and often support to exercise that right, as I described in Chapters 3 and 4).

Before evaluating whether the function of the citizenship ceremony is undermined if accommodations are made in that space, it is first important to set out what accommodations are, as well as which accommodations are generally made and why they are requested. In general terms, an accommodation is a deviation from a regulated or customary practice, requested because, for some reason, the person cannot or does not want to perform the standard practice. Accommodations can be requested for many reasons, including to enable people with physical disabilities to access key public spaces, and in the cases at issue here, to enable those with religious and cultural beliefs to access public services without compromising their felt religious or cultural obligations. As the examples with which I began this chapter suggest, practices that stem from deeply held religious and cultural beliefs produce frequent requests for accommodation across a range of spaces, including citizenship oath ceremonies (Balint and Lenard 2022; Lenard 2020a).

Is there any reason to believe that the ceremony's mutual exchange—the commitment to obey the state's laws in exchange for protection against expulsion—is undermined if cultural and religious accommodations are granted? It does not seem so. There is no prima facie reason to believe that a handshake, or an open face, is *essential* to the exchange that is made. Even without a handshake, the oath ceremony remains a space in which newcomers can offer a public commitment to their new state. When the German court issued its decision that it was permissible to deny citizenship on the grounds that the applicant would not shake hands with a female officiant, it did not escape notice that the decision was issued as COVID-19 spread around the world, and everyone was advised to stay far away from each other. In such times, naturalization has proceeded, even in Germany, without the formal shaking of hands. In response, German officials simply noted the expectation that, in time, handshaking would return to being a central aspect of German culture (so, in this case, the relevant individual would have been granted citizenship if his oath had overlapped with COVID-19 precautionary measures). Similarly, if the showing of faces is deemed important as part of the oath ceremony, it is reasonable to offer occasional women-only ceremonies to permit this; or, if the worry is identification of *who* is taking an oath, identification can transpire prior to the oath-taking by female state authorities. Ultimately, it does not appear that the *exchange* that is marked by the citizenship ceremony would be undermined if handshaking were replaced with an alternative form of mutual recognition or if women-only ceremonies were permitted.

Responding to Objections

This section considers three reasons given for refusals to accommodate cultural and religious practices during a citizenship ceremony and explains why they generally fail. One reason is that accommodation rights are reserved for citizens, so states are not obligated to extend them at the time of the citizenship ceremony. A second reason is that those who are unwilling to participate in the ceremony on the terms set by the welcoming state demonstrate a failure of integration so severe that they deserve to be excluded from membership; a variation on this objection proposes that citizenship access is so important that naturalizing individuals should be willing, anyway, to forego accommodations to prove they understand its value. A third reason is that those who are unwilling to participate in the ceremony may harbor harmful views, sometimes explicitly so, aimed at undermining the state.

Objection 1: Cultural Accommodations Are Citizen-Specific Rights

The first objection to accommodating religious or cultural practices at citizenship ceremonies concedes that states must make cultural and religious accommodations for citizens but suggests that such accommodations may permissibly be reserved for them alone. Thus, accommodations are not required at citizenship ceremonies because those taking oaths are not yet citizens.

Certain rights are permissibly reserved for citizens. For example, in addition to voting and protection against deportation, it may be permissible to restrict access to some benefits or services to citizens, as I explained in Chapter 5; for example, to free non-emergency health care access, to subsidized university or college education, and even to some employment opportunities, such as in the military or intelligence services. But it is not similarly permissible to limit the protection of basic rights to citizens. In particular, the basic rights—including freedom of conscience and religion and rights of due process—are protected for all residents on a territory and not simply citizens. Recall Joppke's argument against some value-based questions on citizenship tests, that they violate the right to freedom of conscience of test-takers. Because this right is not citizen-specific, it must be protected for incoming citizens as much as for current citizens. Similarly, in the case of citizenship ceremonies, freedom of conscience is at stake. Would-be citizens' beliefs about proper dress, modesty, or contact with strangers must be respected as part of a commitment to their freedom of conscience.

In support of this position, it is worth noting the history of accommodations that have been routinely made, in the domain of oath-taking, for both citizens and non-citizens. Take the United States as an example, in which oaths are taken in advance of taking political office or before giving testimony in court. It is common to see oath-takers with their hand on a religious text; historically, this has most often been a Christian bible, but that is not required and never was. Many oath-takers choose an alternative text with religious or cultural significance to them. When US lawmakers were sworn in, in January 2021, lawmakers used at least 12 different such books, including the Quran (Rashida Tlaib swore in on Thomas Jefferson's Quran) and, simply, a copy of the US constitution (Jackson 2019). When Suzi LeVine took the oath required to take up the position of American Ambassador to Switzerland and Lichtenstein in 2014, she swore her oath with a hand on a Kindle, open to the

19th amendment to the US Constitution, which guaranteed the right to vote to women (Rosefield 2014). The law that permits US oath takers to choose a text of significance to them may not seem like an accommodation because it is not a deviation from accepted or mandated practice; rather, it is an accommodative law that permits oath takers to select the text of their choice, as a manifestation of acceptance of religious and cultural difference. But more obvious accommodations are also made, for example, in the case of US citizens who have religious objections to oath-taking, such as Jehovah's Witnesses, who when required to testify in court or take up political office, are permitted to simply affirm their intent to tell the truth or serve their constituents.

These accommodations may be understood as offered to citizens, but they apply to non-citizens testifying in US court cases as well. Moreover, similar modifications are made to the oath of citizenship itself for incoming citizens who are Jehovah's Witnesses, who may similarly affirm their commitment to the United States (Tarovic 2015). The United States is not unusual in this. In Germany, the oath required of political leaders asks them to say: "I swear that I will dedicate my efforts to the well-being of the German people, promote their welfare, protect them from harm, uphold and defend the Basic Law and the laws of the Federation, perform my duties conscientiously, and do justice to all. So help me God." But the last clause is not required of oath-takers and it may be omitted ("Oath of Office" 2021). There is, in other words, historical precedent for respecting and accommodating conscience claims at moments when oath-taking is required, while recognizing that these accommodations do not undermine the oath itself.

Objection 2: The Demand for Accommodations Demonstrates a Failure to Integrate

The second objection to granting citizenship to those who request religious or cultural accommodations to enable participation in naturalization ceremonies is that their need for these accommodations demonstrates a severe failure of integration. A variation on this objection says that even if the practices at issue are matters of conscience, incoming citizens should be willing to forego them for the duration of the oath ceremony, to signal their commitment to the host state and an appreciation for the significant benefits that membership will bring; that is, minorities are not asked to abandon their practices in perpetuity, rather only to refrain from engaging in them at one particular moment. On this objection, the state is treating the citizenship oath ceremony as a kind of ritual of mutual recognition with substantial expressive value, marked by shaking hands or uncovered faces; those who refuse these mechanisms of mutual recognition demonstrate that they have not sufficiently absorbed the values of the state they hope to join as members. This objection is made especially strongly in cases like the one that has motivated this chapter, where the worry is that the refusal to shake hands originates in a belief in the inferiority of women. A state is obligated to protect the rights of *all* citizens, and permitting handshake refusals (on the grounds that these refusals stem from a rejection of gender equality) implies that it is not doing so. According to this objection, social cohesion among a population rests on a willingness of newcomers to demonstrate evidence of assimilation rather than simply integration (Lægaard 2010).

These worries dominate public discourse around the legitimacy of permitting or denying accommodations. In the case of the individual who refused to shake the official's hand, and was therefore denied German citizenship, the court ruled that the denial of citizenship was appropriate and fair because his refusal was evidence of his "fundamentalist concept of culture and values," and moreover that it demonstrated his failure to integrate "into German living conditions." The court continued, explaining that handshakes were "deeply rooted in social, cultural, and legal life" in Germany (Embury-Dennis 2020). In Denmark, a law mandating handshaking as a part of the citizenship ceremony came into effect in January 2019; in its defense, then-Minister of Immigration, Integration and Housing wrote that a handshake is a "visible sign that you've taken Denmark to heart" (Sorensen 2018).[5] In France, a woman of Algerian origin was similarly denied citizenship for refusing to shake hands with an officiant; a court ruled the denial was fair because it revealed her "lack of assimilation" (Breeden 2018).

I do not deny that handshakes are a common greeting in many states, or even that they have a long cultural history, especially in business and other formal contexts as a way of sealing an agreement; the post-oath ceremony handshake analogously does operate to seal an agreement. However, such statements infuse handshaking with an exaggerated meaning and importance. People in handshaking countries, including my own, often replace it with hugs and kisses (in the pre-COVID-19 era), waves, or nods of the head. Although something small may be lost in these cases, whatever is lost does not appear substantial enough to justify retaining the handshake, where the cost is excluding cultural and religious minorities from citizenship. In

Canada, although the decision was ultimately reversed, Zunera Ishaq was initially denied the opportunity to take the oath of citizenship on the grounds that she refused to uncover her face and that the oath taking must be done in plain view of others. Jason Kenney, then-Minister of Citizenship and Immigration Canada, said: "to segregate one group of Canadians or allow them to hide their faces, to hide their identity from us precisely when they are joining our community is contrary to Canada's proud commitment to openness and to social cohesion" (L. Goodman 2014).

These claims about immigrants' failure to integrate go beyond naturalization ceremonies. Over the last twenty years, many leaders have declared that multiculturalism—broadly, the view that multiple cultures can live and work together in a democratic society, in part by accommodating a range of cultural and religious practices—has failed (Joppke 2017; Vertovec and Wessendorf 2010). A more concerted focus on the importance of ensuring that newcomers adopt shared norms and values, as manifest, for example, in the adoption of citizenship tests of the kind considered earlier, has been proposed instead. But what these calls demonstrate is a conviction that there is a strong connection between the adoption of shared values and norms and the ability of immigrants to integrate along the many metrics of integration, which I described in Chapter 7. For those who are declaring that multiculturalism has failed, the claim is that the reason that newcomers struggle to access gainful employment and educational opportunities, or "refuse" to learn the host state's language, is that they do not share the right values and norms; were they required to do so more robustly, they would be able better to integrate into the labor market, and so on.

This conclusion is mistaken, however. Where integration is difficult for newcomers, it is usually not because of their failure to adopt the majority's values, but rather because a wide range of barriers to their integration persist, and host states are not willing or able to support newcomers in overcoming them, and in many cases perpetuate them. Indeed, failure to accommodate these practices, in general and at the moment of naturalization, perpetuates barriers to integration.[6] Consider how political theorists of migration reject immigration policies that are openly racist. One reason to reject racist immigration policies, says Michael Blake, is that they demonstrate disrespect for current citizens who share the race of those who are being excluded (Blake 2002). Because nearly no country in the world is homogenous, he says, countries are effectively barred from adopting racist admission policies out of respect for their own citizens. By analogy, one reason to accommodate cultural and religious practices among incoming citizens, at the citizenship ceremony, is that such practices are present already among citizens, and perhaps even that similar accommodations of these practices are also granted to current citizens in other contexts.

Anti-accommodation policies serve to communicate hostility to would-be citizens by signaling that these practices are not fully welcome. Recall how I described the debate around the legitimacy of citizenship tests: when those tests signal that certain values and norms are so widespread that they in fact define the state, they suggest a homogeneity of values and norms among a population that is generally not in fact present. The same signaling occurs in citizenship ceremonies where certain practices are not permitted, especially when those same practices are permitted among the wider population: the refusal to accommodate suggests a homogeneity of values and norms among a population that is not present. The choice to disallow accommodations throughout the naturalization process can be understood as a lack of respect for those who hold non-dominant norms and values. Overall, then, while refusal of accommodations is defended on the grounds that it encourages immigrants to integrate, that refusal instead acts as a barrier to integration, in part because it is a sign of hostility towards the practices that would-be citizens hold dear.

One might say that where states refuse accommodative practices at the oath stage, and where such accommodative practices are themselves not accepted more generally, there is no moral problem. Naturalizing newcomers are treated just as citizens are, with respect to specific (unaccommodated) cultural practices. Certainly, the consistency in refusing accommodation suggests that those requesting accommodation are not singled out for their being newcomers, and there is some very limited value to that. But, as a holistic evaluation, the failure to adopt accommodative practices is generally an exclusionary choice for the ways it requires minorities to abandon or compartmentalize religious and cultural practices in order to access the full range of goods and services available in a democratic society. I will return to this in the book's conclusion.

Objection 3: Demands for Accommodation Are Correlated with Anti-Democratic Views

A third worry is that candidates for naturalization who request accommodations may, in virtue of their cultural and religious practices, be signaling that they harbor harmful views. There are weaker and stronger versions of this worry. The weaker version claims that demands for accommodation reflect an unwillingness to embrace fully liberal democratic norms and values. Perhaps liberal democratic states will not prove to be robust against, for example, the gender inegalitarian norms that such practices are said to demonstrate. The stronger version states that demands for accommodation travel with extremist views that threaten the stability of liberal democratic institutions; those who demand such accommodations are, therefore, a threat to a state's democratic, constitutional order. Because it is generally viewed as permissible to screen out applicants for entry (and again for naturalization) if they possess extreme views aimed at undermining liberal democratic foundations, then it remains permissible to do so at the oath-taking stage. So, the stronger worry simply extends this already accepted practice of excluding those who threaten the state, to suggest that the request for cultural or religious accommodations is a possible or indeed likely signal that a would-be citizen has these sorts of objectives.

It is vitally important to reject the premise that there exists some sort of necessary connection between the request for cultural and religious accommodations and the more general possession of extremist views. Indeed, the sheer number of citizens across democratic states who engage in the practices that are the subject of discussion here suggests that there is no such connection: citizens who request accommodations, citing the importance of religious and cultural practices, for example in schools or employment, have not proven to be dangers to the state's foundations. Similarly, despite many critics saying that, for example, a woman's choice to cover her face represents a failure to respect gender egalitarianism, that conclusion cannot be inferred from the practice. Indeed, there has been much political theory written on the choices of Muslim women with respect to face and head covering, and many women who engage in these practices believe deeply in the equality of men and women. They choose Muslim practices for themselves as a signal of their faith commitments and nothing more (Laborde 2008; Adrian 2009; Bakht 2020). Moreover, just as in the case of the practice of wearing head or face coverings, the religious refusal to touch members of the opposite sex can derive from reasons other than a belief in the inferiority (of women), and one can be committed to observing religious injunctions against touching the opposite sex while being committed to the view that their rights should be protected. That is to say, while the belief in the inferiority of others is certainly inconsistent with liberal democratic norms, the refusal to shake hands with others on the grounds of their sex is not obviously a manifestation of that belief.

What if, though, it were certain that those who request the accommodations under discussion held anti-egalitarian views? In that case, could democratic states permissibly deny the accommodations (and, perhaps even more, admission to membership)? In these circumstances, permitting the accommodations may appear to amount to an endorsement of those views, and even more to a refusal by the state to protect (mainly women) citizens from the proliferation of anti-egalitarian views. On this view, democratic states are permitted, and may even be required, to hold incoming citizens to a higher moral standard than current citizens are held. Even though such states may be home already to inegalitarian views, it remains the case that the spreading of anti-egalitarian views presents a danger to citizens in general and women in particular. However a democratic state outlines its central values, usually in a constitution, these values are recognized to be in part aspirational, in the sense that they are not always respected by all citizens, in principle or in practice. Therefore, even though there are plenty of anti-egalitarian views among citizens of democratic states, a democratic state is not required to admit anyone who refuses to acknowledge and respect these values; such individuals may, in other words, be permissibly excluded in support of the objective of moving towards better protection of the (especially equality) rights outlined in a state's constitution (or equivalent). The same can be said of would-be citizens who profess commitment to racist views, who could not thereby request accommodations to avoid their having to shake hands with individuals of a different race. In the latter racism case, the issue is clearer because there are no religions that require their adherents to avoid racial mixing.

The case is more complicated where such individuals convey a commitment to abide by the law, in spite of their anti-egalitarian views, or state that their intent is to work within the democratic system to undermine existing commitments to gender egalitarianism or racial equality. Such an individual would be able to gain citizenship in Norway, where the oath is optional and, if taken, requires only that one pledges to abide by the law. Again in this case, while a democratic state may permissibly exclude someone from naturalizing who is explicit about their anti-democratic values, even where they indicate their commitment to abide by the law, they are not *required* by justice to do so. The key message I want to make clear, however, is that while certain views may be objectionable, and therefore permissibly excludable, the religious and cultural practices for which accommodations are sought are not reliable markers of such views.

What if an incoming citizen states their fundamental objection to the oath itself on the grounds that they *do* object to certain statements in it? Consider this example. Individuals naturalizing to Canadian citizenship are asked to take a citizenship oath in which, in addition to committing to abiding by the law, they must say, "I swear (or affirm) that I will be faithful and bear true allegiance to His Majesty King Charles the Third, King of Canada, His Heirs and Successors, and that I will faithfully observe the laws of Canada and fulfil my duties as a Canadian citizen." (Note that until September 8, 2022 this oath referenced "Queen Elizabeth the Second, Queen of Canada, Her Heirs and Successors.") In 2013, three would-be Canadians challenged this requirement in court, arguing that the requirement to affirm or swear a commitment to the British monarchy amounted to a violation of their freedom of conscience. They asked that the relevant portion of the oath be made optional. They did not request accommodations for ancillary practices during the oath-ceremony; they requested that the text of the oath itself be changed so that its content reflected their true beliefs. As well, the applicants, although they asserted a willingness to abide by the Canadian constitution in general, argued that if they took the oath as it was written, they would feel "constrained from advancing their goal of abolishing Canada's constitutional monarchy in favor of a republic" (*McAteer v. Canada (Attorney General)*, 2014 ONCA 578 2013).

In two separate decisions, Canada's right to insist that would-be citizens pledge allegiance to the then Queen was upheld. The judge in the initial decision wrote, "The Applicants' problem is not so much that they take the oath seriously. Rather their problem is that they take it literally," and proposed instead that would-be Canadians treat the oath merely as "an oath to a domestic institution that represents egalitarian governance and the rule of law" (*Toronto Star* 2013, 2015). On appeal, where the decision was upheld, the judgment read: "There is no violation of the appellants' right to freedom of religion and freedom of conscience because the oath is secular and is not an oath to the Queen in her personal capacity but to our form of government of which the Queen is a symbol" (*McAteer v. Canada (Attorney General)*, 2014 ONCA 578 2013).

Of particular note is that, when defending the oath's content, the judge explained that the commitment to the British monarchy was intended to highlight Canada's particular historical connection to the United Kingdom, and moreover that "[t]he evolution of Canada from a British colony into an independent nation and democratic constitutional monarchy must inform the interpretation of the reference to the Queen in the citizenship oath. As Canada has evolved, the symbolic meaning of the Queen in the oath has evolved. The Federal Court of Appeal ... read the reference to the Queen as a reference not to the person but to the institution of state that she represents" (*McAteer v. Canada (Attorney General)*, 2014 ONCA 578 2013).

In advancing their objections to the text of the Canadian oath, the plaintiffs asserted their intention to, in fundamental ways, subvert Canada's basic constitutional structure. Following the ruling that the text of the oath will not change, several would-be Canadians responded by taking the oath and nearly immediately issuing a formal disavowal of their commitments. One of the plaintiffs, Dror Bar-Natan, after taking the citizenship oath immediately handed the officiating judge a letter indicating that he recanted the words he had just said. In his letter, he wrote: "I hereby disavow whatever I thought the first 25 words of the citizenship oath conveyed when I took the oath earlier today" (Barber 2015; Kassam 2016). Bar-Natan has since launched a website where naturalized Canadians can publicly disavow their oath, if they so choose ("Disavowal.ca: No Oath to the Monarchy!" 2021).

This example is instructive. Notice that the would-be Canadians announced *in advance* their intention to advocate for major changes to the Canadian constitutional structure. No modifications to the oath itself were made in response to their requests, but they were nevertheless permitted to naturalize and, furthermore, to pursue major constitutional reform from within the Canadian political community. Although no modifications to the oath were made as was requested, the court decisions do demonstrate a kind of accommodation in practice. By telling people that they are free to swear the oath to the monarchy without actually meaning it (in the literal sense), republican views are accommodated and given space in the naturalization process. By accepting that someone can formally disavow the oath immediately after swearing it—without forfeiting citizenship—an important accommodation has been made.

Crucial in this case is that would-be Canadians stated their intention to work towards generating radical shifts in the welcoming state's governing structure. Nevertheless they were permitted to join the state as full and equal members, presumably because it was believed that they were intending to work within democratic structures to achieve the change they sought. By contrast, those who request cultural or religious accommodations at the citizenship ceremony are accused, generally without evidence, of desiring to change the practices of the state. The Canadian example shows that a robust democratic, egalitarian state can welcome those who are committed to lobbying for significant reform within it. I do not believe that those who are requesting exemptions from certain key aspects of the citizenship ceremony—note that they are willing to *take the oath*—demonstrate a failure to integrate or an intention to undermine the liberal democratic state from within. But for those who are not persuaded by my case, it is important to note as well that liberal democratic states can support newcomers whose views do not align perfectly with the way in which the state conceives its norms and values, so long as they commit to lobbying for change from within established political rules.

Conclusion

In this final chapter, I have examined would-be citizens' requests for accommodation with respect to some of the key performative aspects of citizenship ceremonies. I have argued that, although citizenship ceremonies have important symbolic meaning, the request for accommodations is justified because they do not relate to the content of the oath itself, and the exchange that is made therein. I have characterized the oath ceremony as, in effect, an exchange between an incoming citizen and the state: the incoming citizen commits to abiding by the law and in exchange the state commits to protecting her full range of rights and privileges on an equal basis with all other citizens. I have argued that it is important to see the oath ceremony as one among many steps along the naturalization process, all of which must be assessed for their permissibility, and I have acknowledged that contextual considerations matter significantly.

That is, where the supposed toughening of naturalization processes is intended to exclude minorities, and especially where that exclusion is successful, the permissibility of these tougher processes is suspect. Changes to naturalization procedures that alter the rate of naturalization can be permissible; but, declining rates of naturalization suggest that a contextual assessment of each step along the way is needed in order to ensure the fairness of the naturalization process overall. I have suggested, as well, that there is no reason to believe that a commitment to the practices that motivate requests for accommodation is evidence of severe failure to integrate, nor is there any substantial evidence that those who carry out these practices possess a desire or intent to undermine the democratic basis of the state. Moreover, even where incoming citizens proclaim their intent to lobby for major constitutional changes, they can be admitted so long as their commitment to abide by the law, and operate within it, is made clear.

The trajectory from admission to citizenship, as outlined in the second half of this book, is a bumpy one, full of obstacles, only some of which are permissible. In general, I have tried to do two things over the last four chapters, two things which are flip sides of a coin: one is to outline and largely object to the obstacles that render full inclusion, that is, access to citizenship status, problematically difficult, and another is to argue that, in general, states should avoid the exclusion of those who can make a plausible case for inclusion. Exclusion and inclusion operate together, in other words, and diverse, immigrant-receiving democratic states should aim for more inclusion and, correspondingly, less exclusion.

Conclusion

Inclusion Remains Out of Reach

Democracies exclude both explicitly and implicitly. In *Justice and the Politics of Difference*, Iris Marion Young observed that the commitment to "universal citizenship"—characterized by abstract principles of equality, with no acknowledgment of differences between people, generated all manner of exclusions. So-called universal citizenship as an ideal offered a vision for what citizens are, and what they should do, that women, racial minorities, sexual minorities, differently abled individuals, and the elderly struggled to recognize as leaving space for them (Young 1989). In principle, universal citizenship was meant to be inclusive, committed to the view that all citizens are equal, but a refusal to pay attention to the differences, and specifically the inequalities, among differently situated citizens produced unjust exclusions of all kinds. Since the publication of Young's *Justice and the Politics of Difference*, normative and political progress has been made towards accommodating minorities across many democratic states, and minorities continue to press forward towards even greater inclusion and respect. However, even as some progress has been made towards adopting more fulsome understandings of what inclusion requires, exclusion—much of it problematic—persists.

The ideal of universal citizenship, Young detailed, assumed that democratic politics was best conducted by impartial citizens who left their differences at home to deliberate best policies in neutral ways. But, as she observed and documented, so-called impartial policies have differential effects on citizens in virtue of their multiple identities, and these differential effects were often *disadvantageous*, resulting in the oppression or exclusion of racial, ethnic, sexual, and other minorities who were unable or unwilling to "leave their differences at home" when at the negotiating table. To be treated fairly, she argued, groups often require differentiated rights, many of which should be granted to individuals in virtue of their membership in particular minority groups. She concluded her critique of the concept of universal citizenship—an ideal that she showed had not been attained for many citizens and, she thought, was ultimately unattainable without committing to a form of differentiated citizenship—by offering a vision of city life in which difference is cause for celebration and collaboration, rather than exclusion.

And yet, the inclusionary ideal at the center of democracy, towards which Young had hoped we were moving, remains out of reach. Even as the moral commitment to equality appears to have taken hold (at least among theorists of democracy!), the realization of substantive equality among citizens and residents of democratic states remains out of reach. The political commitment to what Anne Phillips has recently described as "unconditional equality"—whatever the foundation of equality to which we are committed—should be central to democratic decision-making with respect to fair and appropriate inclusion and exclusion (A. Phillips 2021). And yet, it is not.

As this book has come together, the work being done by Black Lives Matter and its many, heterogeneous allies has laid bare what continues to be at stake: the failure of democracies to protect the rights of all citizens on an equal basis. The movement has focused on the injustices to which Black American citizens are subject both on a daily basis and also systemically, but its message resonates with a much wider audience of minoritized citizens whose promised equality remains out of reach. An exhibit at the Smithsonian's National Museum of African American History and Culture, titled "Reconstructing Citizenship," asks its audience, "Who is included in 'We the People'? Whose rights does the law protect?," highlighting the gap between promise and reality for millions of African Americans in the United States (National Museum of African American History and Culture 2021). The 14th Amendment to the United States Constitution officially granted equal citizenship status to its formally enslaved population, but there are many measures along which this status is not yet fully protected for African Americans, nor for many other minority groups in the United States and across democratic states more generally. In writing of the global impact of the Black Lives Matter, E. Tendayi Achiume observed the solidarity expressed globally for working towards dismantling structures of "systemic racism, colonialism, and police brutality in their own countries" (Achiume 2020), forces that work together to deny equal rights protection to far too many. The echoes of the Black Lives Matter movement were heard loud and clear in the global outcry at reports that African-origin students studying in Ukraine were being denied entry at the Polish border as they sought to escape Russian aggression in early 2022 (Adams 2022). Even if membership rules were made fair, and even if border control policies were made fair, domestic exclusion could persist in democratic states that are otherwise in principle committed to inclusion. The longstanding failure of states to properly include their own citizens, which Black Lives Matter highlights, goes beyond the topics discussed in this book.

The purpose of centering exclusion has been to highlight that, for all their commitment to inclusion, democracies engage in extensive exclusion and offer a range of justifications for doing so. However, as I have said repeatedly over the course of this book, full inclusion into a state and society must track subjection to state power, or else that subjection is unjust. Subjection differs from coercion, which, like subjection, stands in need of justification, by extending over time; subjection thereby shapes the lives of those who are subjected across political, economic, and social spaces. Because subjection demands inclusion and precludes exclusion, the theoretical and policy analysis must then shift to determining clear standards for when someone is properly considered to be subjected. States may differ, within reason, on exactly where they draw the line.

I have centered exclusion of citizens and residents from territory and from membership, knowing that even where inclusion to membership and to territory is achieved the democratic ideal will not necessarily have been met. But it is my hope that the consideration of what constitutes wrongful exclusion can show a productive way forward for those who develop admission policies, to both territory and membership. I have adopted the lens of subjection to explain where and when exclusion is wrong; the long-time subjection to state power, without full and robust inclusion into the state, cannot be justified. This analysis moves the question of who merits inclusion to the question of who is subjected. While the lines between subjection, coercion, and merely being affected are not sharp, states can develop standards for just inclusion using these concepts.

Ultimately, my aim has not been a radical or ideal one; I am not aiming to dismantle existing structures, although many may well deserve to be dismantled. I am not offering a new political theory of migration here or a new theory of democracy. Rather, I have deployed a contextual approach to tackle key questions that democracies are facing, and I have centered the exclusion of citizens and residents from territory and membership to show that democracies should be as invested in the principles of just exclusion as they are in the principles of just inclusion. I have focused on the boundaries, that define territory and membership, and which democracies establish to exclude some and include others. These boundaries appear in many places, often far from territorial borders. Exclusion can be justified, or at least permitted, for those who are not subjected by the state and for non-citizen residents who threaten direct harm to the state. Citizens, however, cannot be excluded, although the state does not in all cases need to actively facilitate their return from abroad, and citizens who are believed to have committed crimes can be tried for those offenses.

With a focus on how to achieve fair exclusion, or even sometimes just fairer exclusion, I have highlighted how current policies fail to meet the inclusionary ideal at which democracies purport to aim. Real, existing democracies must make decisions about how best to go forward in messy circumstances. My objective has been to take seriously this messiness, to show the direction in which democracies must go if they insist on pursuing exclusion, which at the very least must be done in a fair way. Sometimes, incremental steps towards full inclusion must be accepted—simply because they bring democracies closer to fair inclusion, even if they do not go far enough, and even if they exclude some others that remain unfairly treated. We must take the victories where we can and press on, and in time we may reach the ideal of inclusion that democracy celebrates.

Notes

Introduction

1. It builds on John Rawls's account of a reflective equilibrium, a deliberative process where "we reflect on and revise our beliefs about an area of inquiry" (Daniels 2020). For Rawls's account of reflective equilibrium, see Rawls (1999, 40–44). For a discussion of the use of reflective equilibrium in contextual political theorizing, see Lægaard (2015) and Miller (2013, ch. 2).
2. Lægaard calls this way of proceeding "applicatory contextualism," which he defines as: "context co-determines the implications of general principles for particular cases since arguments for normative judgments require both normative premises in the form of general principles and empirical premises in the form of factual claims about specific cases that connect general principle to cases" (Lægaard 2019, 956).
3. I hope it is already clear that I have drawn substantial inspiration from Young (2002).
4. The question of how border control may be exerted between relatively poorer states is more complicated, however, and beyond the scope of my introductory discussion here.
5. A notable exception is that Michael Blake believes that family reunification may be a matter of "mercy" rather than justice (see Blake 2019). I will return to the importance of family reunification in Chapter 5.
6. However, note that this statistic only includes long-term non-citizen migrants. It does not include those who engage in circular migration, nor does it account for the increase in more general temporary cross-border mobility in this time period. I thank Rainer Bauböck for this point.
7. This challenge, of protecting the equal rights of minorities in democratic states, has been the focus of my earlier work, including in Balint and Lenard (2022) and Lenard (2012a).

Chapter 1

1. There are additional strategies, as well. See Whelan (1983).
2. Of course, not all laws operate in this way, at least not straightforwardly. Some laws protect entitlements and might be said to increase freedom as a result; although even here, contributions to supporting these programs are generated via taxation regimes, typically, to which all citizens and residents of a state are *subjected*.
3. I owe this way of articulating the challenge to Mollie Gerver.

4. Thank you to Valeria Ottonelli for emphasizing the normative dimension of subjection.
5. I also leave aside the question of the proper response to significant events that are not obviously caused by subjecting agents including for example climate change. I say "not obviously," because of course climate change is caused by various agents, and also multiple agents are responsible for responding to the impacts of climate change.
6. Although, as Rainer Bauböck pointed out me, this right to vote in both EU and UK elections depends on citizenship status, in the sense that it is a right that is available to some resident non-citizens on the basis of specific other citizenships that they possess.
7. For Bauböck, to be specific, local level citizenship ought to be based on residence. As a result, he explains, the granting of local voting rights to non-nationals affirms a local conception of citizenship, against the imposition of national conditions for voting rights that do not apply at local level.
8. So, fundamentally, Bauböck believes that the set of people who are entitled to protection against exclusion is far wider than the set of people who are entitled to citizenship (and correspondingly the right to vote), whereas I believe that there is no way to protect people against exclusion without granting them citizenship, and therefore that the set of people who are entitled to protection against exclusion must be the same as the set of people who are entitled to citizenship. I further elaborate the intimate connection between protection against forced exclusion and citizenship in Chapter 2.

Chapter 2

1. Buckinx and Filindra focus on long-term, mainly economic, irregular migrants, although it seems likely that a large number of failed asylum seekers would also struggle to reintegrate following unwanted deportation—especially if, in spite of their failure to gain refugee status—their lives would be at risk in their home country.
2. I too have emphasized the arbitrary aspects of deportation strategies, although I characterize them differently than does Ellerman. See Lenard (2015).
3. I do not believe, though, that Ellerman would be happy if the probability of deportation were higher! The point is only that the combination of the "blind eye" strategy and political choices to occasionally pursue aggressive deportation strategies is quite unsettling for long-term irregular migrants. If nothing were to change in US policy, then overall, it is better if the probability of deportation remains as low as possible.
4. The vast majority of immigrants to the United States, regular and irregular, are members of visible minorities. National origin is, of course, not a perfect predictor of the color of one's skin, but only thirteen percent of immigrants to the United States are from Canada and Europe (Budiman 2020). Although much commentary, including in this chapter, focuses on the fears of irregular migrants in the United States, irregular migrants globally likewise worry about the possibility of coerced deportation. For a discussion of Venezuelan irregular migrants in Colombia (which ultimately

NOTES 181

granted temporary visas to Venezuelans) and elsewhere in Latin America, who fear deportation, see Otis (2021).
5. One strong reason is that some states do not permit dual citizenship, so some migrants would be forced to give up a citizenship that they value to take on a new one. For a discussion, see Blatter (2011). I do think this worry is enough to defeat a general argument in favor of compulsory naturalization, such as the one advocated by Schutter and Ypi (2015), but not to defeat the general view that citizenship should be made available to those who desire it after a residency period is met.
6. It need not be the case that those who have committed this wrong-doing face *no* penalties for having done so; it is rather my view that if a penalty is (believed to be) warranted, it should not come in the form of deportation or permanent exclusion from citizenship, but rather in the form of fines, community service, or perhaps delayed (but not denied) access to naturalization procedures, and so on.
7. These distinctions are important in international law, but not for what I am arguing here. For more on the distinction, see Massey (2010).
8. Some states have admitted small numbers of Rohingya refugees to their states and granted them citizenship.
9. I do not wish to detract from the efforts being made by a range of international organizations on the ground; however, the lack of international support (economically, but also with respect to offering resettlement spaces) for their work is among the major challenges they face in carrying it out.
10. Because of where most stateless people are located, in the Global South, this solution would impose costs on them that ought to be fairly distributed across all states. The same challenge, of fair distribution of costs, emerges with respect to refugees because most of them seek refuge in countries near their own, and in general these states of refuge are among the less well-off globally.
11. Refugees are not necessarily, and perhaps not even mainly, stateless, however. Many refugees are merely presumed stateless because their state of citizenship is not able or willing to protect their rights, forcing them to flee.

Chapter 3

1. There may well be instances when host states believe that they can protect all those on its territory, but the home state disagrees. I leave aside the question of whether, in such cases, the home state can nevertheless enter the host state's territory to facilitate evacuation of its citizens.
2. For example, there is (or at least should be) a reluctance to remove children from families, even where families may not be able to provide for their children optimally. Support to enable parents to keep their families together ought to be prioritized, even where circumstances are challenging.
3. For example, most countries issue travel advisories when they believe citizens ought not travel to certain, dangerous locations, but will nevertheless offer them support if these citizens find themselves in difficult circumstances abroad.

4. This section is developed from research conducted by three excellent students, Charles Takvorian, Anne-Marie Chevalier and Jeanette Ghislaine Yameogo, over the course of their final project for the term, in my graduate-level course on Ethics in Public Policy in Winter 2021 at the University of Ottawa.
5. Engi Abou-El-Kheir's excellent research assistance as part of the University of Ottawa's Undergraduate Research Opportunity Program formed the basis of this analysis. See also the replies to my original article: Reed-Sandoval (2022), Blake (2022), Khadka (2022), and Bosc and Wadhawan (2022).
6. The idea of representing local jurisdictions is, of course, not as strong in states that elect representatives via party-list systems.
7. A related question is whether states that actively repatriate non-resident citizens in moments of emergency can ask, after the service is provided, for such individuals to repay the cost of providing this emergency service. I leave that aside here, although it was a key question in the Canadian debate during the 2006 Hezbollah–Israel conflict.

Chapter 4

1. For a brief account of perpetual allegiance, see Whelan (1981, 640–641).
2. There is resonance here with Seana Valentine Shiffrin's work arguing that states ought not uphold "unconscionable" contracts, that is, contracts "whose terms are seriously one-sided, overreaching, exploitative, or otherwise manifestly unfair" (see Shiffrin 2000, 205). A citizenship contract that denies the right of citizens to renounce their status (in favor of another) might be described as "unconscionable."
3. In fact, there are many reasons that individuals may desire stateless status, as Jocelyn Kane is documenting in her University of Ottawa PhD thesis examining the arguments given by those who seek stateless status. Among the most convincing claims are those made by Indigenous groups who wish to reject citizenship in colonial states.
4. My thinking on forfeiture here is heavily influenced by Moore (unpublished draft).
5. It is worth noting that deradicalization programs, which aim to re-integrate would-be or actual terrorists into everyday life, more or less operate on the idea that every person can rejoin the community. See, for example, Popp, Canna, and Day (2020).
6. In what follows, I will not consider one important argument for repatriation, namely, that each state's duty to repatriate their foreign fighters stems from their more general duty to participate in the global reduction of terror, and that by refusing repatriation, such states are showing themselves indifferent to this duty, or are exacerbating the risks of global terrorism. David Miller finds this argument to be the most persuasive one made against revocation (see Miller 2016b).
7. There is a clause that permits Norway to detain him for longer if it is believed that he persists in posing a danger to society. For a longer discussion of this case, see Lenard (2020b, ch. 2).
8. I am not qualified to make a legal statement here, beyond noting that Bangladesh denies this claim. See Sakib (2020).

9. Many believe the same is true for prisons, jails, and detention centers in North American and Europe, a claim with which I do not disagree, and so will simply say that there are reasons to believe the conditions in Iraqi jails are even worse than they are in democratic states.
10. Not all foreign fighters wish to return home and face the consequences of their actions; some may well be happy to stay away and avoid punishment.
11. One objection to this strategy that I will leave aside here is that, because the evidence of criminal activity is hard to track down when it has been committed abroad, it may be difficult to convict foreign fighters in domestic courts. This kind of challenge is in part what led the United States to open Guantanamo Bay, imprisoning wrongdoers for years, where the available evidence of their wrongdoing would not be sufficient to satisfy US civilian courts.

Chapter 5

1. For an argument defending special accommodation rights for temporary labor migrants, see Ottonelli and Torresi (forthcoming). A forthcoming symposium in *Law, Ethics and Philosophy* considers the main claims of this book in more detail.
2. For a critique of inferring the intent of temporary labor migrants from the visas they apply for and hold, see Lenard (early view).
3. Of course, one of the main purposes of no-fly lists is to keep potential terrorists out of airplanes rather than to keep them out of the destination countries per se. That is why the no-fly lists affect domestic flights as well as international ones. For more discussion, see Lenard (2020b).
4. There is more disagreement among scholars on the justice of policies that preferentially include migrants on the basis of religious, racial and ethnic characteristics, but I will not consider that debate here.
5. For more, see Dyzenhaus and Moran (2005) and Lee (2003).
6. The justification for such an omission is, presumably, that screening authorities believe that national security would be threatened by revealing these details. Appeal mechanisms can be made available to those who are denied entry without undermining national security, however.
7. For example, see Immigration, Refugees and Citizenship Canada (2004), Kamishi (2021), and Shengen Visa Info (2022).
8. I believe this remains true, presently. See Government of Norway (n.d.).
9. This statement is a bit of a generalization, though, and of course European and North American states that are largely white are increasingly less so, and their citizens (regardless of racial or ethnic origin) benefit from visa-free travel. As well, little evidence suggests that overt Islamophobia plays a role in choices about whether to require visas; according to at least some scholarship, Muslim-majority countries are not (additionally) disadvantaged, although countries that have experienced recent terrorist incidents are. See Luedtke, Byrd, and Alexander (2010, 155).
10. I will not consider the distinction between single entry and multiple entry visas.

11. Elsewhere I have criticized current understandings of family in international law, and have proposed a more flexible procedure for determining who ought to be admitted as "family" (see Morris, Lenard, and Haugen 2021).
12. Michael Blake made this point in a discussion about the importance of prioritizing family reunification at an "author-meets-critics" session on his important book (Blake 2019), at the APA conference in January 2021. There, he pointed out, many specifically LGBTQ+ persons may desire to be separated from their families. I do not disagree with him, and family reunification policies can certainly facilitation oppression in some instances. For example, I worked with a refugee whose abusive husband had secured visas for her and her children to Germany (from their country of refuge) on the basis of family reunification, which she desperately did not want to take up. She was nearly denied safe passage to Canada on the grounds that she had already been offered safety elsewhere. But, as I elaborated in our discussions at APA, family is deeply important to most people (and sometimes this family is the one we are born into and sometimes it is chosen), and so treating reunification in general as a matter of justice (rather than mercy, as Blake proposes) is appropriate.
13. I have now made this point several times. There is inevitable vagueness around the length of time that can permissibly pass before migrants must be able to access various rights and privileges across immigration spaces, but nevertheless a decision must be made. So, the objective is mainly about ensuring that whatever length of time is selected (for migrants to receive any particular good) is within reasonable boundaries. For more on the political relevance of time, see E. F. Cohen (2018).
14. For a discussion of the challenges of the J-1 visa, and how migrants respond to its requirements (including with respect to waiving the mandatory repatriation requirement), see Bartlett (2014).
15. The brain drain literature is rich and varied, and scholars are not agreed with respect to whether sending states can—on a temporary basis—refuse to permit the exit of their skilled professionals (educated at state expense). For a discussion of these questions, see Brock and Blake (2014), Sager (2014) and Oberman (2013).

Chapter 6

1. I would like here to register some discomfort with the use of the term "low-skilled" to describe the employment opportunities that are made available on a temporary basis to migrants. In fact, some of this work is skilled labor (caregiving is skilled work, for example), even if it not well-remunerated in host states. So, here, I use the terms high- and low-skilled because that is standard in the literature; however, it is not always the case that such terms track whether the jobs carried out by migrants require substantial skills.
2. It has been replaced with the similarly named Caregiver Program, now formally a distinct stream of Canada's Temporary Foreign Worker Program (see Drolet 2016).

3. These programs are quite explicit that they are trading access to expedited citizenship for military labor. But, as Alex Sager suggested to me, an underlying logic might also be in operation, that those who participate in the military are, in virtue of their actions, full members of society, and thus denying them citizenship amounts to a kind of incoherence. I do not disagree with the potential for this logic to be in operation, but it is at least not explicitly the motivation or logic for the programs.
4. One might object that the military is, effectively, the state, so the distinction I am drawing does not apply in this case. But because the military issues the contract, and the state separately operates as a kind of overseer, this characterization remains fair.
5. One response might be that temporary labor migrants who transition to permanent status, over time, send less money "home" to developing states, therefore undermining the alleged redistributive benefits of temporary labor migration. But I do not believe that these writers aim to rest their arguments on treating migrants as mere means to reduce wealth inequalities.
6. For a history of immigrants in the US military, see in general Sullivan (2019, chs. 2 and 3).
7. DACA has permitted migrants who arrived as children to remain in the United States on renewable visas, a condition which, among other things, has permitted their holders to work legally.
8. Others moved only to extend visas beyond their expiration date, including in South Africa (Le Roux 2021) and in the UK (Waldron 2020), although at the time of writing a UK Bill to offer such workers "indefinite leave to remain" has been tabled, but not brought forward for discussion (Noland 2021).
9. At least in public discourse, it is frequently claimed that some or even many asylum seekers are not, in fact, in danger but are "mere" economic migrants who are taking advantage of an asylum system to gain access to a healthy labor market. There are ongoing questions among political theorists of migration on whether those escaping severe poverty rather than political persecution ought to be entitled to asylum. With Sarah Song, I prefer to use the language of "necessitous" migrants rather than wade into this dispute more fully; the term includes those who are escaping persecution, violence, and crushing poverty (see Song 2018). See, more generally, Shacknove (1985).
10. For an argument defending the claim that all workers who performed essential duties during the COVID-19 pandemic are entitled to permanent residence (not citizenship, necessarily) because of the gratitude that is owed to them for the work they have done, that is, for the exceptional contributions they have made, see Gerver (2021).
11. I thank Alex Sager for this observation.
12. In general, it is hard to determine what counts as a contribution to the well-being of a particular state, including whether non-residents might be said to contribute sufficiently to a state's well-being to warrant citizenship. But, it seems possible to establish criteria by which to assess contributions and then apply them fairly, even if there remain cases at the boundaries that require further conversation.

Chapter 7

1. This statement is deliberately invoking Michael Walzer's arguments for naturalizing guest workers to avoid two classes of people in a democratic state, those with citizenship and those without, which I considered in Chapter 6. In this case, effective and efficient integration ensures that all citizens are able to access the goods of economic, political, and social society, rather than leaving some of those with citizenship at the margins because they are insufficiently integrated.
2. My way of framing the objective here is inspired by Brownlee (2013), who focused on social deprivation.
3. For an account of the reality that most refugees find themselves in effectively "permanent" temporary situations (i.e., situations that are said to be temporary, but for which no alternative is offered), having escaped their home country, see (Parekh 2016).
4. The question of who is a voluntary migrant is by no means clear and is the subject of considerable ongoing discussion among political theorists. For an example, see Ottonelli and Torresi (2013). An additional complication is that many migrants are voluntary, in the sense that they have chosen to move, but they have not been invited in by the host state, and rather gain entry by irregular means.
5. For example, the United States has offered "Temporary Protected Status" (TPS) to many migrants fleeing natural disasters in Central America, which are renewed repeatedly, but generally does not permit TPS holders to transition to citizenship (see Frelick 2020).
6. It is worth noting that some resettlement states require refugees to pay the cost of their flights. In most cases, refugees are not able to do this immediately, and so are offered low-cost travel loans, which they are asked to repay when they are gainfully employed.
7. A danger is that host states treat refugee arrivals, who sometimes come from vastly different social, cultural, and economic environments, as though their past experience is irrelevant or unimportant in a whole range of ways. For an account of this danger and how best to avoid it, see Haugen, Regan Wills, and Lenard (2020) and Lenard (2016b).
8. The argument I am making over the course of this book is that residents who are subjected to a state's power for more than six months ought to be permitted to begin the process of naturalization to citizenship. However, in the case of refugees, the issue is complicated by the likely result of enforcing such a policy: states neighboring refugee-producing states would be required to naturalize refugees even though they do not possess the resources needed to do so well, and this requirement would in part be caused by the unwillingness of farther-away states to admit and naturalize refugees. In this case, then, the failure to find a permanent home for refugees who are in protracted refugee situations is a global failure, rather than a failure of the state of temporary refuge.
9. There is a separate issue, which is that migrants who are admitted on a temporary basis, but who are eventually permitted to stay permanently, may have "missed" some of the basic orientation and settlement services that are typically available on arrival

NOTES 187

to newcomers who are admitted for permanent residence. Having been denied access to these services initially may have set back their overall integration, even as their integration into the labor market appears assured.

10. On the more general political theory question of how to distribute the responsibilities of refugee support, the possibility that refugees will be of net benefit to a resettling state may seem to shift how refugee admission for resettlement is costed in a responsibility-sharing regime. Whether refugees provide a net benefit ought not to be counted as a relevant factor when determining a just distribution of duties, however. On the one hand, if states see that refugees are a net benefit, they may well want to settle more refugees and feel incentivized to support their resettlement as effectively as possible. But, on the other hand, it may lead to ire directed against refugees who arrive but who are not able to offer economic contributions to the state that has granted them protection. While, on average, refugees may be of economic benefit to resettling states, there will also always be refugees for whom past trauma translates into an inability to work, and they too are entitled to safety. Ultimately, even if a refugee contributes to the economy of a resettling state, the act of resettling reduces the load on other states. This benefit is strongest in a global environment where there are not enough resettlement spots to meet the demand, as is currently the case. See Lenard (2021a).

11. I thank Annamari Vitikainen for this way of articulating the special duty that is owed to persecuted, resettled refugees.

12. The UNHCR has a specific strategy for assessing the vulnerability of refugees in countries of refuge in particular (UNHCR 2015). I assess its prioritization strategy (Lenard 2020c).

13. The result is that it may be justified to resettle LGBTQ+ refugees to cities or countries that are generally tolerant of sexual differences/diversity.

Conclusion

1. However, the global pandemic border closures have been devastating, and I have argued (with Alex Neve) that political theorists must add more nuance to the generally accepted claim that health risks justify border closures (Lenard and Neve 2021).
2. That said, even in these countries, the call to toughen up the tests has been made (and indeed, the tests have been toughened) with the goal of naturalizing only those individuals who prove willing and able to integrate successfully (Cargill 2020; Lenard 2018b).
3. The best case may well be that no tests are required at all, as ultimately even the best tests operate as an obstacle to gaining citizenship. For this argument, see Carens (2010b).
4. This focus is because where oaths are mandatory, an unwillingness to accommodate cultural and religious practices means that some people cannot gain citizenship status at all. But an unwillingness to accommodate cultural and religious practices at voluntary ceremonies is still exclusionary in harmful ways.

5. That Minister, Inger Stojberg, has since been convicted of illegally separating refugee couples in Danish asylum centers (see Erdbrink and Nielsen 2021).
6. There are many reasons to think, on the contrary, that the accommodation of cultural and religious practices across a range of political, social, and economic spaces facilitates integration. For an argument defending this claim, see my contribution to Balint and Lenard (2022).

Bibliography

Abizadeh, Arash. 2008. "Democratic Theory and Border Coercion: No Right to Unilaterally Control Your Own Borders." *Political Theory* 36, no. 1: 37–65.

Abizadeh, Arash. 2010. "Democratic Legitimacy and State Coercion: A Reply to David Miller." *Political Theory* 38, no. 1: 121–130. https://doi.org/10.1177/0090591709348192.

Abizadeh, Arash. 2012. "On the Demos and Its Kin: Nationalism, Democracy, and the Boundary Problem." *American Political Science Review* 106, no. 4: 867–882.

Achiume, E. Tendayi. 2020. "Black Lives Matter and the UN Human Rights System: Reflections on the Human Rights Council Urgent Debate." *EJIL: Talk!* (blog). December 15. https://www.ejiltalk.org/black-lives-matter-and-the-un-human-rights-system-reflections-on-the-human-rights-council-urgent-debate/.

Ackerly, Brooke A. 2018. *Just Responsibility: A Human Rights Theory of Global Justice*. Oxford: Oxford University Press.

Adams, Char. 2022. "'Life Is More Important': Africans in Ukraine Lead Their Own Rescue Efforts." *NBC News*. March 7. https://www.nbcnews.com/news/nbcblk/black-african-students-ukraine-are-leading-rescue-efforts-rcna18531.

Adrian, Melanie. 2009. "France, the Veil and Religious Freedom." *Religion, State and Society* 4 (December).

Anderson, Scott. 2021. "Coercion." In *The Stanford Encyclopedia of Philosophy*, edited by Edward N. Zalta, Summer 2021. Metaphysics Research Lab, Stanford University. https://plato.stanford.edu/archives/sum2021/entries/coercion/.

Anglican Diocese of Canada. 2015. *A Guide to Refugee Sponsorship for Vancouver Island*. https://dq5pwpg1q8ru0.cloudfront.net/2020/10/29/17/34/14/139eb7fd-59f3-4cae-b37e-6f108a82ec41/refugee_sponsorship_manual.pdf.

Arendt, Hannah. 1963. *Eichmann in Jerusalem*. London: Penguin.

Attas, Daniel. 2000. "The Case of Guest-Workers: Exploitation, Citizenship and Economic Rights." *Res Publica* 6: 73–92.

Australian Government. 2021. "Health." https://immi.homeaffairs.gov.au/help-support/meeting-our-requirements/health.

Bakan, Abigail, and Daiva Stasiulis. 1994. "Foreign Domestic Worker Policy in Canada and the Social Boundaries of Modern Citizenship." *Science and Society* 58, no. 1: 7–33.

Bakht, Natasha. 2020. *In Your Face: Law, Justice, and Niqab-Wearing Women in Canada*. Toronto: Delve Books.

Balint, Peter, and Patti Tamara Lenard. 2022. *Debating Multiculturalism: Should There Be Minority Rights?* Oxford, New York: Oxford University Press.

Banerjee, Rupa, Philip Kelly, and Ethel Tungohan. 2017. "Accessing the Changes to Canada's Live-in Caregiver Program: Improving Security or Deepening Precariousness?" *Pathways to Prosperity*. http://p2pcanada.ca/files/2017/12/Assessing-the-Changes-to-Canadas-Live-In-Caregiver-Program.pdf.

Banting, Keith, Thomas J. Courchene, and F. Leslie Seidle, eds. 2007. *Belonging?* Montreal, Kingston: McGill-Queen's University Press. https://www.mqup.ca/belonging--products-9780886452018.php.

Barber, John. 2015. "Canadian Republic Advocates Hope New Government Has Less 'Loyalty to Royalty.'" *The Guardian*. December 3. http://www.theguardian.com/world/2015/dec/03/canada-republicans-trudeau-queen-elizabeth.

Barbieri, William A. 1998. *Ethics of Citizenship: Immigration and Group Rights in Germany*. North Carolina: Duke University Press.

Barder, Owen, and Euan Ritchie. 2018. "Spending Money on Refugees Is an Investment, Not a Cost." *Refugees Deeply*. January 15. https://www.newsdeeply.com/refugees/community/2018/01/15/spending-money-on-refugees-is-an-investment-not-a-cost.

Barry, Christian, and Luara Ferracioli. 2015. "Can Withdrawing Citizenship Be Justified?" *Political Studies* 64, no. 4: 1055–1070.

Bartlett, Lora. 2014. *Migrant Teachers: How American Schools Import Labor*. Cambridge, MA: Harvard University Press.

Bauböck, Rainer. 2009. "The Rights and Duties of External Citizenship." *Citizenship Studies* 13, no. 5: 475–499. https://doi.org/10.1080/13621020903174647.

Bauböck, Rainer. 2015. "Morphing the Demos into the Right Shape. Normative Principles for Enfranchising Resident Aliens and Expatriate Citizens." *Democratization* 22, no. 5: 820–839. https://doi.org/10.1080/13510347.2014.988146.

Bauböck, Rainer. 2018a. "Refugee Protection and Burden-Sharing in the European Union." *Journal of Common Market Studies* 56, no. 1: 141–156.

Bauböck, Rainer. 2018b. "Democratic Inclusion: A Pluralist Theory of Citizenship." In *Democratic Inclusion: Rainer Bauböck in Dialogue*, edited by Rainer Bauböck, 3–102. Manchester: Manchester University Press. https://www.manchesteropenhive.com/view/9781526105257/9781526105257.00007.xml.

Bauböck, Rainer, and Liav Orgad. 2019. *Cities vs States: Should Urban Citizenship Be Emancipated from Nationality?* EUI: Global Citizenship Observatory. https://globalcit.eu/cities-vs-states-should-urban-citizenship-be-emancipated-from-nationality/.

Bauböck, Rainer, and Vesco Paskalev. 2015. "Cutting Genuine Links: A Normative Analysis of Citizenship Deprivation." *Georgetown Immigration Law Journal* 30, no. 1: 47–104.

Bauböck, Rainer, Mourao Permoser, Julia, and Ruhs, Martin. 2022. "The Ethics of Migration Policy Dilemmas." *Migration Studies* 10, no. 3: 427–441.

Baynes, Chris. 2018. "US Army Quietly Discharging Immigrant Recruits That Were Promised Citizenship." *The Independent*. July 6. https://www.independent.co.uk/news/world/americas/us-army-discharge-immigrant-recruits-citizenship-trump-administration-a8434166.html.

BBC News. 2018. "Muslim Couple Denied Swiss Citizenship over No Handshake." *BBC News*. August 18. https://www.bbc.com/news/world-europe-45232147.

Beckman, Ludvig. 2014. "The Subjects of Collectively Binding Decisions: Democratic Inclusion and Extraterritorial Law." *Ratio Juris* 27, no. 2: 252–270. https://doi.org/10.1111/raju.12038.

Bender, Felix. 2021. "Enfranchising the Disenfranchised: Should Refugees Receive Political Rights in Liberal Democracies?" *Citizenship Studies* 25, no. 1: 56–71.

Bennhold, Katrin. 2008. "A Veil Closes France's Door to Citizenship." *New York Times*. July 19.

Bevelander, Pieter, and Ravi Pendakur. 2014. "The Labour Market Integration of Refugee and Family Reunion Immigrants: A Comparison of Outcomes in Canada and Sweden." *Journal of Ethnic and Migration Studies* 40, no. 5: 689–709.

Birnie, Rutger. 2020. "Citizenship, Domicile and Deportability: Who Should Be Exempt from the State's Power to Expel?" *Citizenship Studies* 24, no. 3: 371–388. https://doi.org/10.1080/13621025.2020.1722412.

Blake, Michael. 2001. "Distributive Justice, State Coercion, and Autonomy." *Philosophy & Public Affairs* 30, no. 3: 257–296.

Blake, Michael. 2002. "Discretionary Immigration." *Philosophical Topics* 30, no. 2: 273–289.

Blake, Michael. 2010. "Equality without Documents: Political Justice and the Right to Amnesty." *Canadian Journal of Philosophy* 40 (January): 99–122. https://doi.org/10.1080/00455091.2010.10717656.

Blake, Michael. 2014. "The Right to Exclude." *Critical Review of International Social and Political Philosophy* 17, no. 5: 521–537. https://doi.org/10.1080/13698230.2014.919056.

Blake, Michael. 2019. *Justice, Migration, and Mercy*. Oxford: Oxford University Press.

Blake, Michael. 2022. "Temporary Migration Bans, Gender, and Exploitation: A Response for Patti Lenard (2021), Commentary for 'The Ethics of Migration Policy Dilemmas' Project." *Migration Policy Centre (MPC)*. https://migrationpolicycentre.eu/docs/dilemmas/dilemmas_project_3rd_response_blake.pdf.

Blatter, Joachim. 2011. "Dual Citizenship and Theories of Democracy." *Citizenship Studies* 15, no. 6–7: 769–798.

Bloemraad, Irene. 2006. *Becoming a Citizen: Incorporating Immigrants and Refugees in the United States and Canada*. Los Angeles: University of California Press.

Blouin, Louis. 2022. "Ottawa Preparing to Charter 3 Flights for Ukrainian Refugees." *CBC*. May 11. https://www.cbc.ca/news/politics/charter-ukranian-refugees-1.6448984.

Bo, Bente Puntervold. 1998. "The Use of Visa Requirements as a Regulatory Instrument for the Restriction of Migration." In *Regulation of Migration: International Experiences*, edited by Anita Böcker, Kees Groenendijk, Tetty Havinga, and Paul Minderhoud, 191–204. Amsterdam: Het Spinhuis Publishers.

Borger, Julian. 2021. "New Claims of Migrant Abuse as Ice Defies Biden to Continue Deportations." *The Guardian*. February 2. https://www.theguardian.com/us-news/2021/feb/02/ice-immigration-migrants-asylum-seekers-abuse-allegations.

Bosc, Igor, and Neha Wadhawan. 2022. "The Moral Exigency of Free Mobility. A Response for Patti Lenard (2021), Commentary for 'The Ethics of Migration Policy Dilemmas' Project." *Migration Policy Centre (MPC)*. https://migrationpolicycentre.eu/docs/dilemmas/dilemmas_project_2nd_response_bosc_wadhawan.pdf.

Bosniak, Linda. 2013. "Amnesty in Immigration: Forgetting, Forgiving, Freedom." *Critical Review of International Social and Political Philosophy* 16, no. 3: 344–365.

Bosniak, Linda. 2020. "Territorial Presence as a Ground for Claims: Some Reflections." *Etikk i Praksis—Nordic Journal of Applied Ethics* 2 (December): 53–70. https://doi.org/10.5324/eip.v14i2.3490.

Bouie, Jamelle. 2018. "ICE Unbound." *Slate*. January 30. https://slate.com/news-and-politics/2018/01/ice-is-out-of-control.html.

Bowcott, Owen. 2010. "Asylum Deportation Flights Need Rights Monitors, EU Says." *The Guardian*. March 14. http://www.theguardian.com/world/2010/mar/14/european-union-border-frontex-deportation.

Bradley, Megan. 2008. "Back to Basics: The Conditions of Just Refugee Returns." *Journal of Refugee Studies* 21, no. 3: 285–304. https://doi.org/10.1093/jrs/fen023.

Bradley, Megan. 2013. *Refugee Repatriation*. Cambridge, UK: Cambridge University Press. https://www-cambridge-org.proxy.bib.uottawa.ca/core/books/refugee-repatriation/785779965E047A947FE69B8EF6E1E10C.

Breeden, Aurelien. 2018. "No Handshake, No Citizenship, French Court Tells Algerian Woman." *New York Times*. April 21. https://www.nytimes.com/2018/04/21/world/europe/handshake-citizenship-france.html.

Brickner, Rachel K., and Christine Straehle. 2010. "The Missing Link: Gender, Immigration Policy and the Live-in Caregiver Program in Canada." *Policy and Society* 29, no. 4: 309–320. https://doi.org/10.1016/j.polsoc.2010.09.004.

Brock, Gillian. 2009. *Global Justice: A Cosmopolitan Account*. Oxford: Oxford University Press.

Brock, Gillian. 2020. *Justice for People on the Move: Migration in Challenging Times*. Cambridge, UK: Cambridge University Press.

Brock, Gillian, and Michael Blake. 2014. *Debating Brain Drain: May Governments Restrict Emigration?* Oxford: Oxford University Press.

Brownlee, Kimberley. 2013. "A Human Right Against Social Deprivation." *The Philosophical Quarterly* 63, no. 251: 199–222.

Brubaker, Rogers. 1992. *Citizenship and Nationhood in France and Germany*. Cambridge, MA: Harvard University Press.

Brunnersum, Sou-Jie. 2020. "COVID: France Fast-Tracks Citizenship for Frontline Workers." *DW.com*. December 23. https://www.dw.com/en/covid-france-fast-tracks-citizenship-for-frontline-workers/a-56042284.

Buckinx, Barbara, and Alexandra Filindra. 2015. "The Case against Removal: Jus Noci and Harm in Deportation Practice." *Migration Studies* 3, no. 3: 393–416. https://doi.org/10.1093/migration/mnu072.

Budiman, Abby. 2020. "Key Findings about U.S. Immigrants." *Pew Research Center* (blog). https://www.pewresearch.org/fact-tank/2020/08/20/key-findings-about-u-s-immigrants/.

Cabrera, Luis. 2010. *The Practice of Global Citizenship*. Cambridge: Cambridge University Press.

Calder, Gideon, Phillip Cole, and Jonathan Seglow, eds. 2009. *Citizenship Acquisition and National Belonging: Migration, Membership and the Liberal Democratic State*. Basingstoke: Palgrave Macmillan.

Canadian Orientation Abroad. 2020. *Canadian Orientation Abroad Participant Workbook*. Ottawa: International Organization for Migration. https://publications.iom.int/books/canadian-orientation-abroad-participant-workbook.

Carens, Joseph H. 1987. "Aliens and Citizens: The Case for Open Borders." *Review of Politics* 49, no. 2: 251–273.

Carens, Joseph H. 1992. "Refugees and the Limits of Obligation." *Public Affairs Quarterly* 6: 31–44.

Carens, Joseph H. 2000. *Culture, Community and Citizenship: A Contextual Exploration of Justice as Evenhandedness*. Oxford: Oxford University Press.

Carens, Joseph H. 2004. "A Contextual Approach to Political Theory." *Ethical Theory and Moral Practice* 7, no. 2: 117–132.

Carens, Joseph H. 2005. "The Integration of Immigrants." *Journal of Moral Philosophy* 2, no. 1: 29–46.

Carens, Joseph H. 2008. "Live-in Domestics, Seasonal Workers, and Others Hard to Locate on the Map of Democracy." *Journal of Political Philosophy* 16, no. 4: 419–445.
Carens, Joseph H. 2009. "The Case for Amnesty." *Boston Review* 34, no. 3: 7–10.
Carens, Joseph H. 2010a. *Immigrants and the Right to Stay*. Cambridge: MIT Press.
Carens, Joseph H. 2010b. "The Most Liberal Citizenship Test Is None at All." In *How Liberal Are Citizenship Tests?*, edited by Rainer Bauböck and Christian Joppke, 19–20. EUI: European Union Democracy Observatory on Citizenship.
Carens, Joseph H. 2013. *The Ethics of Immigration*. Oxford: Oxford University Press.
Cargill, Clinton. 2020. "The Trump Administration Just Made the Citizenship Test Harder. How Would You Do?" *The New York Times*. December 3. https://www.nytimes.com/interactive/2020/12/03/us/citizenship-quiz.html.
Carlson, Kerstin Bree. 2021. "What to Do about Islamic State Supporters Still in Syria? Denmark's Decision Sets a Worrying Trend." *The Conversation*. June 2. http://theconversation.com/what-to-do-about-islamic-state-supporters-still-in-syria-denmarks-decision-sets-a-worrying-trend-161971.
Castles, Stephen. 1985. "The Guests Who Stayed—The Debate on 'Foreigners Policy' in the German Federal Republic." *International Migration Review* 19, no. 3: 517–534.
Celikates, Robin. 2013. "Democratic Inclusion: Citizenship or Voting Rights?" *Krisis* 1: 30–34.
Chávez, Karma R. 2011. "Identifying the Needs of LGBTQ Immigrants and Refugees in Southern Arizona." *Journal of Homosexuality* 58, no. 2: 189–218. https://doi.org/10.1080/00918369.2011.540175.
Chin, Rita. 2007. *The Guest Worker Question in Postwar Germany*. Cambridge: Cambridge University Press.
Christiano, Thomas. 2004. "The Authority of Democracy." *Journal of Political Philosophy* 12, no. 3: 266–290.
Cohen, Elizabeth F. 2018. *The Political Value of Time: Citizenship, Duration, and Democratic Justice*. Cambridge, UK: Cambridge University Press.
Cohen, Elizabeth F. 2020. *Illegal: How America's Lawless Immigration Regime Threatens Us All*. New York: Basic Books.
Cole, Phillip. 2000. *Philosophies of Exclusion: Liberal Political Theory and Immigration*. Edinburgh: Edinburgh University Press.
Cole, Phillip, Tendayi Bloom, and Katherine Tonkiss, eds. 2017. *Understanding Statelessness*. London: Routledge.
Coolsaet, Rik, and Thomas Renard. 2020. "Foreign Fighters and the Terrorist Threat in Belgium." *Egmont Institute*. January 10. https://www.egmontinstitute.be/foreign-fighters-and-the-terrorist-threat-in-belgium/.
Corntassel, Jeff. 2012. "Re-Envisioning Resurgence: Indigenous Pathways to Decolonization and Sustainable Self-Determination." *Decolonization: Indigeneity, Education & Society* 1, no. 1: 86–101.
Czaika, Mathias, and Eric Neumayer. 2017. "Visa Restrictions and Economic Globalisation." *Applied Geography* 84: 75–82. https://doi.org/10.1016/j.apgeog.2017.04.011.
Damsholt, Tine. 2018. "'I Didn't Think I Would Be Emotional until I Started Saying the Oath'—Emotionalising and Ritualising Citizenship." *Journal of Ethnic and Migration Studies* 44, no. 16: 2701–2716. https://doi.org/10.1080/1369183X.2017.1389038.
Daniels, Norman. 2020. "Reflective Equilibrium." In *The Stanford Encyclopedia of Philosophy*, edited by Edward N. Zalta, Summer 2020. Metaphysics Research Lab,

Stanford University. https://plato.stanford.edu/archives/sum2020/entries/reflective-equilibrium/.

Deonanan, Regan, and Benjamin Ramkissoon. 2018. "Remittances and Economic Development: Evidence from the Caribbean." *Social and Economic Studies* 67 (September): 95–132.

Department of Homeland Security. 2017. "ICE ERO Immigration Arrests Climb Nearly 40%." https://www.ice.gov/features/100-days.

Dhaliwal, Sukhwant, and Kirsten Forkert. 2015. "Deserving and Undeserving Migrants." *Soundings* 61, no. 61: 49–61. https://doi.org/10.3898/136266215816772205.

"Disavowal.ca: No Oath to the Monarchy!" 2021. http://disavowal.ca/.

Drolet, Natalie. 2016. "An Overview of Canada's New Caregiver Program: A Shift From Permanence to Precariousness." *Canada's Immigration and Citizenship Bulletin* 27, no. 6: 104.

Dyzenhaus, David, and Mayo Moran, eds. 2005. *Calling Power to Account: Law, Reparations, and the Chinese Canadian Head Tax*. Toronto: University of Toronto Press. https://doi.org/10.3138/9781442671669.

Edmond, Charlotte. 2020. "Global Migration, by the Numbers." *World Economic Forum*. January 10. https://www.weforum.org/agenda/2020/01/iom-global-migration-report-international-migrants-2020/.

Efthymiou, Dimitrios E. 2020. "EU Immigration, Welfare Rights and Populism: A Normative Appraisal of Welfare Populism." *Global Justice: Theory Practice Rhetoric* 12, no. 2: 161–188. https://doi.org/10.21248/gjn.12.02.202.

El-Assal, Kareem, and Alexandra Miekus. 2020. "Quebec Offers Immigration Pathway to 'Guardian Angels.'" *CIC News*. August 14. https://www.cicnews.com/2020/08/quebec-offers-immigration-pathway-to-guardian-angels-0815463.html.

Ellerman, Antje. 2014. "The Rule of Law and the Right to Stay: The Moral Claims of Undocumented Migrants." *Politics and Society* 42, no. 3: 293–308.

Embury-Dennis, Tom. 2020. "Man Denied German Citizenship for Refusing to Shake Woman's Hand at Naturalisation Ceremony." *The Independent*. October 19. https://www.independent.co.uk/news/world/europe/handshake-german-citizenship-doctor-court-baden-wurttemberg-b1152776.html.

Erdbrink, Thomas, and Jasmina Nielsen. 2021. "Former Immigration Minister in Denmark Sentenced to Prison for Separating Couples." *The New York Times*. December 13. https://www.nytimes.com/2021/12/13/world/europe/denmark-immigration-minister-migrants-prison.html.

Erman, Eva. 2014. "The Boundary Problem and the Ideal of Democracy." *Constellations* 21, no. 4: 535–546. https://doi.org/10.1111/1467-8675.12116.

Espejo, Paulina Ochoa. 2016. "Taking Place Seriously: Territorial Presence and the Rights of Immigrants." *Journal of Political Philosophy* 24, no. 1: 67–87. https://doi.org/10.1111/jopp.12061.

Espejo, Paulina Ochoa. 2020. *On Borders: Territories, Legitimacy, and the Rights of Place*. Oxford, UK: Oxford University Press.

European Network on Statelessness. 2019. "Getting to 100%: New Video on the Importance of Ending Gender Discrimination in Nationality Laws." *European Network on Statelessness*. March 28. https://www.statelessness.eu/updates/blog/getting-100-new-video-importance-ending-gender-discrimination-nationality-laws.

European Network on Statelessness. 2021. "Statelessness Index." https://index.statelessness.eu/countries.

Evans, Margaret. 2021. "Mother of Canadian Girl Freed from ISIS Detention Camp in Syria Earlier This Year Released." *CBC*. June 28. https://www.cbc.ca/news/world/mother-isis-camp-irbil-1.6082900.

Favell, Adrian. 1998. *Philosophies of Integration: Immigration and the Idea of Citizenship in France and Britain*. Basingstoke: Palgrave.

Ferracioli, Luara. 2017. "Citizenship Allocation and Withdrawal: Some Normative Issues." *Philosophy Compass* 12, no. 12: 1–9.

Festenstein, Matthew. 2005. *Negotiating Diversity: Culture, Deliberation, Trust*. Cambridge: Polity Press.

Fine, Sarah. 2010. "Freedom of Association Is Not the Answer." *Ethics* 120, no. 2: 338–356. https://doi.org/10.1086/649626.

Foreign Affairs Manual. 2018. "Loss and Restoration of US Citizenship." https://fam.state.gov/FAM/07FAM/07FAM1210.html#M1215.

Forsdyke, Sara. 2009. *Exile, Ostracism, and Democracy: The Politics of Expulsion in Ancient Greece*. Princeton, NJ: Princeton University Press.

France 24. 2019a. "Repatriate or Reject: What Countries Are Doing with IS Group Families." *France 24*. June 11. https://www.france24.com/en/20190611-repatriation-families-islamic-state-group-jihadists-children.

France 24. 2019b. "Paris Attacks Suspect Charged over Brussels Suicide Bombings." *France 24*. August 12. https://www.france24.com/en/20190812-paris-attacks-charged-brussels-suicide-bombings-terrorism-islamic-state-group-abdeslam.

Fratzke, Susan, and Lena Kainz. 2019. "Preparing for the Unknown: Designing Effective Predeparture Orientation for Resettling Refugees." Migration Policy Institute. https://www.migrationpolicy.org/sites/default/files/publications/MPIE_PredepartureOrientation-FINAL.pdf.

Frelick, Bill. 2020. "What's Wrong with Temporary Protected Status and How to Fix It: Exploring a Complementary Protection Regime." *Journal on Migration and Human Security* 8, no. 1: 42–53. https://doi.org/10.1177/2331502419901266.

Gerver, Mollie. 2018. *The Ethics and Practice of Refugee Repatriation*. Edinburgh: Edinburgh University Press.

Gerver, Mollie. 2021. "The Case for Permanent Residency for Frontline Workers." *American Political Science Review* 16, no. 1: 87–110. https://doi.org/10.1017/S0003055421000708.

Gibney, Matthew J. 2004. *The Ethics and Politics of Asylum: Liberal Democracy and the Response to Refugees*. Cambridge: Cambridge University Press.

Gibney, Matthew J. 2006. "A Thousand Little Guantanamos: Western States and Measures to Prevent the Arrival of Refugees." In *Migration, Displacement, Asylum: The Oxford Amnesty Lectures 2004*, edited by K. Tunstall, 139–169. Oxford: Oxford University Press.

Gibney, Matthew J. 2013. "Should Citizenship Be Conditional? The Ethics of Denationalization." *The Journal of Politics* 75, no. 3: 646–658.

Gibney, Matthew J. 2017. "Denationalization." In *The Oxford Handbook of Citizenship*, edited by Ayelet Shachar, Rainer Bauböck, Irene Bloemraad, and Maarten Peter Vink, 358–379. Oxford, UK: Oxford University Press. https://doi.org/10.1093/oxfordhb/9780198805854.013.16.

Gilabert, Pablo. 2012. *From Global Poverty to Global Equality*. Oxford: Oxford University Press.

Goldberg, Andreas C., and Simon Lanz. 2019. "Living Abroad, Voting as If at Home? Electoral Motivations of Expatriates1." *Migration Studies*, no. mnz018 (May). https://doi.org/10.1093/migration/mnz018.

Goodin, Robert E. 2007. "Enfranchising All Affected Interests, and Its Alternatives." *Philosophy and Public Affairs* 35, no. 1: 20–68.

Goodin, Robert E. 2016. "Enfranchising All Subjected, Worldwide." *International Theory* 8, no. 3: 365–389. https://doi.org/10.1017/S1752971916000105.

Goodman, Lee-Anne. 2014. "Kenney on Twitter Defends Ban on Niqabs at Citizenship Ceremonies." *CBC News Online*. October 17. https://www.cbc.ca/news/politics/jason-kenney-defends-niqab-ban-at-citizenship-ceremonies-on-twitter-1.2803642.

Goodman, Sara Wallace. 2011. "Controlling Immigration through Language and Country Knowledge Requirements." *West European Politics* 34, no. 2: 235–255.

Government of Norway. n.d. "The Result of Your Application." https://www.norway.no/en/kosovo/services-info/visitors-visa-res-permit/visitors-visa/result-app/.

Government of the Netherlands. 2019. "Do I Need to Start Civic Integration before I Arrive in the Netherlands?" *Do I Need to Start Civic Integration before I Arrive in the Netherlands?* December 24. https://www.government.nl/topics/immigration-to-the-netherlands/question-and-answer/topics/immigration-to-the-netherlands/question-and-answer/do-i-need-to-start-civic-integration-before-i-arrive-in-the-netherlands.

Gustavsson, Gina, and David Miller. 2020. *Liberal Nationalism and Its Critics: Normative and Empirical Questions*. Oxford, UK: Oxford University Press.

Hampshire, James. 2011. "Liberalism and Citizenship Acquisition: How Easy Should Naturalisation Be?" *Journal of Ethnic & Migration Studies* 37, no. 6: 953–971. https://doi.org/10.1080/1369183X.2011.576197.

Hanley, Jill, Eric Shragge, Andre Rivard, and Jahhon Koo. 2012. "Good Enough to Work? Good Enough to Stay!" In *Legislated Inequality. Temporary Labour Migration in Canada*, edited by Patti Tamara Lenard and Christine Straehle, 245–271. Montreal, Kingston: McGill-Queen's University Press.

Hansen, Randall. 2010. "Citizenship Tests: An Unapologetic Defense." *European Union Democracy Observatory on Citizenship* (blog). http://eudo-citizenship.eu/citizenship-forum/255?start=7.

Harder, Niklas, Lucila Figueroa, Rachel M. Gillum, Dominik Hangartner, David D. Laitin, and Jens Hainmueller. 2018. "Multidimensional Measure of Immigrant Integration." *Proceedings of the National Academy of Sciences* 115, no. 45: 11483–11488. https://doi.org/10.1073/pnas.1808793115.

Harles, John C. 1997. "Integration before Assimilation: Immigration, Multiculturalism and the Canadian Polity." *Canadian Journal of Political Science* 30, no. 4: 711–736.

Hartmann, Jörg. 2016. "Do Second-Generation Turkish Migrants in Germany Assimilate into the Middle Class?" *Ethnicities* 16, no. 3: 368–392. https://doi.org/10.1177/1468796814548234.

Haugen, Stacey, Emily Regan Wills, and Patti Tamara Lenard. 2020. "Creating Canadians through Private Sponsorship." *Canadian Journal of Political Science* 53, no. 3: 560–576.

Hayduk, Ronald. 2006. *Democracy for All: Restoring Immigrant Voting Rights in the United States*. New York: Taylor & Francis.

Haynal, George, Michael Welsh, Louis Century, and Sean Tyler. 2013. *The Consular Function in the 21st Century*. University of Toronto: Munk School of Global Affairs.

Heijer, Maarten den. 2018. "Visas and Non-Discrimination." *European Journal of Migration and Law* 20, no. 4: 470–489. https://doi.org/10.1163/15718166-12340039.

Herzog, Ben. 2010. "Dual Citizenship and the Revocation of Citizenship." In *Democratic Paths and Trends*, edited by Barbara Wejnert, 18:87–106. Bingley: Emerald Group Publishing.

Hidalgo, Javier. 2015. "Resistance to Unjust Immigration Restrictions." *Journal of Political Philosophy* 23, no. 4: 450–470.

Hidalgo, Javier. 2019. "The Ethics of Resisting Immigration Law." *Philosophy Compass* 14, no. 12: 1–10. https://doi.org/10.1111/phc3.12639.

Hing, Bill Ong. 2007. "The Case for Amnesty." *Stanford Journal of Civil Rights & Civil Liberties* 3, no. 2: 233–284.

Hollifield, James F., Philip L. Martin, and Pia M. Orrenius. 2014. "The Dilemmas of Immigration Control." In *Chapter 1. The Dilemmas of Immigration Control*, edited by James F. Hollifield, Philip L. Martin, and Pia M. Orrenius, 3–34. Redwood City, CA: Stanford University Press. https://doi.org/10.1515/9780804787352-004.

Howard, Jeffrey. 2020. "The Public Role of Ethics and Public Policy." In *Routledge Handbook of Ethics and Public Policy*, edited by Annabelle Lever and Andrei Poama. New York: Routledge.

Howard, Marc Morjé. 2005. "Variation in Dual Citizenship Policies in the Countries of the EU." *International Migration Review* 39, no. 3: 697–720.

Hubbard, Ben, and Constant Méheut. 2020. "Western Countries Leave Children of ISIS in Syrian Camps." *The New York Times*. May 31. https://www.nytimes.com/2020/05/31/world/middleeast/isis-children-syria-camps.html.

Human Rights Watch. n.d. "Rohingya." https://www.hrw.org/tag/rohingya.

Ibrahim, Azeem, and Myriam François. 2020. "Foreign ISIS Children Deserve a Home." *Foreign Policy* (blog). June 18. https://foreignpolicy.com/2020/06/18/islamic-state-foreign-fighters-children-syria-camps-repatriation/.

Ignatieff, Michael. 2004. *The Lesser Evil: Political Ethics in an Age of Terror*. Toronto: Penguin Canada.

Ilcan, Suzan, Kim Rygiel, and Feyzi Baban. 2018. "The Ambiguous Architecture of Precarity: Temporary Protection, Everyday Living and Migrant Journeys of Syrian Refugees." *International Journal of Migration and Border Studies* 4, no. 1–2: 51–70. https://doi.org/10.1504/IJMBS.2018.091226.

ILO. 2016. "A Migrant Centred Approach to Remittances (Labour Migration)." https://www.ilo.org/global/topics/labour-migration/policy-areas/remittances/lang--en/index.html.

ILO. 2021. "Statistics on International Labour Migration." *ILOSTAT* (blog). June 30. https://ilostat.ilo.org/topics/labour-migration/.

Immigration, Refugees and Citizenship Canada. 2004. "Letter of Invitation." Service Initiation. February 17. https://www.canada.ca/en/immigration-refugees-citizenship/services/visit-canada/letter-invitation.html.

Institute on Statelessness and Inclusion. 2016. "Civil Society Submission on the Right of Every Child to Acquire a Nationality under Article 7 CRC." *Committee on the Rights of the Child*, July 1. https://files.institutesi.org/CRC_Lebanon_2016.pdf.

IRCC. 2018. "Medical Inadmissibility." December 21. https://www.canada.ca/en/immigration-refugees-citizenship/services/immigrate-canada/inadmissibility/reasons/medical-inadmissibility.html.

"ISIS Foreign Fighters after the Fall of the Caliphate." 2020. *Armed Conflict Survey* 6, no. 1: 23–30. https://doi.org/10.1080/23740973.2020.1761611.

Jackson, Amanda. 2019. "Muslim and Jewish Holy Books among Many Used to Swear-in Congress." *CNN.* January 3. https://www.cnn.com/2019/01/03/us/congress-swear-in-religious-books-trnd/index.html.

Jacobs, Emma. 2020. "Canada Is Granting Residency to Some Asylum-Seekers Working in Pandemic Health Care." *The World.* August 25. https://www.pri.org/stories/2020-08-25/canada-granting-residency-some-asylum-seekers-working-pandemic-health-care.

Joppke, Christian. 2014. "Europe and Islam: Alarmists, Victimists, and Integration by Law." *West European Politics* 37, no. 6: 1314–1335. https://doi.org/10.1080/01402382.2014.929337.

Joppke, Christian. 2016. "Terror and the Loss of Citizenship." *Citizenship Studies* 20, no. 6–7: 728–748.

Joppke, Christian. 2017. *Is Multiculturalism Dead? Crisis and Persistence in the Constitutional State.* Cambridge: Polity Press.

Joppke, Christian, ed. 2010. *How Liberal Are Citizenship Tests?* Florence, Italy: European Union Democracy Observatory on Citizenship.

Joppke, Christian, and Ewa T. Morawska. 2002. *Toward Assimilation and Citizenship: Immigrants in Liberal Nation-States.* New York: Springer.

Kalicki, Konrad. 2020. "Trading Liberty: Assisted Repatriation in Liberal Democracies." *Government and Opposition* 55 (4): 711–731. https://doi.org/10.1017/gov.2020.15.

Kalir, Barak. 2017. "Between 'Voluntary' Return Programs and Soft Deportation." In *Return Migration and Psychosocial Wellbeing*, edited by Zana Vathi and Russell King, 56–71. London: Routledge. https://www.taylorfrancis.com/chapters/edit/10.4324/9781315619613-4/voluntary-return-programs-soft-deportation-barak-kalir?context=ubx&refId=2324cc9a-ca7d-4a51-ad6d-86ad0b102644.

Kamishi, Lum. 2021. "Invitation Letter for Australia Visa—2022 Samples." *Visaguide. World.* https://visaguide.world/tips/australia-visa-invitation-letter/.

Kamm, Frances Myrna. 1985. "Equal Treatment and Equal Chances." *Philosophy & Public Affairs* 14, no. 2: 177–194.

Karki, Ram. 2021. "Statelessness among Resettled Bhutanese Refugees in Europe: An Unresolved Problem." European Network on Statelessness. June 10. https://www.statelessness.eu/updates/blog/statelessness-among-resettled-bhutanese-refugees-europe-unresolved-problem.

Kassam, Ashifa. 2016. "Royal Rejection: Naturalised Canadians Recant Oath of Allegiance to Queen." *The Guardian.* March 31. http://www.theguardian.com/world/2016/mar/31/naturalized-canadians-recant-oath-to-queen-royal-monarchy.

Kennedy, Rachael. 2019. "British ISIS Schoolgirl Found in Syria Says She Wants to Go Home." *Euronews.* February 14. https://www.euronews.com/2019/02/14/i-don-t-regret-coming-here-says-british-schoolgirl-who-ran-away-to-join-isis.

Khadka, Upasana. 2022. "There Are Better Options That Exit Bans to Protect Migrant Workers Abroad: A Response to Patti Lenard (2021), Commentary for 'The Ethics of Migration Policy Dilemmas' Project." *Migration Policy Centre (MPC).* https://migrationpolicycentre.eu/projects/dilemmas-project/.

Kingston, Rebecca. 2005. "The Unmaking of Citizens: Banishment and the Modern Citizenship Regime in France." *Citizenship Studies* 9, no. 1: 23–40.

Kolers, Avery. 2009. *Land, Conflict, and Justice: A Political Theory of Territory.* New York: Cambridge University Press.

Koning, Edward A. 2011. "Ethnic and Civic Dealings with Newcomers: Naturalization Policies and Practices in Twenty-Six Immigration Countries." *Ethnic and Racial Studies* 34, no. 11: 1974–1994.

Kukathas, Chandran. 2004. "Contextualism Reconsidered: Some Skeptical Reflections." *Ethical Theory and Moral Practice* 7, no. 2: 215–225. https://doi.org/10.1023/B:ETTA.0000032808.92466.f5.

Kukathas, Chandran. 2005. "Contextualism Reconsidered: Some Skeptical Reflections." *Ethical Theory and Moral Practice* 7: 215–225.

Kukathas, Chandran. 2021. *Immigration and Freedom. Immigration and Freedom*. Princeton, NJ: Princeton University Press. https://doi.org/10.1515/9780691215389.

Kymlicka, Will. 1996. *Multicultural Citizenship: A Liberal Theory of Minority Rights*. Oxford: Oxford University Press.

Kymlicka, Will. 1998. *Finding Our Way: Rethinking Ethnocultural Relations in Canada*. Oxford: Oxford University Press.

Kymlicka, Will. 2001. *Politics in the Vernacular: Nationalism, Multiculturalism, and Citizenship*. Oxford: Oxford University Press.

Kymlicka, Will, and Alan Patten, eds. 2003. *Language Rights and Political Theory*. Oxford: Oxford University Press.

Laborde, Cécile. 2008. *Critical Republicanism: The Hijab Controversy and Political Philosophy*. Oxford: Oxford University Press.

Lægaard, Sune. 2010. "Immigration, Social Cohesion, and Naturalization." *Ethnicities* 10, no. 4: 452–469. https://doi.org/10.1177/1468796810378324.

Lægaard, Sune. 2015. "Multiculturalism and Contextualism: How Is Context Relevant for Political Theory?" *European Journal of Political Theory* 14, no. 3: 259–276. https://doi.org/10.1177/1474885114562975.

Lægaard, Sune. 2019. "Contextualism in Normative Political Theory and the Problem of Critical Distance." *Ethical Theory and Moral Practice* 22, no. 4: 953–970. https://doi.org/10.1007/s10677-019-10026-6.

Lafleur, Jean-Michel, and María Sánchez-Domínguez. 2015. "The Political Choices of Emigrants Voting in Home Country Elections: A Socio-Political Analysis of the Electoral Behaviour of Bolivian External Voters." *Migration Studies* 3, no. 2: 155–181. https://doi.org/10.1093/migration/mnu030.

Landström, Yrsa. 2021. "Remaining Foreign Fighters: Fear, Misconceptions and Counterproductive Responses." In *Understanding the Creeping Crisis*, edited by Arjen Boin, Magnus Ekengren, and Mark Rhinard, 51–67. Cham: Springer International Publishing. https://doi.org/10.1007/978-3-030-70692-0.

Lazar, Seth. 2009. "The Nature and Disvalue of Injury." *Res Publica* 15, no. 3: 289–304.

Le Roux, Willem. 2021. "New South African Visa Concessions." *SAvisas.Com* (blog). March 27. https://www.savisas.com/blog/new-visa-concessions-announced-march-2021/.

Lee, Erika. 2003. *At America's Gates: Chinese Immigration During the Exclusion Era, 1882–1943*. Chapel Hill: University of North Carolina Press.

Leerkes, Arjen, Rianne van Os, and Eline Boersema. 2017. "What Drives 'Soft Deportation'? Understanding the Rise in Assisted Voluntary Return among Rejected Asylum Seekers in the Netherlands." *Population, Space and Place* 23, no. 8: 1–11. https://doi.org/10.1002/psp.2059.

Leistner, Alexandra. 2021. "Disenfranchised and Unheard, Germany's Turks Remain an Island." *Euronews.* September 25. https://www.euronews.com/2021/09/25/disenfranchised-and-unheard-germany-s-turks-remain-an-island.

Lenard, Patti Tamara. 2007. "Shared Public Culture: A Reliable Source of Trust." *Contemporary Political Theory* 6, no. 4: 385–404.

Lenard, Patti Tamara. 2010. "What Can Multicultural Theory Tell Us about Integrating Muslims in Europe?" *Political Studies Review* 8, no. 3: 308–321.

Lenard, Patti Tamara. 2012a. *Trust, Democracy and Multicultural Challenges.* University Park: Pennsylvania University State Press.

Lenard, Patti Tamara. 2012b. "Why Temporary Labour Migration Is Not a Satisfactory Alternative to Permanent Migration." *Journal of International Political Theory* 8, no. 1–2: 172–183. https://doi.org/10.3366/jipt.2012.0037.

Lenard, Patti Tamara. 2014. "Residence and the Right to Vote." *Journal of International Migration and Integration* 16, no. 1: 119–132.

Lenard, Patti Tamara. 2015. "The Ethics of Deportation in Liberal Democratic States." *European Journal of Political Theory* 14, no. 4: 464–480.

Lenard, Patti Tamara. 2016a. "Democracies and the Power to Revoke Citizenship." *Ethics & International Affairs* 30, no. 1: 73–91.

Lenard, Patti Tamara. 2016b. "Resettling Refugees: Is Private Sponsorship a Just Way Forward?" *Journal of Global Ethics* 12, no. 3: 300–310.

Lenard, Patti Tamara. 2016c. "Temporary Labour Migration and Global Inequality." In *The Ethics and Politics of Immigration: Core Issues and Emerging Trends*, edited by Alex Sager, 85–102. New York: Rowman & Littlefield.

Lenard, Patti Tamara. 2018a. "Democratic Citizenship and Denationalization." *American Political Science Review* 112, no. 1: 99–111.

Lenard, Patti Tamara. 2018b. "Wither the Canadian Model? Evaluating the New Canadian Nationalism (2006–2015)." In *Diversity and Contestations over Nationalism in Europe and Canada*, edited by John Erik Fossum, Riva Kastoryano, and Birte Siim, 211–236. Palgrave Studies in European Political Sociology. London: Palgrave Macmillan UK. https://doi.org/10.1057/978-1-137-58987-3_8.

Lenard, Patti Tamara. 2019. "How Do Sponsors Think about 'Month 13'?" *Refuge: Canada's Journal on Refugees* 35, no. 2: 65–74. https://doi.org/10.7202/1064820ar.

Lenard, Patti Tamara. 2020a. "Culture." In *The Stanford Encyclopedia of Philosophy*, edited by Edward N. Zalta, Winter 2020. Metaphysics Research Lab, Stanford University. https://plato.stanford.edu/archives/win2020/entries/culture/.

Lenard, Patti Tamara. 2020b. *How Should Democracies Fight Terrorism?* Cambridge, UK: Polity Press.

Lenard, Patti Tamara. 2020c. "The Ethics of Citizen Selection of Refugees for Admission and Resettlement." *Journal of Applied Philosophy* 37, no. 5: 731–745. https://doi.org/10.1111/japp.12412.

Lenard, Patti Tamara. 2021a. "How Exceptional? Welcoming Refugees the Canadian Way." *American Review of Canadian Studies* 51, no. 1: 78–94. https://doi.org/10.1080/02722011.2021.1874230.

Lenard, Patti Tamara. 2021b. "Restricting Emigration for Their Protection? Exit Controls and the Protection of (Women) Migrant Workers." *Migration Studies* (November): mnab045. https://doi.org/10.1093/migration/mnab045.

Lenard, Patti Tamara. early view. "Unintentional Residence and the Right to Vote." *Journal of Applied Philosophy.* https://doi.org/10.1111/japp.12513.

Lenard, Patti Tamara, and Daniel Munro. 2012. "Extending the Franchise to Non-Citizen Residents in Canada and the United States: How Bad Is the Democratic Deficit?" In *Imperfect Democracies: Comparing the Democratic Deficit in Canada and the United States*, edited by Patti Tamara Lenard and Richard Simeon. Vancouver: UBC Press.
Lenard, Patti Tamara, and Alex Neve. 2021. "The Pandemic, Borders and Refugees." *Centre for International Policy Studies* (blog). March 18. https://www.cips-cepi.ca/2021/03/18/the-pandemic-borders-and-refugees/.
Lenard, Patti Tamara, and Christine Straehle. 2010. "Temporary Labour Migration: Exploitation, Tool of Development, or Both?" *Policy and Society* 29, no. 4: 283–294.
Lenard, Patti Tamara, and Christine Straehle. 2011. "Temporary Labour Migration, Global Redistribution and Democratic Justice." *Politics, Philosophy & Economics* 11, no. 2: 206–230.
Lenard, Patti Tamara, and Christine Straehle. 2012a. "Temporary Labour Migration, Global Redistribution and Democratic Justice." *Philosophy, Politics and Economics* 11, no. 2: 206–230.
Lenard, Patti Tamara, and Christine Straehle. 2012b. "Temporary Labour Migration, Global Redistribution, and Democratic Justice." *Politics, Philosophy & Economics* 11, no. 2: 206–230. https://doi.org/10.1177/1470594x10392338.
Lever, Annabel. 2016. "Racial Profiling and the Political Philosophy of Race." In *The Oxford Handbook of the Philosophy of Race*, edited by Naomi Zack, 425–435. Oxford: Oxford University Press. https://www.oxfordhandbooks.com/view/10.1093/oxfordhb/9780190236953.001.0001/oxfordhb-9780190236953-e-7.
Lim, Sokchea, and Hem C. Basnet. 2017. "International Migration, Workers' Remittances and Permanent Income Hypothesis." *World Development* 96 (August): 438–450. https://doi.org/10.1016/j.worlddev.2017.03.028.
"Lowering the Bar." 2021. *The Economist*. June 24.
Lu, Catherine. 2017. *Justice and Reconciliation in World Politics*. Cambridge, UK: Cambridge University Press.
Luedtke, Adam, Douglas G. Byrd, and Kristian P. Alexander. 2010. "The Politics of Visas." *Whitehead Journal of Diplomacy and International Relations* 11, no. 1: 147–164.
Macedo, Stephen. 2011. "When and Why Should Liberal Democracies Restrict Immigration?" In *Citizenship, Borders, and Human Needs*, edited by Rogers M. Smith, 301–323. Philadelphia: University of Pennsylvania Press. https://doi.org/10.9783/9780812204667.301.
Macedo, Stephen. 2020. "After the Backlash: Populism and the Politics and Ethics of Migration." *The Law & Ethics of Human Rights* 14, no. 2: 153–180. https://doi.org/10.1515/lehr-2020-2018.
Macklin, Audrey. 1994. "On the Inside Looking In: Foreign Domestic Workers in Canada." In *Maid in the Market*, edited by W. Giles and S. Arat-Koc, 13–39. Halifax: Fernwood Press.
Macklin, Andrey. 2015. "The Return of Banishment: Do the New Denationalisation Policies Weaken Citizenship?" In *Debating Transformations of National Citizenship*, edited by Rainer Bauböck, 163–172. New York: Springer.
Macklin, Audrey, and François Crépeau. 2010. *Multiple Citizenship, Identity and Entitlement in Canada*. Ottawa: IRPP.
Malkopoulou Anthoula. 2017. "Ostracism and Democratic Self-defense in Athens." *Constellations* 24, no. 4: 623–636. https://doi.org/10.1111/1467-8675.12285.

Massey, Hugh. 2010. "UNHCR and De Facto Statelessness." *United Nations High Commissioner for Refugees*. https://www.unhcr.org/4bc2ddeb9.pdf.

Mau, Steffen, Fabian Gülzau, Lena Laube, and Natascha Zaun. 2015. "The Global Mobility Divide: How Visa Policies Have Evolved over Time." *Journal of Ethnic and Migration Studies* 41, no. 8: 1192–1213. https://doi.org/10.1080/1369183X.2015.1005007.

Mayer, Robert. 2005. "Guestworkers and Exploitation." *Review of Politics* 67, no. 2: 311–334.

McAteer v. Canada (Attorney General), 2014 ONCA 578. 2013. Court of Appeal for Ontario.

MEE. 2020. "Russia Repatriates Orphans of Suspected Islamic State Fighters in Syria." *Middle East Eye*. February 7. http://www.middleeasteye.net/news/russia-repatriates-26-islamic-state-linked-children-syria.

Mena, Kelly. 2021. "New York City Gives Noncitizens Right to Vote in Local Elections." *CNN*. December 9. https://www.cnn.com/2021/12/09/politics/nyc-noncitizens-local-elections-voting-rights/index.html.

Mencütek, Zeynep S. 2015. "External Voting: Mapping Motivations of Emigrants and Concerns of Host Countries." *Insight Turkey* 17, no. 4: 145–169.

Mendoza, José Jorge. 2015. "Enforcement Matters: Reframing the Philosophical Debate over Immigration." *Journal of Speculative Philosophy* 29, no. 1: 73–90.

Menjívar, Cecilia, Andrea Gómez Cervantes, and Daniel Alvord. 2018. "The Expansion of 'Crimmigration,' Mass Detention, and Deportation." *Sociology Compass* 12, no. 4: e12573.

Michalowski, Ines. 2010. "Citizenship Tests and Traditions of State Interference with Cultural Diversity." In *How Liberal Are Citizenship Tests?*, edited by Rainer Bauböck and Christian Joppke, 5–8. Robert Schuman Centre for Advanced Studies: European University Global Citizenship Observatory.

Miller, David. 2005. "Immigration: The Case for Limits." In *Contemporary Debates in Applied Ethics*, edited by Andrew Cohen and Christopher Wellman, 193–207. Malden: Blackwell Publishers.

Miller, David. 2009. "Democracy's Domain." *Philosophy & Public Affairs* 37, no. 3: 201–228.

Miller, David. 2012. "Are Human Rights Conditional?" *CSSJ Working Papers Series, SJ020*. https://www.politics.ox.ac.uk/materials/centres/social-justice/working-papers/SJ020_Miller_Are%20Human%20Rights%20Conditional%20final%20draft.pdf.

Miller, David. 2013. *Justice for Earthlings: Essays in Political Philosophy*. Cambridge: Cambridge University Press.

Miller, David. 2016a. "Boundaries, Democracy, and Territory." *The American Journal of Jurisprudence* 61, no. 1: 33–49.

Miller, David. 2016b. "Democracy, Exile, and Revocation." *Ethics & International Affairs* 30, no. 2: 265–270.

Miller, David. 2016c. *Strangers in Our Midst: The Political Philosophy of Immigration*. Cambridge, MA: Harvard University Press.

Miller, David. 2020. "Reconceiving the Democratic Boundary Problem." *Philosophy Compass* 15, no. 11: 1–9. https://doi.org/10.1111/phc3.12707.

Milton, Abul Hasnat, Mijanur Rahman, Sumaira Hussain, Charulata Jindal, Sushmita Choudhury, Shahnaz Akter, Shahana Ferdousi, Tafzila Akter Mouly, John Hall, and Jimmy T. Efird. 2017. "Trapped in Statelessness: Rohingya Refugees in Bangladesh."

International Journal of Environmental Research and Public Health 14, no. 8: 942. https://doi.org/10.3390/ijerph14080942.
Ministry of Children, Equality and Social Inclusion. 2014. The Norwegian Nationality Act. Redaksjonellartikkel. Government. No. regjeringen.no. December 14. https://www.regjeringen.no/en/topics/immigration-and-integration/kd/statsborgerloven/id2343481/.
Modood, Tariq, and Simon Thompson. 2018. "Revisiting Contextualism in Political Theory: Putting Principles into Context." *Res Publica* 24, no. 3: 339–357. https://doi.org/10.1007/s11158-017-9358-1.
Monbiot, George. 2014. "Orwell Was Hailed a Hero for Fighting in Spain. Today He'd Be Guilty of Terrorism." *The Guardian*. February 10. http://www.theguardian.com/commentisfree/2014/feb/10/orwell-hero-terrorism-syria-british-fighters-damned.
Monforte, Pierre, Leah Bassel, and Kamran Khan. 2019. "Deserving Citizenship? Exploring Migrants' Experiences of the 'Citizenship Test' Process in the United Kingdom." *The British Journal of Sociology* 70, no. 1: 24–43. https://doi.org/10.1111/1468-4446.12351.
Moore, Margaret. 2015. *A Political Theory of Territory*. New York: Oxford University Press.
Moore, Margaret. unpublished draft. "Territorial Rights and Forfeiture Theory."
Morris, Stéfanie, Patti Tamara Lenard, and Stacey Haugen. 2021. "Refugee Sponsorship and Family Reunification." *Journal of Refugee Studies* 34, no. 1 (December): 130–148. https://doi.org/10.1093/jrs/feaa062.
Nagel, Thomas. 1973. "Equal Treatment and Compensatory Discrimination." *Philosophy & Public Affairs* 2, no. 4: 348–363.
Napier-Moore, Rebecca. 2017. *"Protected or Put in Harm's Way?" Report*. International Labour Organization. http://www.ilo.org/asia/publications/WCMS_555974/lang--en/index.htm.
Näsström, Sofia. 2011. "The Challenge of the All-Affected Principle." *Political Studies* 59, no. 1: 116–134. https://doi.org/10.1111/j.1467-9248.2010.00845.x.
National Museum of African American History and Culture. 2021. "Reconstructing Citizenship." June 29. https://nmaahc.si.edu/explore/exhibitions/reconstruction/citizenship.
Nethery, Amy, and Stephanie J. Silverman, eds. 2015. *Immigration Detention: The Migration of a Policy and Its Human Impact*. New York: Routledge.
Noland, Natalie. 2021. "France Is Getting Progressive with Its Immigration. Others Should Too." *Northeastern University Political Review* (blog). March 12. https://www.nupoliticalreview.com/2021/03/12/france-is-getting-progressive-with-its-immigration-others-should-too/.
"Oath of Office." 2021. *Wikipedia*. https://en.wikipedia.org/w/index.php?title=Oath_of_office&oldid=1002439281.
Oberman, Kieran. 2013. "Can Brain Drain Justify Immigration Restrictions?" *Ethics* 123, no. 3: 427–455. https://doi.org/10.1086/669567.
Oberman, Kieran. 2016. "Immigration as a Human Right." In *Migration in Political Theory: The Ethics of Movement and Membership*, edited by Sarah Fine and Lea Ypi, 32–56. Oxford: Oxford University Press.
Oers, Ricky van. 2020. "Deserving Citizenship in Germany and The Netherlands. Citizenship Tests in Liberal Democracies." *Ethnicities* 21, no. 2 (October): 271–288. https://doi.org/10.1177/1468796820965785.

OHCHR. 1989. "Convention on the Rights of the Child." OHCHR. https://www.ohchr.org/en/instruments-mechanisms/instruments/convention-rights-child.

OHCHR. 2021. "Syria: UN Experts Urge 57 States to Repatriate Women and Children from Squalid Camps." February 8. https://www.ohchr.org/EN/NewsEvents/Pages/DisplayNews.aspx?NewsID=26730&LangID=E.

Orgad, Liav. 2014. "Liberalism, Allegiance, and Obedience: The Inappropriateness of Loyalty Oaths in a Liberal Democracy." *Canadian Journal of Law & Jurisprudence* 27, no. 1: 99–122. https://doi.org/10.1017/S084182090000624X.

Orgad, Liav. 2016. *The Cultural Defense of Nations: A Liberal Theory of Majority Rights*. Oxford: Oxford University Press.

O'Sullivan, Maria. 2019. *Refugee Law and Durability of Protection: Temporary Residence and Cessation of Status*. New York: Routledge.

Otis, John. 2021. "'A Huge Opportunity': Venezuelan Migrants Welcome Colombia's New Open-Door Policy." *NPR*. February 26. https://www.npr.org/2021/02/26/971776007/a-huge-opportunity-venezuelan-migrants-welcome-colombias-new-open-door-policy.

Ottonelli, Valeria, and Tiziana Torresi. 2012. "Inclusivist Egalitarian Liberalism and Temporary Migration: A Dilemma." *Journal of Political Philosophy* 20, no. 2: 202–224.

Ottonelli, Valeria, and Tiziana Torresi. 2013. "When Is Migration Voluntary?" *The International Migration Review* 47, no. 4: 783–813.

Ottonelli, Valeria, and Tiziana Torresi. forthcoming. *The Right Not to Stay*.

Owen, David. 2011. "Transnational Citizenship and the Democratic State: Modes of Membership and Voting Rights." *Critical Review of International Social and Political Philosophy* 14, no. 5: 641–663. https://doi.org/10.1080/13698230.2011.617123.

Owen, David. 2016. "Refugees, Fairness and Taking up the Slack: On Justice and the International Refugee Regime." *Moral Philosophy and Politics* 3, no. 2: 141–164.

Owen, David. 2020. *What Do We Owe to Refugees?* Cambridge, UK: Polity Press.

Parekh, Serena. 2016. *Refugees and the Ethics of Forced Displacement*. London: Routledge.

Parekh, Serena. 2020. *No Refuge: Ethics and the Global Refugee Crisis*. Oxford: Oxford University Press.

Peach, Ceri. 2007. "Muslim Population of Europe: A Brief Overview of Demographic Trends and Socioeconomic Integration, with Particular Reference to Britain." In *Muslim Integration: Challenging Conventional Wisdom in Europe and the United States*, edited by Steffen Angenendt, Paul. M. Barrett, Jonathan Laurence, Ceri Peach, Julianne Smith, and Tim Winter, 7–32. Washington, DC: Center for Strategic and International Studies.

Pedroza, Luicy. 2019. *Citizenship Beyond Nationality: Immigrants' Right to Vote Across the World*. Philadelphia: University of Pennsylvania Press.

Penninx, Rinus. 2019. "Problems of and Solutions for the Study of Immigrant Integration." *Comparative Migration Studies* 7, no. 1: 13. https://doi.org/10.1186/s40878-019-0122-x.

Pevnick, Ryan. 2009. "Social Trust and the Ethics of Immigration Policy." *Journal of Political Philosophy* 17, no. 2: 146–167.

Phillips, Anne. 2021. *Unconditional Equals*. Princeton, NJ: Princeton University Press.

Phillips, Robert Lu. 2021. "A Tribunal for ISIS Fighters—A National Security and Human Rights Emergency." *Just Security* (blog). March 30. https://www.justsecurity.org/75544/a-tribunal-for-isis-fighters-a-national-security-and-human-rights-emergency/.

Popp, George, Sarah Canna, and Jeff Day. 2020. "Common Characteristics of 'Successful' Deradicalization Programs of the Past." *Defense Technical Information Center: NSI Reachback*. https://apps.dtic.mil/sti/pdfs/AD1092721.pdf.

Pritchett, Lant. 2006. *Let Their People Come: Breaking the Gridlock on International Labor Mobility*. Washington, DC: Center for Global Development.

Rae, Bob. 2018. "Tell Them We're Human" What Canada and the World Can Do About the Rohingya Crisis." *Global Affairs Canada*. https://www.international.gc.ca/world-monde/assets/pdfs/rohingya_crisis_eng.pdf.

Rawls, John. 1999. *A Theory of Justice (Revised Edition)*. Cambridge: Belknap Press of Harvard University Press.

Reed-Sandoval, Amy. 2016. "The New Open Borders Debate." In *The Ethics and Politics of Immigration: Core Issues and Emerging Trends*, edited by Alex Sager, 13–28. Lanham: Rowman & Littlefield.

Reed-Sandoval, Amy. 2022. "Are Exit Controls for Women Migrant Workers Justified in Theory? A Response for Patti Lenard (2021), Commentary for 'The Ethics of Migration Policy Dilemmas' Project." *Migration Policy Centre (MPC)*.

Risse, Mathias, and Richard Zeckhauser. 2004. "Racial Profiling." *Philosophy & Public Affairs* 32, no. 2: 131–170.

Rosefield, Hannah. 2014. "A Brief History of Oaths and Books." *The New Yorker*. June 20. https://www.newyorker.com/books/page-turner/a-brief-history-of-oaths-and-books.

Rosenberg, Cynthia B. 2018. "IMMIGRATION LAW FOCUS: Dishonorable Discharge?" Maryland State Bar Association—MSBA. August 5. https://www.msba.org/immigration-law-focus-dishonorable-discharge/.

Roy van Zuijdewijn, Jeanine de, and Edwin Bakker. 2004. *Returning Western Foreign Fighters: The Case of Afghanistan, Bosnia and Somalia*. International Centre for Counter-Terrorism: The Hague. https://www.icct.nl/download/file/ICCT-De-Roy-van-Zuijdewijn-Bakker-Returning-Western-Foreign-Fighters-June-2014.pdf.

Ruhs, Martin. 2010. "Migrant Rights, Immigration Policy and Human Development." *Journal of Human Development and Capabilities* 11, no. 2: 259–279.

Ruhs, Martin. 2013. *The Price of Rights*. New Jersey: Princeton University Press.

Ruhs, Martin, and Philip Martin. 2008. "Numbers vs. Rights: Trade-Offs and Guest Worker Programs." *International Migration Review* 42, no. 1: 249–265.

Sager, Alex. 2014. "Reframing the Brain Drain." *Critical Review of International Social and Political Philosophy* 17, no. 5: 560–579.

Sager, Alex. 2017. "Immigration Enforcement and Domination: An Indirect Argument for Much More Open Borders." *Political Research Quarterly* 70, no. 1: 42–54.

Sakib, SM Najmus. 2020. "Bangladesh Will Not Accept ISIS Girl Shamima Begum." *Anadolu Agency*. February 16. https://www.aa.com.tr/en/asia-pacific/bangladesh-will-not-accept-isis-girl-shamima-begum/1735373.

Salter, Mark B. 2006. "The Global Visa Regime and the Political Technologies of the International Self: Borders, Bodies, Biopolitics." *Alternatives: Global, Local, Political* 31, no. 2: 167–189.

Saunders, Natasha. 2017. *International Political Theory and the Refugee Problem*. New York: Routledge.

Scheffler, Samuel. 2007. "Immigration and the Significance of Culture." *Philosophy and Public Affairs* 35, 2: 93–125.

Schneider, Jens, and Maurice Crul, eds. 2014. *Theorising Integration and Assimilation*. New York: Routledge.

Schuck, Peter H. 1997. "Refugee Burden-Sharing: A Modest Proposal." *Yale Journal of International Law* 22: 243–297.

Schutter, Helder De, and Lea Ypi. 2015. "Mandatory Citizenship for Immigrants." *British Journal of Political Science* 45, no. 2: 235–251. https://doi.org/10.1017/S000712341 4000568.

Selm, Joanne Van. 2014. "Refugee Resettlement." In *The Oxford Handbook of Refugee and Forced Migration Studies*, edited by Elena Fiddian-Qasmiyeh, Gil Loescher, Katy Long, and Nando Sigona, 512–524. Oxford, UK: Oxford University Press. https://doi.org/10.1093/oxfordhb/9780199652433.013.0014.

Senyshyn, Olha, Ksenia Tchern, and Irina Maimust. 2022. "How IRCC Can Improve the Canada-Ukraine Authorization for Emergency Travel (CUAET)." *Canadian Immigration Lawyers Association (CILA)* (blog). May 2. https://cila.co/how-ircc-can-improve-the-canada-ukraine-authorization-for-emergency-travel-cuaet/.

Shachar, Ayelet. 2011. "Picking Winners: Olympic Citizenship and the Global Race for Talent Part IV: Business, Labor, and the Economy." *Immigration and Nationality Law Review* 32: 523–574.

Shachar, Ayelet. 2020. *The Shifting Border*. Manchester: Manchester University Press.

Shachar, Ayelet, and Ran Hirschl. 2014. "On Citizenship, States, and Markets." *Journal of Political Philosophy* 22, no. 2: 231–257. https://doi.org/10.1111/jopp.12034.

Shacknove, Andrew E. 1985. "Who Is a Refugee?" *Ethics* 95, no. 2: 274–284.

Shah, Nasra M. 2006. "Restrictive Labour Immigration Policies in the Oil-Rich Gulf: Effectiveness and Implications for Sending Asian Countries," May 15–17, 1–20. https://www.un.org/en/development/desa/population/events/pdf/expert/11/P03_Shah.pdf.

Shalit, Avner de-. 2019. *Cities and Immigration: Political and Moral Dilemmas in the New Era of Migration*. Oxford, New York: Oxford University Press.

Sharp, Daniel. 2020. "Immigration and State System Legitimacy." *Critical Review of International Social and Political Philosophy*, 1–11. https://doi.org/10.1080/13698 230.2020.1860416.

Shengen Visa Info. 2022. "Invitation Letter for Schengen Visa—Letter of Invitation for Visa Application." https://www.schengenvisainfo.com/invitation-letter-schengen-visa/.

Shiffrin, Seana Valentine. 2000. "Paternalism, Unconscionability Doctrine, and Accommodation." *Philosophy & Public Affairs* 29, no. 3: 205–250. https://doi.org/10.1111/j.1088-4963.2000.00205.x.

Shin, Patrick S. 2009. "The Substantive Principle of Equal Treatment." *Legal Theory* 15, no. 2: 149–172. https://doi.org/10.1017/S1352325209090090.

Shivakoti, Richa. 2020. "Protection or Discrimination? The Case of Nepal's Policy Banning Female Migrant Workers." In *Urban Spaces and Gender in South Asia*, edited by D. U. Joshi and C. Brassard, 17–34. Switzerland: Springer.

Shivakoti, Richa, Sophie Henderson, and Matt Withers. under review. "The Migration Ban Policy Cycle: A Comparative Analysis of Restrictions on the Emigration of Women Domestic Workers."

Shklar, Judith N. 1991. *American Citizenship: The Quest for Inclusion*. Cambridge, MA: Harvard University Press.

Siegelberg, Mira L. 2020. *Statelessness: A Modern History*. Cambridge, MA: Harvard University Press.

Simpson, Leanne Betasamosake. 2016. "Indigenous Resurgence and Co-Resistance." *Critical Ethnic Studies* 2, no. 2: 19–34. https://doi.org/10.5749/jcritethnstud.2.2.0019.

Song, Sarah. 2012. "The Boundary Problem in Democratic Theory: Why the Demos Should Be Bounded by the State." *International Theory* 4, no. 1: 39–68.
Song, Sarah. 2016. "The Significance of Territorial Presence and the Rights of Immigrants." In *Migration in Political Theory: The Ethics of Movement and Membership*, edited by Sarah Fine and Lea Ypi, 225–247. Oxford University Press.
Song, Sarah. 2018. *Immigration and Democracy*. New York: Oxford University Press.
Sorensen, Martin Selsoe. 2018. "Denmark, With an Eye on Muslims, Requires New Citizens to Shake Hands." *The New York Times*. December 20. https://www.nytimes.com/2018/12/20/world/europe/denmark-muslims-handshake-law.html.
Soysal, Yasemin Nuhoğlu. 1994. *Limits of Citizenship: Migrants and Postnational Membership in Europe*. Chicago: University of Chicago Press.
Spiro, Peter J. 2019. "The Equality Paradox of Dual Citizenship." *Journal of Ethnic and Migration Studies* 45, no. 6: 879–896. https://doi.org/10.1080/1369183X.2018.1440485.
Statistics Canada. 2019. "Asylum Claimants." May 17. https://www150.statcan.gc.ca/n1/pub/89-28-0001/2018001/article/00013-eng.htm.
Staufenberg, Jeff. 2016. "Switzerland Denies Citizenship to Muslim Girls Who Refused to Swim with Boys." *The Independent*. July 1. https://www.independent.co.uk/news/world/europe/switzerland-citizenship-muslim-girls-refuse-swim-boys-islam-immigration-europe-a7111601.html.
Stemplowska, Zofia. 2016. "Doing More than One's Fair Share." *Critical Review of International Social and Political Philosophy* 19, no. 5: 591–608.
Stevenson, Verity. 2020. "Program to Grant Residency to Asylum Seekers Who Work in Health Care Excludes Hundreds, Advocates Say." *CBC*. August 15. https://www.cbc.ca/news/canada/montreal/excluded-from-asylum-seekers-program-residency-1.5687184.
Stilz, Anna. 2010. "Guestworkers and Second-Class Citizenship." *Policy and Society* 29, no. 4: 295–307.
Sullivan, Michael J. 2019. *Earned Citizenship*. New York: Oxford University Press.
Supreme Court of Canada. 2019. *Frank v. Canada (Attorney General)*, 2019 SCC 1, [2019] 1 S.C.R. 3. Supreme Court of Canada.
Tarovic, Helen L. 2015. "Naturalization and the Modified Oath for Jehovah's Witnesses." April 25. https://www.avvo.com/legal-guides/ugc/naturalization-and-the-modified-oath-for-jehovah-s-witnesses.
The Local. 2019. "Denmark Passes Law Enabling Withdrawal of Jihadists' Citizenship." *The Local Denmark* (blog). October 24. https://www.thelocal.dk/20191024/denmark-passes-law-enabling-withdrawal-of-jihadists-citizenship/.
The Local. 2021. "Thank You France, for Offering Me Citizenship to Recognise My Work during the Pandemic." *The Local France* (blog). January 4. https://www.thelocal.fr/20210104/thank-you-france-for-offering-me-citizenship-to-recognise-my-work-during-the-pandemic/.
The Ombudsman. n.d. "Ombudsmans Role in Matters Concerning Foreign Nationals." *Non-Discrimination Ombudsman*. https://syrjinta.fi/en/ombudsmans-role-in-matters-concerning-foreign-nationals.
Toronto Star. 2013. "Mandatory Citizenship Oath to the Queen Ruled Constitutional." *Toronto Star*. September 20. https://www.thestar.com/news/gta/2013/09/20/wouldbe_citizens_required_to_swear_allegiance_to_queen_court_says.html.
Toronto Star. 2015. "Oath to Queen Stays as Citizenship Requirement after Supreme Court Decision." February 26. https://www.thestar.com/news/canada/2015/02/26/

oath-to-queen-stays-as-citizenship-requirement-as-supreme-court-wont-hear-appeal.html.
Tungohan, Ethel. 2012. "Reconceptualizing Motherhood, Reconceptualizing Resistance." *International Feminist Journal of Politics* 15, no. 1: 39–57.
Ullah, Akm Ahsan. 2011. "Rohingya Refugees to Bangladesh: Historical Exclusions and Contemporary Marginalization." *Journal of Immigrant & Refugee Studies* 9, no. 2: 139–161. https://doi.org/10.1080/15562948.2011.567149.
UN Press Release. 2017. "Greater Cooperation Needed to Tackle Danger Posed by Returning Foreign Fighters." November 28. https://www.un.org/press/en/2017/sc13097.doc.htm.
UNHCR. 2015. "Guidelines on International Protection No. 11: Prima Facie Recognition of Refugee Status." https://www.refworld.org/docid/555c335a4.html.
UNHCR. 2019. "Resettlement." 2019. https://www.unhcr.org/resettlement.html.
United Nations. 1948. "Universal Declaration of Human Rights." http://www.un.org/en/universal-declaration-human-rights/.
United Nations. 2022. "UNHCR Chief Condemns 'Discrimination, Violence and Racism' against Some Fleeing Ukraine." *UN News*. March 21. https://news.un.org/en/story/2022/03/1114282.
United Nations High Commissioner for Refugees. 2019. *Handbook on Procedures and Criteria for Determining Refugee Status under the 1951 Convention and the 1967 Protocol Relating to the Status of Refugees*. Geneva: UNHCR. https://www.unhcr.org/publications/legal/3d58e13b4/handbook-procedures-criteria-determining-refugee-status-under-1951-convention.html.
USCIS. 2020. "Naturalization Oath of Allegiance to the United States of America." July 5. https://www.uscis.gov/citizenship/learn-about-citizenship/the-naturalization-interview-and-test/naturalization-oath-of-allegiance-to-the-united-states-of-america.
USCIS. 2021. "Naturalization Through Military Service." February 23. https://www.uscis.gov/military/naturalization-through-military-service.
Valentini, Laura. 2013. "Justice, Disagreement and Democracy." *British Journal of Political Science* 43, no. 1: 177–199. https://doi.org/10.1017/S0007123412000294.
Vandoorne, Saskya, Samantha Beech, and Ben Westcott. 2018. "'Spiderman' Granted French Citizenship after Rescuing Child from Paris Balcony." *CNN*. May 28. https://www.cnn.com/2018/05/28/asia/paris-baby-spiderman-rescue-intl/index.html.
Verba, Sidney, Kay Lehman Schlozman, and Henry E. Brady. 1995. *Voice and Equality: Civic Volunteerism in American Politics*. Cambridge: Harvard University Press.
Vertovec, Steven, and Susanne Wessendorf, eds. 2010. *The Multicultural Backlash: European Discourses, Policies, Practices*. London: Routledge.
Vitikainen, Annamari. 2020. "LGBT Rights and Refugees: A Case for Prioritizing LGBT Status in Refugee Admissions." *Ethics & Global Politics* 13, no. 1: 64–78. https://doi.org/10.1080/16544951.2020.1735015.
Waldron, Daniel. 2020. "Home Office U-Turn on UK Visa Extensions for Migrant NHS Workers." *Workpermit.com*. November 21. https://workpermit.com/news/home-office-u-turn-uk-visa-extensions-migrant-nhs-workers-20201121.
Walzer, Michael. 1983. *Spheres of Justice: A Defense of Pluralism and Equality*. New York: Basic Books.
Weerasinghe, Sanjula, and Abbie Taylor. 2015. "On the Margins: Noncitizens Caught in Countries Experiencing Violence, Conflict and Disaster." *Journal on Migration and Human Security* 3, no. 1: 26–57. https://doi.org/10.1177/233150241500300102.

Weil, Patrick. 2012. *The Sovereign Citizen*. Philadelphia: University of Pennsylvania Press.

Weinstock, Daniel. 2004. "Four Kinds of (Post)Nation Building." In *The Fate of the Nation-State*, edited by Michel Seymour, 51–68. Montreal, Kingston: McGill-Queen's University Press.

Wellman, Christopher Heath. 2008. "Immigration and Freedom of Association." *Ethics* 119, no. 1: 109–141.

Wellman, Christopher Heath. 2012. "The Rights Forfeiture Theory of Punishment." *Ethics* 122, no. 2: 371–393.

Whelan, Frederick G. 1981. "Citizenship and the Right to Leave." *American Political Science Review* 75, no. 3: 636–653.

Whelan, Frederick G. 1983. "Prologue: Democratic Theory and the Boundary Problem." In *Nomos 25: Liberal Democracy*, edited by J. R. Pennock and J. W. Chapman, 13–47. New York: New York University Press.

Wilkinson, Lori. 2017. "The Labour Market Experiences of Refugees in Canada." In *Structural Context of Refugee Integration in Canada and Germany*, edited by Annette Korntheuer, Débora Maehler, and Paul Pritchard, 93–99. Manheim: LEIBNIZ Institute for the Social Sciences and GEISIS.

Wolff, Jonathan. 2020. *Ethics and Public Policy: A Philosophical Inquiry*. New York: Routledge.

Youn, Soo. 2019. "Thousands Protest ICE across Cities Targeted for Weekend Raids." *ABC News*. July 14. https://abcnews.go.com/US/thousands-protest-ice-cities-targeted-weekend-raids/story?id=64312657.

Young, Iris Marion. 1989. *Justice and the Politics of Difference*. Princeton: Princeton University Press.

Young, Iris Marion. 2002. *Inclusion and Democracy*. Oxford: Oxford University Press.

Index

For the benefit of digital users, indexed terms that span two pages (e.g., 52–53) may, on occasion, appear on only one of those pages.

Abizadeh, Arash, 26, 31–32
Achiume, E. Tendayi, 176–77
admission / entry
   denial of, as "life-changing," 30
   non-entry policies, 17–18
   "numbers and rights" trade-off (Ruhs and Martin), 110, 115–16, 118
   numerical targets for, 109–10
   point-based systems for selection for, 109–10
   requirements, 156
Afroyim, Beys, 75
Afroyim v. Rusk, 80
All-Affected Principle, 24–26, 67
All-Subjected Principle, 21, 24–26, 28–29
   defined (Näsström), 32
   defining boundaries, 23
   and entitlement to stay, 35–36
   and "equal influence," 32
   and forced exclusion, 37
   and participatory democratic rights, 32–33
assimilation
   versus integration, 138–39
   objective of, 138–39
asylum seekers, 11–12
   defined, 126
   political theory of, 134–37

banishment / expulsion / exile / ostracism, 14–15, 19–20, 27, 77–78
basic rights, protecting, 164
Bauböck, Rainer, 34–35, 64, 65–66
Beckman, Ludvig, 31–32
Begum, Shamima, 81–84, 85. *See also* jihadi brides
Biden, Joe, 42–43

Birnie, Rutger, 45
Black Lives Matter movement, 1, 14–15, 176–77
Blake, Michael, 7–8, 167–68
Block, Gillian, 116–17, 118
borders
   closed, 2
   control of, 9, 11, 12
   control of, and refugees, 99
   control of, imperfect, 38–39 (*see also* admission / entry)
   moral relevance of inequalities, across, 8–13
   open, 2, 12–13 (*see also* Carens, Joseph)
   placement of, 8–9
   and wealth inequalities, 8–9
Bosniak, Linda, 47–48
Breivik, Anders, 82
Brock, Gillian, 117, 118, 124–25
Buckinx, Barbara, 41–42

"Canada–Ukraine Authorization for Emergency Travel," 18–19
Canadian Live-in Caregiver Program, 111, 121–22
Carens, Joseph, 3, 8–9, 101
Chinese Exclusion Act (USA, 1882-1952), 94–95
Chinese Immigration Act (Canada, 1923), 94–95
Christiano, Thomas, 5
citizens abroad
   and consular assistance, 55–59
   duty to protect, 69
   host state obligations toward, 55, 56, 64, 71
   labor migrants, 63–65

citizens abroad (cont.)
   labor migrants, exploiting temporary, 64
   obligations of citizenship state toward, 55–56, 62, 64
   "remedial duty" toward, 62, 71
   and right of return, 55–59, 70, 71
   rights of, 87–107
   and subjection, 55
   temporary bans on labor migrants, 63–64
citizenship. *See also* naturalization: requirements
   and accommodation rights, 155, 162–63
   and anti-accommodation policies, 168
   ceremonies, 155–60
   conditional, 73–74
   contracts, 112–14, 116
   "contribution," 108–9, 110–11, 124–30, 142–43
   "of convenience," 69
   criteria for, 130–31
   cultural exclusions, 19
   denying, 10
   earning, 108–9
   evaluating entitlement to, 130–31
   exclusion from, 18–19
   forfeiting, as punishment, 74–78
   as full inclusion, 85–86
   inalienable, 72–73
   as an "inalienable, unconditional, and non-forfeitable" right, 71–78, 86
   laboring for, 108–31
   and labor migration, 109–25
   and language tests, 19
   main benefit of, 162
   military labor for expedited, 120–21, 122–23, 185n.3
   and naturalization, 108
   objections to accommodation rights, 163–73
   permissibility of ceremonies for, 160–63
   and perpetual allegiance, 72
   post-national, 52, 53
   practicality of, 52–53
   and residency, 108, 130–31, 153
   and right to nationality, 49–50
   revocation of, 14–15, 20, 71–72
   shared institutions and culture, 52–53
   social contact theory of, 73–74
   and subjection, 36–37
   tests, 154
   unconditional, 84 (*see also* citizenship: revocation of)
   "universal" (Young), 175–76
   voluntarily relinquishing, 73
Cohen, Elizabeth, 18, 43
conscience, freedom of, 5, 164
Convention on the Reduction of Statelessness, 49–50
Convention on the Rights of the Child, 62
Crépeau, François, 69–70

Dahl, Robert, 32
Deferred Action for Childhood Arrival (DACA) program, 122
democracy
   aims of a just, 1
   basic rights of, 76
   defined, 5
   and equality, 5
   and the harms of exclusion, 5–8
   and justice, 5
   "liberty rights in," 74–75
democratic boundary problem, 24–25
denationalization, 69–70, 78. *See also* dual citizens: denationalizing wrongdoing
   defined, 19–20
   permissible, 71–72
denaturalization, 14–15, 87–107
   defined, 19–20
deportation
   and border control, 38–40
   defined, 38
   "domicile principle of non-deportability," 45
   fair, 47
   harms of, 40–48
   involuntary (forced), 40–41
   and racial profiling, 43
   rates of, 42–43
   as a strategy for border control, 43–44
discrimination, 14–15
   ethic, racial, cultural in admission, 11–12

INDEX

host state, 151
dual citizens, 68–70, 72, 181n.5
  basic rights protection for, 84–85
  denationalizing wrongdoing, 78–80
  resistance to recognizing, 80
  and right of return, 69
  rights of, 132–52

Ellerman, Antje, 41–43, 44–45
Erman, Eva, 32, 37
Espejo, Paulina Ochoa, 44–45
exclusion
  from citizenship, 13–15 (*see also* naturalization: requirements)
  citizen versus non-citizen, 14–15
  harmful versus wrongful, 6–7
  membership, and citizenship, 52
  protection from social, 149–51
  territorial, 13–15, 16–17, 18
  territorial, and citizenship, 52
  types of, 1
  typology of, 13
exploitation, of temporary migrant labor, 116, 129–30

family
  defined (Universal Declaration of Human Rights), 101
  forced separation from, 102–3
  reunification, 179n.5, 184n.12
  unity, as a basic right, 11–12, 101
Filindra, Alexandra, 41–42, 180n.1
foreign fighters, 18
  children of, 59–62
  and denationalization, 81–83
  and involuntary statelessness, 83
  and repatriation, 83–84, 86, 182n.6
  returning, 80–85

gender identity. *See* LGBTQ+ refugees
Geneva Convention on Refugees, 11–12
Gerver, Mollie, 40–41
Gibney, Matthew, 17–18, 49–50, 72
Goodin, Robert, 31–32
Guantanamo Bay, 183n.11

Hansen, Randall, 157–58, 159–60

Howard, Jeffrey, 3
humanitarian disasters, 3, 55–56, 57, 58–59, 62, 64–65, 71, 72, 83–84, 91–92, 132–33, 143

Immigration and Refugee Protection Act, 87–107
Indigenous Land Back movement, 1, 14–15
integration
  versus assimilation, 138–39
  defined by social and political scientists, 141
  host state obligations toward, 138
  labor market, 133–34, 137, 141–43
  and language competence, 158–59
  local, 135
  objective of, 133–34
  political theory of, 137–40
  versus resettlement, 152
International Labour Organization (ILO), 110
International Organization of Migration, 145
internment / detainment camps, 60, 79–80, 82–83
Ishaq, Zunera, 153–54

jihadi brides, 60. *See also* Begum, Shamima
Joppke, Christian, 75, 159–60, 164
justice
  democratic, 5
  and equality, 5
  immigration, requirements of, 5–6
Justice and the Politics of Difference (Young), 175

Kymlicka, Will, 27, 28–29
  "societal culture," 27, 28–29

Legault, François, 108–9, 125–26
legitimacy, criteria for, 11–12
  Democratic, Principle of, 26
LGBTQ+ refugees, 149–52. *See also* discrimination
  host state obligations toward, 150–51
  resettling, 151–52

loyalty
  dual nationals and, 78–79
  immigrants and, 79–80

Macklin, Audrey, 69–70
Macron, Emmanuel, 109
majority rule, protecting against the harms of, 5
marriage, and association, 7–8
migration
  contextualist methodology for, 3–5 (*see also* Carens, Joseph)
  "existential insecurity" of, 41–42
  forms of, 2
  and global inequalities, 9–10
  "guest worker" programs, 114–15
  irregular, 44–46
  labor, 110, 119–20
  major questions of, 2
  "necessitous" (Song), 185n.9
  surveillance (of migrants), 17–18, 39–40
  temporary labor, 114–17
  transitioning from temporary to permanent status, 106, 107
  unaddressed questions around, 3
  voluntary, 186n.4
Military Accessions Vital to National Interest (MAVNI), 111–12, 120–21, 122, 123
Miller, David, 24–25, 31–32, 76–77, 182n.6
movement / travel, right to, 8–9, 13–20, 57
"Muslim ban," 94–95

Näaström, Sofia, 31–32
naturalization, 45
  and anti-egalitarianism, 170
  ceremonies attendant on, 10, 14
  criteria for, 132
  dangers of exceptional programs for, 127–28
  defined, 108
  expedited, by contribution (*see* citizenship: "contribution")
  oath, 153

  oath, allegiance-based, 160–61, 171–72
  oath, elements of, 161
  oath, purpose of, 161–62
  objective of the process of, 159–60
  proposed timeline for, 51, 186n.8
  requirements, 14, 50–51, 154, 155–60
  for stateless peoples, 50
Naturalization for Military Service program (NMS), 111
no-fly lists, 94, 183n.3
"non-refoulement," duty of, 11–12

Ottonelli, Valeria, 89–90, 118

passports, and citizenship, 51–52
Phillips, Anne, 175–76

racism, 14–15
  systemic, 176–77
Rawls, John, 94
Reed-Sandoval, Amy, 2
  "classical immigration debate," 2
  coercion, 26
reflective equilibrium, 179n.1
Refugee Convention relating to the Status of Refugees, 126, 135
refugees
  defined, 134, 139–40
  host state obligations toward, 134–35
  net benefit of, 187n.10
  pathways to resolve the situation of, 135
  political theory of, 134–37
repatriation, 55–56, 105–6
  of children, 60–62
  voluntary versus coercive, 40–41
resettlement
  duties of, 140–49
  and integration, 143
  objective of, 133–34, 141, 143–44
  and the right to work, 147–49
  unmet duty of, 136–37
  versus voluntary migration, 139–40
residency
  versus citizenship in voting rights, 33–36

long-term, 66
permanent, 154
regularizing long-term non-citizens, 11–12

safe arrival
  and basic orientation duties, 145–46
  duties of, 144, 145
  host state obligations toward, 145–46
safe pathway, duties of, 144
Sager, Alex, 39–40, 185n.3
Shachar, Ayelet, 17–18, 39–40
Song, Sarah, 26, 31, 44–45, 93–94, 116–17, 118, 124–25
statelessness, 40–48
  choosing, 72–73
  "de facto" versus "de jure," 48–49
  defined, 48–49
  harm of, 49–50
  loss of protective rights with, 72–73
  presumption of, 181n.11
  voluntary, 72, 182n.3
subjection, 20–22, 23–27
  and affect, 25–26
  and citizenship status, 153
  versus coercion, 177
  defined, 20–21
  deliberative political process for, 31–32
  "enough-time" criterion, 29–30
  exceptions to, 23
  and forced exclusion, 36–37
  and inclusion, 32
  justification, 31–36
  "life-changing," 30, 35–36
  "life-shaping," 27–29, 38
  political entitlements of, 31–37
  triggering justification (Song), 31
Sullivan, Michael, 129–30

"Temporary Protected Status" (TPS), 15, 18–19, 186n.5
temporary refuge, 135–36, 141
  defined, 147
  and the right to work, 147–49
terrorism, 14–15, 75–76, 80–81
Torresi, Tiziana, 89–90, 118

tourists, 24, 28–29, 64–65, 89, 101, 156

United Nations High Commissioner for Refugees (UNHCR), 135
Universal Declaration of Human Rights, 14–15, 101
  Article 13, 56–57
  Article 15, 49–50

Valentini, Laura, 5
visas, 14, 16–17
  access to services, especially medical, and, 100–1
  American J-1, 105–6
  criteria for short-term, 91–92
  denial of, for non-citizens, 55–70
  and discrimination, 93–95
  eligibility conditions, 87
  eligibility requirements, 72–78
  ethics of requirements for short-term, 91–92
  expiration, 42–43
  extending temporary, 18–19
  and family movement, 101–3
  general global procedures for, 88–90, 91, 92
  health-based exclusions for, 93–94
  labor migrants, 104–5
  and movement, 100
  national security based exclusions for, 94
  proof of financial resources, 96, 100
  "prove that you are includable" criteria for, 95–99
  "prove you are not excludable" criteria, 93–95
  purpose of visit, 96
  renewable, for DACA migrants, 185n.7
  and rights restrictions, 100–6
  and the right to work, 100, 103
  short-term, 89–90
  short- versus long-term, 89, 104
  and social services access, 100
  and transition to permanency, 100
  waivers for, 88–89
voting rights, 162
  for citizens abroad, 63–65

voting rights (*cont.*)
    denial of, 15
    extent of, for citizens abroad, 66
    and long-term citizens
        abroad, 66
    and residency, 65, 66–68

Walzer, Michael, 46–47, 114–15
wealth, unequal distribution of, 8–9
Wellman, Christopher Heath, 7–8
Wolff, Jonathan, 3–4

Young, Iris Marion, 175